My Life and I

More Handheld Classics

Algernon Blackwood, *The Unknown. Weird Writings, 1900–1937*

Ernest Bramah, *What Might Have Been. The Story of a Social War* (1907)

D K Broster, *From the Abyss. Weird Fiction, 1907–1940*

John Buchan, *The Runagates Club* (1928)

John Buchan, *The Gap in the Curtain* (1932)

Melissa Edmundson (ed.), *Women's Weird. Strange Stories by Women, 1890–1940*

Melissa Edmundson (ed.), *Women's Weird 2. More Strange Stories by Women, 1891–1937*

Zelda Fitzgerald, *Save Me The Waltz* (1932)

Marjorie Grant, *Latchkey Ladies* (1921)

Inez Holden, *Blitz Writing. Night Shift & It Was Different At The Time* (1941 & 1943)

Inez Holden, *There's No Story There. Wartime Writing, 1944–1945*

Margaret Kennedy, *Where Stands A Wingèd Sentry* (1941)

Rose Macaulay, *Non-Combatants and Others. Writings Against War, 1916–1945*

Rose Macaulay, *Personal Pleasures. Essays on Enjoying Life* (1935)

Rose Macaulay, *Potterism. A Tragi-Farcical Tract* (1920)

Rose Macaulay, *What Not. A Prophetic Comedy* (1918)

James Machin (ed.) *British Weird. Selected Short Fiction, 1893–1937*

Vonda N McIntyre, *The Exile Waiting* (1975)

Elinor Mordaunt, *The Villa and The Vortex. Supernatural Stories, 1916–1924*

John Llewelyn Rhys, *England Is My Village, and The World Owes Me A Living* (1939 & 1941)

John Llewelyn Rhys, *The Flying Shadow* (1936)

Malcolm Saville, *Jane's Country Year* (1946)

Helen de Guerry Simpson, *The Outcast and The Rite. Stories of Landscape and Fear, 1925–1938*

Jane Oliver and Ann Stafford, *Business as Usual* (1933)

J Slauerhoff, *Adrift in the Middle Kingdom*, translated by David McKay (1934)

Amara Thornton and Katy Soar (eds), *Strange Relics. Stories of Archaeology and the Supernatural, 1895–1954*

Elizabeth von Arnim, *The Caravaners* (1909)

Sylvia Townsend Warner, *Kingdoms of Elfin* (1977)

Sylvia Townsend Warner, *Of Cats and Elfins. Short Tales and Fantasies* (1927–1976)

Sylvia Townsend Warner, *T H White. A Biography* (1967)

My Life and I

Confessions of an Unliberated Housewife, 1966–1980

by Betty Bendell

with an introduction by Kate Macdonald

Handheld Classic 33

This edition published in 2023 by Handheld Press
72 Warminster Road, Bath BA2 6RU, United Kingdom.
www.handheldpress.co.uk

ISBN 978-1-912766-70-3

1 2 3 4 5 6 7 8 9 0

Series design by Nadja Guggi and typeset in Adobe Caslon Pro
and Open Sans.

Printed and bound in Great Britain by Short Run Press, Exeter.

Contents

Acknowledgements

Kate Macdonald would like to thank Anna and Richard Tjepkema for all their help in sending copies of published magazine and newspaper articles from Betty's private archive, and for information about Betty's life. Much of the information about Betty's career in the Introduction comes from an interview Richard filmed with her in 1996. Thanks are also due to Stella Collins and her sister for their early work in researching the artwork of Belinda Lyon.

Kate Macdonald is a literary historian and publisher, and has published scholarly research on Victorian and First World War periodicals. She is a visiting research fellow at the Oxford International Centre for Publishing at Oxford Brookes University.

Introduction

KATE MACDONALD

I am a child of *Good Housekeeping* magazine, from the generation of British children who grew up in the 1960s and 1970s. As a little girl I was too young to understand why my mother and her friends dressed differently from my teachers and old ladies in the city we lived in. But I studied the advertisements for clothes, shoes and household appliances in my mother's magazines, absorbing the coded messages about how women should live, and what they could wear. My mother liked to reread old magazines, and resolutely kept her collection of fashion magazines for years on shelves in the downstairs cupboard that I would often raid and read until I left home for university.

Vogue was an alluring fairy-tale treat, but it was expensive, and rarely seen in our house. *Family Circle* would appear in phases for six months at a time and then disappear. I remember occasional sightings of *She*, a glamorous large-format women's magazine on strangely shiny paper. In times of magazine drought I had to make do with the features in the *Radio Times*, and its inexplicable adverts for dowdy clothes I could not imagine anyone actually wearing. But *Good Housekeeping* was our constant, the magazine my mother read for pleasure all her life. I was fascinated by the *GH* Look for a Lifestyle makeover feature, which supplied even more coded messages about how ordinary women could manage their busy lives and still wear high fashion and on-trend hairstyles, but my real reason for reading *GH* so addictively was Betty Bendell.

Betty Bendell wrote the My Life And I column for *GH* from 1968 to 1980. I grew up reading her stories about daily life with her family of four and her exuberantly recounted everyday accidents and embarrassments. The episodes she related were brief, occasionally charming and once or twice actually tear-jerkingly sad. But nearly always her columns were laugh-out-loud funny. She would reliably make me snort with laughter at a joke, a turn of phrase, at her unexpected verbal juxtapositions, at her comic timing. She had a glorious capacity to pull off the unexpected and the socially shocking that made me weep with laughter. When I was old enough to be interested in why and how her writing was so funny (for me, at least), I would try taking the jokes apart to see how she did it, studying her syntax and word choice. She taught me how self-deprecation worked, and how to draw back from socially unacceptable boasting with a pinprick and a pratfall. From her I learned what bathos and high farce looked like in practice, long before I discovered that Monty Python used the same techniques (at more or less the same time), and years before I learned the technical terms at university. She was simply a supremely funny writer, with an impeccable sense for when to stop and when to keep going.

✕

Betty Eileen Bendell was born in Wimbledon in south London on 28 September 1929. She joined the Women's Royal Naval Service after the Second World War, entering the Education section, and edited the WRNS section of the camp magazine, often writing all the articles under different names. She met her husband David Rapkins in Scotland, where they were both based. He was a Royal Navy photographer, and they married in 1957. They had two children, Anna and Daniel, and emigrated to Canada twice to be near David's family, for the second and last time in late 1975. Between these upheavals the family lived in Goring-on-Thames and in Henley, where George Harrison was a neighbour.

Betty wrote articles and helped with the editing of the county magazine *Oxfordshire Roundabout*. Her confidence in her writing was boosted in 1966 when she won a *Daily Telegraph* writing competition. She went on to write continuously for a range of magazines, including *Annabel, Woman, Homes and Gardens, The Lady, The Countryman* and *Heal's Fourposter Magazine*. But she was most well-known for her long series of articles in *Good Housekeeping* and *Family Circle*.

Betty met an editor of *Good Housekeeping* at a party who suggested that she submit some 'filler' articles. Betty bought a copy of *GH*, carefully counted the words needed, and sent in a sample article. *GH* requested some more fillers, and then Betty was invited to write a gardening column. After reading Betty's deadpan account of casually lifting up a dead tree from the front garden, GH decided that she 'simply could not help being funny'. Their readers were dissatisfied with the syndicated political satirist Art Buchwald writing the *GH* humour column, because he was a man and because he was American. (*GH* orginally began as an American magazine, and its separate British title was overseen by the American managing editor.) Betty was asked to supply six columns for 'My Life And I'. Since they didn't ask her to stop, she said, she carried on writing for *GH* for thirteen more years. At the peak of her career she was writing a regular column for three separate magazine publishers and her columns were syndicated in magazines around the world. Her British readership would also have known her from the women's monthly magazine *Family Circle*, where her columns, published between 1970 and 1977, were slightly racier, with a livelier reader in mind.

Betty's readers loved her: her column was regularly cited as a readers' favourite in the magazine, and she was reckoned to be one of the top five woman magazine writers of her day. Some of her columns were published in 1974 in a book, *Home and Dry*, but it was poorly advertised and vanished from sight. But on her emigration to Canada in 1977, Betty's magazine career changed direction. She continued to write for *GH* for a few more years, and her columns featured new episodes about the trials and fascinating details of settling into Canadian culture, but she was losing touch with her *GH* readers. British English and its idioms were changing. In the new era of punk, *The Hitchhiker's Guide to the Galaxy*, *Evita*, the return of food rationing (briefly) and strikes, when she wrote from Canada Betty was in danger of seeming no longer on top of the daily details of her readers' lives in Britain. Eventually *GH* ended the column.

Betty then worked as an editor for the Canadian Scouting Association and wrote for Canadian magazines, such as *Nature Canada*, *Canadian Geographic* and *Habitabec*. She was invited to write a regular column, 'Settling In', for the *Perth Courier*, which she did for 18 years. After retirement in 2012 (at the age of 83) her life filled up joyfully with writing, gardening, her writers' circle, country cottage life and grandchildren. Betty died in July 2021, three years after her husband David. They had been married for 61 years.

※

Humour produces an extremely personal response. I hope the columns in this collection of what I think is the best of Betty Bendell, from *GH* and other magazines, will delight and amuse readers. They have been chosen also for their value as social history, fashion history and their absolute embeddedness in the Britain of the late 1960s to 1980. They offer new perspectives on the lives of women of her time and class, with a different kind of approach – reportage and memoir rather than fiction – from that of the much earlier *Diary of a Provincial Lady* by E M Delafield (1930). Betty recorded her era from the perspective of a woman at home, a mother and a wife, and occasionally as an office worker. She was in the school playground, at the parties, in the garden, on holiday, in the shops, or queuing at the butcher's or in the supermarket. She went dancing, walking, picnicking, shopping (a lot), visited beauty salons and speculated wildly about the lives of her friends and neighbours. She learnt to drive (almost). She thought about applying to do a horticultural course, but was not encouraged by the thought of being called to work as a grave-digger.

She made her own clothes: one gloriously tragic column relates the process of making a garment perfectly by hand (incidentally showing later generations how home sewing, home tailoring even, was quite normal for this period), only to find that:

> On its padded hanger the finished coat looked like something out of *Vogue*. There was just one problem though. It looked ghastly on *me*. (157)

Betty spoke for anyone who has sewn an unwise choice of garment, describing the pride in good dressmaking done well mixed with the chagrin of being unable to wear the wretched thing.

But Betty was not a slave to her treadle sewing machine. Many of her columns refer to hunting for the perfect new outfit – classically Seventies Lurex, chiffon trousers, a cream leather coat, even a velvet suit – as an alternative to the tyranny of an old brown dress fit only for housework. She bought herself clothes to cheer herself up, to wear to the many, many parties she and her husband were invited to, or because she had realised that she had neglected her wardrobe for too long and needed sparkles and oomph again, possibly with a new lipstick or an exciting new hairstyle. Some of the sartorial details she tosses in as a casual aside are startlingly alien now, but were apparently routine to women of her generation:

> Now that I suppose most of us wear tights, we no longer have to face that moment of truth when, leaping up from a casual legs-crossed sitting position, we found that the back suspender on one leg had attached itself to the front suspender on the other. (71)

And the wigs! The instances of Betty buying and wearing wigs as a completely normal part of her personal wardrobe, without the imperative of religious observance that some other women would have had, remind us how glamorous the period could be, with its joyful embrace of artifice for the sheer pleasure of looking different and acting a part.

The parties she attended seem to have been so much *fun*.

Before marriage I did find that good old Chanel No 5 worked wonders. In fact at one party a young man followed me all evening on his knees, on the strength of it. (44)

I once went to a Christmas party in black stockings and a red dress. By some strange coincidence, the dress fitted me all over, the black stockings were in fashion and I was the star turn from the moment I inadvertently flung my Martini backwards into the fireplace. (19)

Sedate ladies in directoire knickers run themselves up chiffon culottes for her parties. Heavy men in local government leap into floral polo shirts. Harassed American fathers start clicking their fingers and making cha-cha noises as soon as they cross over the threshold.

I, not to be outdone, put on a pair of ear-rings like ceramic bathroom tiles and paint my toe-nails silver. ('You look as if a snail has crawled over your feet,' says Anna.) (21)

Somehow the presence of children in close attendance during the preparation for and even at the parties makes them seem jolly friends-and-family affairs rather than louche and sweaty. Readers may wonder why some things are not mentioned in these columns (homosexuality, say, or reports of domestic abuse), or why stories avoid subjects that might be contentious. She skates briefly over an unpleasant episode of sexual harassment by her landlord (251), and a threat of rape on a boat (216) in comic anecdotes, but the rarity of this subject in her vast output of published writing shows that it was not particularly desired by her magazine clients.

GH, and her other magazines, would have had guidelines for its writers, and avoidance of controversy would also have been pragmatic for a comic column. Betty never wrote about religion or politics, the two most contentious subjects in British life, and only once mentioned fox-hunting. She only mentioned class issues in terms of encountering posh people in her past life, never in the present. Betty and David as characters are classless and infinitely relatable inhabitants of Middle England, as *GH* wanted them to be.

Betty was skilled in almost all the domestic arts: sewing and cooking, also gardening, interior decoration, making do and mending and hoarding useful items. She craved colour to enliven her surroundings: a purple tea caddy and a green washing-up bowl, and up-to-the-minute tea-towels from Heals and other trendy London shops. She visited the Design Centre in London to source the right kind of lighting fixture, and was enraged when her local supplier borrowed her catalogue, ordered its stock for himself and flooded the local market, destroying the exclusivity of her advanced good taste. She wrote about aspiring to go to art galleries, though didn't describe what she saw there (possibly to avoid libel, or to avoid being seen as too elitist). She often mentions reading in bed (Iris Murdoch was her most-cited choice of author). Her passion for language is obvious throughout these columns, and sometimes she expresses this directly:

> Let us feel able to make full, confident use of such mellifluous words as mellifluous. And clew and cleat and clerestory. And possibly even plumose. Let us get as far away as possible from sentences such as:
>   'Er, well, I mean, like, you know.'
>   Let us not grope for words. Let us *plunge* with etymological assurance. (116)

Cinema was a background entertainment in her family life, as were radio and television: not described in detail, but indicated as part of a normal everyday life. She could have but never did mention programmes such as *The Eurovision Song Contest*, *The Archers*, *The Onedin Line* or *Top of the Pops*, which would have been completely familiar to her, but by not being specific about particular programmes she avoided endorsement: this also may have been a requirement by her client magazines. She doesn't completely avoid brand names, but they are rare sightings. Only once is she critical about popular entertainment: 'Have you ever watched Saturday evening television? Roll on Sunday.' (54)

Betty also never wrote about amateur theatricals, so these were presumably not part of her life. However she mines the drama in her everyday encounters with gusto, playing a part enthusiastically for the reader's entertainment. She palpitates with excitement when the most handsome upholsterer she has ever seen strides through her door, and is only brought back to reality by the beady-eyed remarks of her pre-teen daughter. (This episode shows that Betty clearly also had a good grounding in the idioms of Georgette Heyer.) She revels in mild flirtations at parties, recalls the attractions and terminal failings of past boyfriends, and writes a little warily, but proudly, about the advances younger women appear to make on her husband.

Her columns show her enthusiasm about her husband, as well as her exasperation. He may be handsome, kind, steady and reliable, with a tremendous moustache, but his quick fixes include hammering a nail into a hot-water pipe, and he once sent her a supremely tactless Valentine's Day card.

> One year, early in marriage, I received a card. 'Here is my heart ...' it said. Mistily I turned the page. '... Why don't you tear it out and eat it, you old vulture?' it went on.
> 'Look, I've said I'm sorry,' said my spouse an hour later, a heavily lived-through hour for all concerned. 'I honestly thought you'd laugh. Like you did when I bought you the rolling pin done up like a bunch of flowers.' (105)

Perhaps laughing was all you could do in the early 1970s, when the joke gift of a rolling-pin simply reflected the fact that a woman's work was expected to be in the home and unpaid.

It's quite extraordinary that the words 'feminism', 'feminist' and (women's) 'liberation' never appear in Betty's writing. She was writing when second-wave feminism was rising, *Spare Rib* magazine and Virago Press were established, and when the Sex

Discrimination Act was passed in the UK. She ignored, or avoided, mentioning these specific examples, even if their effects filtered through into more subtle acknowledgements of new feminist desires, undetected by the *GH* censors, or simply permitted, since they were so meek and mild. The most radical political gestures in Betty's writing referred to women's sexual freedom (although she also never mentions contraception). She frequently jokes about securing the attentions of devastatingly dishy men, but also remarks that she is not personally interested in taking a lover, suggesting that this was an accepted part of the social scenes she moved in, or at least talking about the possibility was.

Taking a job was also quite normal, and certainly more acceptable to admit in public, but it was much less normal in this period to keep working once you had children if your husband could support the family. Betty writes occasionally about office jobs she had before her children arrived, or once they were off her hands, but in most of her columns she is at home with the children, and naturally from time to time she longed to escape. On one occasion, when she devised complex ways to have a day out in London on her own, she ruefully anticipated that she would probably use that 'Me-time' to buy new wellies for her children. Pointing out that she chose to buy children's boots when she should have been enjoying herself was one of the ways Betty was careful to balance a feminist desire for freedom and self-expression with the expectations of her *GH* readership.

Betty's columns remind us of the sheer physical labour she expected to tackle just to keep her house in order. The details of her normal housework routine may be daunting for many readers: waxing floors weekly, cleaning carpets, paintwork, the oven and behind the boiler, the tyranny of dusting Venetian blinds, *always* doing the cooking for *all* the meals. Many columns begin with Betty musing with her hands in the washing-up, or while surveying all the housework that is yet to be done. She bought the new zingy green washing-up bowl to cheer herself and her kitchen up (and it was ruined by David using it for engine oil). In 1973 she realises the joys of a new vacuum cleaner, and how her life will be changed by getting a deep-freeze. (*GH* advertisers must have loved that issue, which represents Betty's closest flirtation with generic product endorsement.) She spends the minutes before the first guests at a party arrive by madly cleaning the radiators and lunging at cobwebs. Never mind that many of us have actually done some or all of this work: this is how she represented herself, an Everywoman, as The One Who Does The Cleaning.

Turning to the other permanences in her life, Betty's children are as much a presence in her columns as her husband. They are much-loved and their caustic responses to the hapless mother that Betty presented herself as are hugely entertaining. One of the delights of Betty's writing is that she refuses to be sentimental. In an early article for *Mother* magazine, she wrote about her eighteen-month-old son in quite startling terms. The juxtaposition of a toddler and the vocabulary of drunkenness make an unforgettable image: 'his rosy face leering at us through the bars of the cot ... wild laughter and boozy singing in the next room' (14). Was this what the readers of *Mother* expected? It certainly reads true to life, but in 1969, was this the kind of instruction that magazines for parents expected to promote? Betty does not seem to have written for them again.

Betty was clearly a devoted mother, but her loudly expressed relief on being able to escape the drudgery of the home on day trips to London, or even to have time to herself once her youngest began full-time school might read as heartless to those who have never been trapped in a house with toddlers. For the rest of us, we empathised, because Betty articulated what her readers would have been reproved for thinking. The drudgery of motherhood for her was solely its service element: the picking-up-after and the providing for, with endless picky food requirements as well as immediately sourcing nature project materials or making a complicated party dress in 24 hours. What Betty loved about motherhood comes through in her pride in how her children grow up, the interests and skills they develop, their successes and extraordinary clevernesses.

Betty was delightfully honest about her complete uninterest in sport, even when her children were competing. Her anxious observation of the 'little, slow-moving hump, still under the canvas long after the end of the obstacle race' (60) at Anna's school sports day is a perfectly timed moment of sympathy in a column battling with the hearty sporting ethos, for a child who is no good at sports but keeps at it doggedly.

This sympathy comes through again in a pair of articles that she and David wrote for the gloriously-named *Tail-Wagger Magazine* in the 1960s, about their daughter Anna's discovery and adoption of a baby fox. The humour is tamped down a touch, but their (or Betty's) control of narrative structure and economy with words is the same. What comes across in these articles is a Betty who responds with wonder and emotion to the miracle of finding a fox cub left abandoned after its mother's death and raising it with the good advice of neighbours and the vet. Betty was not a natural inhabitant of the wilder world: she loves her garden and their allotment, but she was not a hiker or a sailor or an explorer in environments more radical than a different kind of supermarket system. Yet the adventure of Chuckles the fox, who went away when he wanted to, and the delight of his return, produced some of the most moving paragraphs Betty wrote. She retreated after this onto safer ground, and focused her writing on laughing at the world and marvelling at civilisation as she knew it.

1 My Dollyrocking Days Are Over

Oxford Roundabout, October 1966

There comes a time in every woman's life when she flings open the door of her clothes closet and realises that it is crammed with a load of old rubbish. Men may curl their lip at this but consider for a moment what we are up against. It isn't just a matter of wear and tear. Or even of extra inches on the waistline. There is also the depressing fact that, as we get older, fashions get younger.

Well my moment of truth dawned the other day. I wouldn't say that I have reached *full-blown* maturity exactly. But I certainly won't be seen around in full skirts or puffed sleeves any more.

My daughter's dressing-up box benefited mightily that day. She couldn't believe her luck when I sadly tossed her a fabulously expensive crinoline petticoat, which alas, now makes me look like a Christmas tree. This was swiftly followed by a billowing red taffeta evening dress, worn once and saved for eight years just in case a formal invitation came my way again. If it ever does now I certainly won't be turning up in billowing taffeta. Armfuls of skirts, stoles and nameless sartorial misfits were carted away and I studied the result.

At least the wardrobe looked tidy. Austere, even. Now, I'm not one to go berserk over fashion, but even I could see that the remaining collection of clothes was pretty pitiful. The best that could be said of them was that they still fitted me and would see me through the housework.

I decided to tackle the problem scientifically. Two dresses to be cleaned. One coat to be dyed. Several hems to be hoisted. Pause for reassessment.

Just then a wedding invitation arrived – not just any merry old do in the backwoods, but a Courrèges bespattered London affair. The time had come to Buy A New Outfit.

After going into a huddle with the housekeeping accounts I decided that I might just get away with it. Towards the end of the month I could always do intricate culinary things with the odd breast of lamb. So much for financial backing.

The next step was to survey the current trends. And this is where I found myself up against it. Dipping into various glossy magazines I was amazed at the number of exceedingly leggy girls sprawling about in shaggy fur coats and stockings like hand-knitted totem poles. Mondrian prints seemed to crop up quite often too, but I would really rather hang these on the wall. My figure leans towards the pre-Raphaelite anyway.

Nevertheless, I trotted out to the shops and tried on a few outfits just to get into the swing of things. It became all too obvious that my dollyrocking days are over, but I refuse to think of myself as *matronly*. I even went so far as to rush up to a capable looking assistant and cry: 'I put myself entirely in your hands.' Unfortunately it wasn't her day for enthusiasm. Briefly frisking me with a pair of disenchanted eyes, she led me to the thin end of the rack and left me to choose between a draped crêpe with dickie front in Air Force blue and a wraparound cotton housedress in brooding shades of brown. I wouldn't be surprised if it bore a label saying 'Comfy for Mum', but I didn't wait to find out.

Sneaking off to the Mod end of the department I tried on a black and white PVC mac. Worn with a leather peaked cap I was immediately transformed from homespun to sinister.

Then I read that those beaded dresses from the Charleston era were being snapped up in second-hand clothes shops by the really avant garde. The trouble is they are a bit too much like the stuff I have only just managed to discard. Oh well, there's nothing else for it. I shall just have to take my daughter on one side and see if she will *lend* me something from her dressing-up box.

2   A Really Super Supermarket

Heal's Fourposter Magazine, June 1967

Recently, one of our village shops decided to go Self Service. Whoopee, I thought, progress at last, as I edged my way round squads of busy little men heaving display stands to and fro.

Of course I didn't expect it to be *quite* like its transatlantic counterpart and I fell to musing on our regular Saturday morning shopping sprees in Canada. Over there the first ingredient is space. This is something our high street lacks for a start. It was obviously built to accommodate two sedan chairs passing each other at a dignified canter.

But to return to Canadian shopping … as I say, the planners simply take a huge chunk of space and turn it into a car park. A car park so vast that if you don't take a bearing or leave a trail of pebbles you may never find your car again. Along one or two sides of this are the shops, carefully selected to include a bank, a restaurant, a hairdresser, a Woolworth's, a departmental store and a supermarket. You see the cunning of it – first you cash a cheque, then eat a meal to lull the senses, then a hairdo to lift the morale, then a few small purchases in Woolworth's as a sort of curtain raiser to the really big spending to come.

Sometimes the supermarket is so all-inclusive that they don't bother with the other shops. We had one like this near us. Just a few acres of car park in the middle of nowhere with this immense, gleaming cube in the middle. All made of glass it was, and fitted with a magical device which recorded the degree of sunshine so that, as the glass warmed up, *acres* of loosely woven curtain net glided across to filter the sun's glare.

As one approached, the doors swung open to a *wooing* sort of music. Now I know we have some worthy supermarkets over here these days but I have yet to find one where you can actually lose your nearest and dearest for hours at a time. This place was like that. They had a dear little cinema with continual cartoons, for parking one's children; a fair-sized snack bar for parking one's husband and miles and miles of shopping lanes to coast up and down. I used to sneak off into a quiet byway, scoot my trolley blissfully past blueberry pie and ice cream in twenty-eight flavours. Past chili con carne, pizza and chicken chow mein. Even HP sauce and English cheddar. Like world travel in microcosm it was.

Eventually I would pull myself together and collect food and family to make for one of the twenty or thirty or maybe even forty cash registers – one always marked Express for folk with five or less purchases – a good idea we don't seem to have caught onto over here yet.

We unload our food onto a conveyor belt and as it trundles off it is checked out by our cashier and packed into cartons by her two helpers. We either pick up a tab and scribble our address and hand it to the girl as we pay, or else we collect a large metal disc with a hook attached. If we take the first course we arrive home to find the cartons *waiting* on the porch. If we settle for the disc, which has a number on it, we go and find our car – if we can remember where we left it. We then hook the disc on our side window and, as we slowly cruise past the entrance, a young man calls out 'back or boot?' With incredible speed of thought we understand him to mean 'do you want your groceries loaded on the back seat or in the boot?' With equally incredible speed the young man has unhooked our disc, found our trolley with identical disc attached, and is loading us up – and we don't even have to stop the car!

To get back to our village high street, we now have our local supermarket. The other morning I gave it a whirl. The staff all stood around looking uneasy and wondering what to lean on. There were two shopping aisles all of 8 feet long. About three minutes later, when I got to the one lonely cash desk a row of dejected mums were all unloading simultaneously. The lady in the middle, (who may well have paid for my cornflakes) seemed ready first and, with a swan-like dive, the cashier swooped on the button marked Total. The cash door sprang open and caught her a very nasty blow on the forehead. Don't *ask* me why she had her forehead down there, or why, for that matter, she was on our side of the counter.

Somehow I don't think our village is quite ready for a really *Super* Supermarket.

3 Who Wants A Perfect Wife Anyway?

Good Housekeeping, August 1968

I have just wrapped my wedding anniversary present to my husband and hidden it under my side of the bed. I will thus be able to produce it tomorrow with the minimum of early morning effort. He will lie there all drowsy and suddenly – *whoosh* – a parcel will appear from thin air. I have even vacuum-cleaned under the bed so that the gift will not arrive in a cloud of fluff. I have secretly practised the required arm movements to achieve this feat of sleight of hand. My coordination early in the day is chancey.

He will be pleased with his new pyjamas. They are large without being gargantuan. I once saw 'Extra Large' on a label and, mindful of the constant ricochet of bursting buttons, brought home the roomiest nightwear ever to come off the production line. He was hurt. He is big, but not that big.

What manner of wife is this, you may ask, who plans tomorrow's presentation down to the last arm manoeuvre but who doesn't seem to have any idea of her husband's measurements? I would like to be able to say that I am all things to all men. (I would *love* to be able to say that.) In fact, I oscillate ineptly between wild enthusiasm and baffled despair.

I occasionally go to stay with an old schoolfriend. She is, quite categorically, *the* perfect housewife. She is well groomed, well organized and well adjusted. Her home sparkles. Her children are delightful. She does useful work in her community. She not only sews a fine seam, she makes her husband's overcoats!

She has a Kenwood mixer and makes use of *all* the attachments.

'Lemonade, anyone?' she says, popping a lemon into the mixer and pressing a switch.

'Works out at threepence a bottle,' says her husband smugly whilst we sit, a few seconds later, sipping the most refreshing squash ever tasted.

But I think I'm most impressed by the way she cleans her cooker. Not just a quick wipe round when she thinks of it. Oh no. She *unscrews* it daily. Right down to its frightful entrails. With a gleaming little silver screwdriver attached to the wall by a gleaming little silver clip,

I could go on and on about this friend. Suffice it to say that she can sit all evening at her knitting machine and still look sexy.

Now why can't I be like that? I do try, but no sooner am I launched on one project that everything else begins to pile up around me. The trouble is, that I am inclined to go to extremes.

If I decide to look glamorous I must become nothing less than a Marlene Dietrich, which takes time with my limited potential. And while I am upstairs doing lustrous things to my eyelids, the acres of Norwegian apple cake and miles of cheese straws I whipped up earlier in the day are slowly burning to a crisp in the kitchen. By the time I languorously trail down in my lamé, the inside of the oven looks like Wookey Hole Cave. It doesn't need a screwdriver. It needs a chisel.

When throwing a children's party I spend hours creating donkeys with detachable tails and treasure-hunts of unbelievable subtlety. (All the guests really want is an unlimited supply of potato crisps.)

While these preparations are going on the house becomes festooned with cobwebs. We live in one of those old places full of character and dark places and our spiders are workers. So, mustering a great surge of energy, I tear round the house doing arabesques with mop and duster.

'Right,' I think, staggering kitchenwards. 'Now to bake the birthday cake.' And do you know, there are even spiders' webs in the oven!

I used to say it was unlucky to kill spiders and would make endless trips outdoors with my gingerly outstretched dustpan. Now, keeping my fingers crossed, I track them down with a mallet.

Recently I did discover one splendid household hint which I gladly pass on to others struggling towards perfection. Namely, that if the floors throughout the house are kept really clean and shining, then everything else (except me) looks better. For weeks now I have been down on my knees applying layers of liquid wax and polish. The floors look lovely. The only snag is that for the next few weeks all my time is going to be taken up getting my knees back into shape.

Never mind. Tomorrow is my ninth wedding anniversary and somehow or other I must get the place tidied up a bit, cope with the children, prepare an extra special dinner, make myself a long knee-enveloping evening skirt, chase a few cobwebs and finish up looking like Marlene Dietrich.

With nine years of experience behind me, it ought to be easy. But I am not over-confident.

4 Let's All Be Individualists

My Life And I, *Good Housekeeping*, October 1968

In the days when burnt orange meant failed marmalade rather than a colour we all seem to have in our living-rooms, I set out to buy new stair carpet.

All over Britain people were treading their turkey-red or leafy-brown staircases. I wanted to be different.

'I know,' I said, 'We'll have olive green. It will be a breakthrough.'

Painstakingly I went around the shops describing the colour in terms of US Army officers' uniforms. 'A kind of *brownish* green,' I would say with an encouraging smile. So the assistant would dart off behind some kind of private arras, and I would hear my request repeated to the accompaniment of hearty laughter and long pauses.

Then a much senior man would drift out. 'Do you mean *brown*, Madam, or *green*?' he would say, enunciating with precision.

Eventually we tracked down something which sounded right and which had to be specially ordered. It turned out to be dark moss, but at least our stairs were different for a while. Then, suddenly, all over the country, shops were flooded with a complete range of moss-to-olive-green carpeting.

The last straw came when the baker peered knowingly over my shoulder and said 'I see you've got the same stair carpet as your friend next door!'

I don't really get *peevish* about this sort of thing but my goodwill did wear a trifle thin over the wall-light incident.

Finding nothing but individual candle sconces locally I headed for the Design Centre, found a rather unusual lighting fixture, and sent away to the manufacturers for details. Then I ordered it through our local shop.

When I went to collect it the shopkeeper was looking pleased with himself. He liked it so much, he said, that he had ordered several dozen. His window was crammed full of them. All exactly the same as mine. Oh, and by the way, could he keep my catalogue please?

Nowadays, various children and pets later, I don't worry so much about these things. The burnt-orange overtones in our living-room carpet mostly *are* marmalade and the stair carpet is lumpy with secreted Lego bricks.

Children, of course, are deeply suspicious of anything which makes them the least bit different from their contemporaries.

'But I've *got* to wear knee-length socks,' they say. 'Everyone in our class wears them.'

And they fling aside several pairs of rotten old new tights and umpteen snowy white socks which, despicably, reach no further than mid-calf.

I met a thoroughly hounded school mum the other day.

'It's my seven-year-old,' she burst out. 'She got black patent tee-strap shoes, and brown leather sandals, and red ballet slippers and a pair of those Dr Scholl wooden things. All absolutely unworn. Apparently you're just *nobody* at the moment if you aren't slopping around in rubber flip-flaps.'

There is little point in explaining flip-flaps. Like French skipping, the craze has either swept through your neighbourhood, or it hasn't.

But once we begin to grow up, there is a certain *panache* in cultivating some slight streak of individuality, if it is only a case of switching to green ink for writing our thank you letters. Or even, these days, of just *writing* them.

Personally, I love to meet unusual people. The lady in the floppy Leghorn hat who *knows* that she is really Charlotte

Bronte; the motherly soul who always keeps matches in the tin marked Prunes, 'for safety, dear'; the racy one who flings open her cocktail cabinet and says 'Would you rather have Tizer or my own potato sherry?' (Give the wrong answer and you join the other reeling guests.)

I especially like the lady who said to me the other day, 'Do you take lovers?' She wasn't actually offering me them one at a time – like a sugar-lump – but she said it in exactly the same conversational tone.

So let's all make life more interesting for everybody by lining our curtains with purple satin. Or by wearing a feather boa round the house. (We can always dust things with the end of it.) Or by taking playful karate lunges at the postman.

When people say, 'Which one is Mary Brown?', let the reply be 'Oh, she's the brunette who's so good at playing the comb and paper,' or perhaps 'The blonde who does taxidermy in her greenhouse.' Even, 'That redhead who knits her own dishcloths.'

As for me, well I'm way ahead at the moment because there's a fox asleep in our living-room.

But that's another story.

5   Life In Daniel's Den

Mother, November 1968

Lately, the awful truth has been dawning away at the back of my mind. There are gentle, sensitive children and there are others. And I am pretty sure my sixteen-month-old son Daniel is flexing himself in readiness to become one of the others.

For the first few months he lay around flashing the odd tooth and guzzling food and drink to excess. Once his co-ordination was up to it, he unpicked and ate the lining of his pram as a curtain-raiser, and then practised acrobatic tactics on his harness. Many is the time we've peeped fondly out of the kitchen window, to find him standing there on the lawn in his bootees, suspended from the pram by one hook, in a nonchalant, semi-detached way.

When he was about nine months, a friend gave us a baby-stroller, a sort of canvas bucket seat in a metal frame on wheels. It seemed a good idea at the time, but Daniel soon discovered its potential and spent most of the summer strolling round the garden eating roses.

Then we acquired a playpen. Peace at last, I thought, as I put my feet up. With a ripple of milk-fed muscle, Daniel tucked the thing under his arm and lurched off to twiddle the Light Programme into obscurity, eat a couple of cigarettes and probe deeply into the cat's ear with a ball-point pen.

Gradually, over the next few months, our living-room changed from a dog-eared, but cosy flopping-out place for all the family, into a big, bare adventure playground. We didn't actually put down asphalt, but we did find it necessary to remove the carpet and replace it with easily-wiped tiles. I don't like our particular choice of tiles much, but perhaps it is just as well, because no amount of wiping ever catches up with all the thickly-spread substances and dragged furniture marks they have to contend with when Daniel plays.

At about twelve months our son developed two other characteristics which didn't exactly help me in the gentle art of child-raising. One was the continual removal of all clothing attached to the lower half of his person and the other was his decision to do without sleep.

No matter how early or late we crept into the nursery, there was his rosy face leering at us through the bars of the cot.

After lunch he would spend a comparatively quiet hour or so back in his cot trying to figure out how to let the side down and make a quick get-away. Some time ago I noticed that he was watching me intently as I slid the two metal catches into place. I've outwitted him so far by waving teddy-bears about and clicking the thing into position at great speed when he is looking the other way – but it's only a matter of time.

At present we do know where he is once he is bedded down – although often at night we are awakened in the small hours by wild laughter and boozy singing in the next room.

'At least he's a *cheerful* little chap,' says my husband, who sees him only briefly at breakfast-time on weekdays. But he has to agree, as weekends draw to a close, that cheerfulness isn't everything.

Have you ever settled down to a peaceful Sunday crossword puzzle, closed your eyes for a moment of deep thought, and opened them to find that the crossword has been torn out and *eaten*?

Have you ever found a plate of bread and butter under the hearthrug?

Or had a loaded ashtray emptied into your handbag? Or discovered all your family's toothbrushes down the lavatory?

'Never mind,' says my husband. 'At least it shows an alert, original mind. Perhaps he's going to be a genius.'

Back at work, however, he is subjected to enthusiastic stories from a colleague with a ten-month-old who already speaks in *sentences*.

'Come on, say dad-dad,' we coax.

'Bye-bye,' says Daniel.

'No, *dad-dad*,' we stress.

'Mum-mum,' says our genius decisively, before shunting off outside to eat the cat's dinner.

Bath time comes round and in he goes clutching boats, beakers and, as an afterthought, the bathmat.

'Let *go*, Daniel,' I pant, but the bathmat is definitely in by now, so there seems little point in rescuing it. Instead, I make unsuccessful attempts to remove cement-hard cereal from various nooks and crannies on his person. Meanwhile, the beakers are coming into their own. Daniel is bailing out!

His grandmother pops in to share the bathtime fun, but retires hastily with a lapful of bathwater.

Just think, we sigh, as we flop down damply in our sad relic of a living-room, soon he'll be eighteen months old – and *that*, I am told, is when the fun *really* begins.

6 At A Disadvantage

My Life And I, *Good Housekeeping*, November 1968

I was peacefully potting up geraniums the other day when I found myself needing more broken crocks for drainage purposes. Seizing a cracked flowerpot I rushed outside and dashed it to the ground.

I suddenly became aware that my husband and two other men were watching me guardedly.

'Need more crocks,' I jabbered, 'for pots, you see.'

It didn't help the situation. They all moved off down the garden talking loudly about chicken-wire.

One of these men, a handsome, inscrutable type, has dropped in on three occasions since then to discuss community matters. The discussions have all been conducted in the friendliest possible way but I am left with an uneasy feeling that he sees me as some kind of nut. The first time he knocked at our door I was under the dining-room table in mortal coil with the vacuum cleaner. The second visit found me swathed in my *muu-muu* and reading a seed catalogue out loud, *quite violently*, to my husband. (One has to stress things rather to husbands, to capture even minimal attention sometimes.) During his third visit I just happened to be running from room to room trying to trace a mysterious clicking noise.

'Can't you hear it?' I puffed, as I sped past him. He is a polite man. He turned and studied our bookcase in a fairly rapt way. At that moment the clicking stopped and it didn't seem worth going into lengthy explanations.

There are mornings when I awake cool and refreshed – could there be more *oxygen* around on those mornings?

These are the times when I not only do the housework in my false eyelashes but I actually get them on straight. Even my dusters seem cleaner and more golden on these mornings. (You should see them on my off-days.)

'If only …' I think, as I toss crisp, hardly worn things into the washing-machine … 'if only people would drop in today!' But of course, as we all know to our cost, they never do.

No. They come on onion-pickling day when my face is all runny. Or when I am reluctantly trying out those really terrible slippers someone sent for my birthday.

I wouldn't mind so much if they *sometimes* caught me at a disadvantage. Even quite shining housewives have been known to cry, 'My God, it's them already!' as we stand, like bollards, on the other sides of their front doors.

But it does seem hard that, for me, there are people who *always* arrive when our place looks like The House of Usher. For that matter there is a brother-in-law who comes to see us sometimes and *each time* he drops in we are having steak and kidney pie for dinner. We don't have it very often and he comes only rarely, but the two events invariably coincide.

'I like this one even better than the last one, he says with commendable tact, but I get the impression that he feels a bit sorry for my husband.

The other day some friends said to me: 'Come on, climb into your mac and come into town with us.'

It must have been a good day for baby-minders because the next thing I knew, I was sitting, all unencumbered, on the 10.15 to Paddington.

I don't know about you, but in our house there is usually a great deal of dashing to and fro with hair-rollers and shoe-brushes and newly ironed blouses the night before A Day Out.

On this particular morning, pleased as I was to be making unexpected whoopee, I was sadly aware that it was one of my wrinkled, *frizzy* days.

We must pause here and cast our thoughts back to the distant past when I used to think it was *fun* to sit on newspapers in the gallery of the Albert Hall at Prom time. Not only was I fairly desperate about Beethoven, but there was this smouldering boy-friend – a sort of Alan Badel at his most Proud and Prejudiced. (Oh, the pinched nostrils. Oh, the heavy-lidded eyes.)

We now return to the wispy-haired, London-bound present, because this was the day I bumped into the same boy-friend (who looked *even better* than I remembered him). And oh, my dears, he stared thoughtfully over his shoulder, shook his head sadly and walked away.

I told someone about this and she had a similar, sad story to tell. Her 'old-smoulderer' turned up one day and she invited him in. Just as they sat down together a great blob of marmalade slid down from her hair and landed in his coffee cup.

I would like to think that perhaps, just once, even Helen of Troy stepped backwards into a bucket of paste. Or that Don Juan leapt passionately over a balcony and landed in something nasty.

It would only be *fair*.

7 Party Time Is Here Again

My Life And I, *Good Housekeeping*, December 1968

I once went to a Christmas party in black stockings and a red dress. By some strange coincidence, the dress fitted me all over, the black stockings were in fashion and I was the star turn from the moment I inadvertently flung my Martini backwards into the fireplace.

'By heavens,' said an intense-looking male guest to our host, 'I've always wanted to meet a girl like that!'

Interpreting this as praise, I went from strength to strength and I do believe I ended the evening on a table top doing some sort of impromptu tap dance to Ravel's *Bolero*.

I never saw the intense guest again, which was probably just as well, because, who knows, perhaps we would have married and I would have been doomed to a life of dancing on table tops.

When we are single there is always the faint hope that we will go to parties and be confronted by one of the Richard Burtons of this world. With any luck he will begin to breathe heavily the moment we enter the room and, from then on, life will be a row of asterisks, to say the least.

But once we are married, we haven't *time* for all that heavy breathing even supposing we do intercept the odd morale-boosting mating call.

And what's the use anyway?

These days most of my panting is from sheer exhaustion and all my energy is directed toward making baby-sitting arrangements. False eyelashes are dabbed on recklessly at the last moment, beads are lassoed into position, and we are off.

Usually I prance into parties and am immediately trapped by a lady who thinks that I am somebody else.

'My dear, I saw you in your sloop on Saturday,' she screams.

'Oh, that old thing,' I murmur with a deprecating laugh. What *can* she mean, I am wondering wildly. The conversation veers off but the new tack is no less bewildering.

'Wasn't it terrible about poor Ethel?' We all shake our heads sadly and then I am pounced upon by an elderly guest who insists that I hear about her leg. Eventually it is time to go home and I know *all* about her leg.

Meanwhile my husband has inadvertently flung his Martini at someone's *au pair* who has come as Pola Negri and who can't possibly be as decadent as she looks. At least I hope she can't.

Our own parties tend to be family affairs. Nothing very racy happens unless you include ancient aunts who mistake the advocaat for custard and have to be helped upstairs.

Every year I incorporate several shillings-worth of mistletoe into the décor and I wait around for something *pagan* to happen but it never does. Not to me anyway.

I used to make quite ornate rings to hang in the hall but, while everyone else frolicked about under them, I would be trudging off to put away coats or to stir things in the kitchen. Even supposing I am ever tracked down out there, it is hard to scintillate over rapidly thickening white sauce.

And anyway there are too many children about at Christmas and they *watch* you, intently, the moment you flirt even the tiniest bit.

'Mummy, why are you laughing so much,' they pipe up, 'you look silly.'

One friend of mine throws super parties and seems to have an unlimited assortment of bunk beds for visiting children. This last fact alone would give her a high friendship rating but she also has a way with her which brings out the best in her guests.

Sedate ladies in directoire knickers run themselves up chiffon culottes for her parties. Heavy men in local government leap into floral polo shirts. Harassed American fathers start clicking their fingers and making cha-cha noises as soon as they cross over the threshold.

I, not to be outdone, put on a pair of ear-rings like ceramic bathroom tiles and paint my toe-nails silver. ('You look as if a snail has crawled over your feet,' says Anna.)

My dress is an African print with strange African sentences incorporated into the design. And the first person I meet *is* an African, who *reads* my dress and stands in a doorway, shaking with laughter for the rest of the evening.

Never mind. It is a marvellous party. But I do hope the message I am wearing is something really witty – and not just an advert for Congolese custard powder.

As you can tell, my confidence is not what it was in those distant days of dancing on table tops.

8 There Is A Verb To Chine

My Life And I, *Good Housekeeping*, January 1969

'My mother always makes her own brawn,' said my husband warmly as I stood staring down into the old, slitty eye of half a pig's head. 'There are limits,' I said, and I went out and bought a quarter of a pound, ready made, for ninepence. It was good brawn, which was a narrow escape for me because I am the sort who can't even handle pigs' trotters without feeling I am actually shaking hands with the pig.

Somehow or other, in my formative years, I didn't have much opportunity to study meat cookery. In fact, the only cookery book I took with me into marriage was a floury little wartime primer full of clever things to do with those flavourless economy rissoles.

In my naive way I asked a butcher once why he didn't put labels on the various joints so that inexperienced wives would know flank from silverside. I think I picked the wrong man because he became quite threatening with his cleaver and a whole shopful of housewives turned and curled their lips at me in unison while I backed nervously out into the street.

After that I became furtive on the subject and would point airily at pieces of beef, or lamb, or, quite possibly, pork, and take them home and hope for the best. This made mealtimes something of a surprise for all concerned.

In those days I always seemed to stand behind someone who was knowledgeably ordering things like a hand and spring, or loudly demanding a saddle. I felt very inferior. And I was amazed to learn that there is a verb to chine. I had always thought the word was a noun found along the cliffs at Bournemouth.

In desperation I went to a lecture given by a local butcher and made copious notes as he held great livers aloft like boxing gloves. But I wasn't really at ease about meat cookery and when we found ourselves for a time in Canada, my husband joined the local hunting set. It was *agony* to open the refrigerator and be confronted by the latest bag of fur and feather, lolling there waiting to be stripped and dealt with.

One English lady used to buy whole cows to last the winter, which is where freezers really come into their own. 'How do you divide it up?' I asked, peering down into the vaporous depths. How, I wondered, does one select a joint from so much solid flesh?

'Well actually,' she said, blushing, 'we just chip bits off as we need them and hope for the best.'

Things gradually sorted themselves out with the aid of cookery books, particularly the ones containing pictures of browsing cattle with discreet little arrows showing exactly where the unsuspecting beast carried his sirloin.

Fish I found relatively easy to cope with. I can even catch them sometimes if someone else will bait my hook. But then one doesn't feel personally involved with a fish. Buying them is fairly simple, too. You choose the one with the brightest eyes (like puppies). If it also happens to wag its tail, so much the fresher.

Of course, I've had my setbacks. I did get rather carried away with herbs at one stage, and many's the meat loaf we've eaten that smelled like a poultice. And too much thyme on the pork chops can get rather gritty. ('I still don't think that *was* thyme,' says my husband, darkly.)

Then there was that moment of truth when I flung aside a one and threepenny tin of oxtail soup and resolved to economize by making my own. 'I'll have to order them specially,' the butcher pointed out.

'Make it two,' I said, in ringing tones. I was *terribly* enthusiastic about the idea. I still think there was a mix-up somewhere. Could they really have cost me sixteen shillings?

Big, brown earthenware pots have given a picturesque quality to my efforts and I can get quite worked up these days as I mull over my moussaka. But I do still have my blind spots. Skinning a tongue is one of them. There is also a terribly macabre little paragraph in one of my cookery books which says 'Soak half a calf's brain in water till all blood is removed. Take the skin off gently plus any fibres.'

Gently! Ye gods, I have to take a couple of aspirin before I can even read about it.

And the very first Arab who sits down opposite me at a dinner party and deems it a compliment to lob me a sheep's eye will see me running out into the night, screaming my head off.

9 The Girl With A Fox

Tail-Wagger Magazine, March 1969

Other people have stray cats or dogs follow them home but with my daughter Anna it isn't that simple. Last week it was three of the saddest donkeys I've ever seen, stringing along behind her elbow as we strolled in the New Forest. Only a fairly hefty five-barred gate prevented them, I am sure, from climbing into the back of the car with us. Low-voiced, she whispered her farewells into big receptive ears. A sort of donkey Esperanto passed between them – the kind of language that comes easily to a small, serious girl of seven who loves animals.

Our cat will come and lean against me at mealtimes, but Anna is the one he really loves, the one whose bed he sleeps on when I pretend I haven't really noticed, or hides under when his popularity is at a low ebb.

Horses take to her, and big, slow Jess, the retriever next door, pads along beside her when we go to the shops. Even tiddlers seem to leap willingly into her fishing-net on soggy, streamside afternoons, and I've got used to doing without my other washing-up bowl now that it has become a makeshift pond for various jerky little water creatures.

So I wasn't really surprised when a baby fox cub lurched up to her and sat barking beseechingly on her foot. We were out for a walk on a nearby hillside and I, who had expected to come back with a few wild flowers, had not thought that we would gather up a tiny, mysterious bundle of abandoned earth-grey fur.

Gingerly we picked it up. It was about three or four weeks old, a bit muddy and very nearly ready to give up the unequal struggle for survival. Looking anxiously round, I caught sight of a woman pegging out washing in the valley below us. We weren't too sure if he was a fox or a puppy so we called to the woman to see if anyone was likely to claim him.

She didn't know anything about it. She sounded exasperated. It had kept them all awake, she said, crying through the night – out on the hillside.

So we headed for home with Foxy held close to my daughter's anorak. A man cutting grass looked up and his eyes focused sharply.

'It seems that we have found a fox,' I said with a light laugh.

'It seems you have indeed,' he said with a great guffaw.

At seven you are content to have a baby fox cradled in your arms. It is warm and you are full of love and life unrolls before you without complications. But I foresaw all kinds of difficulties. It had been out all night so it was probably an orphan. We had passed cartridge shells on our walk. We subsequently discovered that the Hunt had caught its mother. So the first problem was food.

A neighbour who bred dogs provided us with milk powder and cereal. We added fresh yolk of egg and my neighbour unhesitatingly cut one finger from her rubber washing-up gloves, pierced a hole in the tip and stretched the open end over a tablespoon. In this way we had a rough and ready feeding apparatus which, with several willing hands to help, worked quite well. Straw was fetched and, all unknowingly, my husband sacrificed a thick woollen pullover which was warm for foxes but of a rather hideous design for husbands. Feeding would be necessary at two-hourly intervals. Children, fox lovers one and all it seemed, materialised from all directions and formed fairly orderly queues down by our shed. Eventually we said no more visitors, my daughter went reluctantly to bed and my husband came home and found out about his pullover. Luckily he too turned out to have a soft spot for foxes. At eleven pm, with a torch held under my chin, I gave Foxy his last feed of the day and we all went to bed.

It was an awful night. The fox-cub, curled up in his pullover cocoon, didn't utter a sound but for the rest of us it was a restless time of wondering. Was he warm enough? Should we go down and feed him again? Would he still be alive in the morning?

At five-thirty am Anna was out in dressing-gown and gum boots. 'Mummy, it's still breathing.' What a relief.

At six-thirty my husband was mixing Foxy's breakfast and the house began to echo with the rubbery rustlings of many wellington boots.

I am not renowned for my early rising but soon I too am peering sleepily into the shed. The air smells very foxy. The pullover will never be the same. But the tiny creature is alive and two misty grey eyes peer up at me from above the long, delicate snout.

Sometimes, when my husband leaves for work, I ask him to bring home little exotic extras from the market: mushrooms perhaps or a couple of green peppers. Today it is different.

'Don't forget the flea powder,' I call from the porch.

The word soon get around in village communities.

'There goes the girl with a fox,' whispers a small boy and Anna walks tall in the village High Street.

I make telephone calls to various people who know about foxes and my daughter pulls off quite a good business deal – a bale of straw for half a crown. Granny sends a postal order – she is another unexpected fox lover – and we start thinking of a good name for him. It is a dog fox so we reluctantly reject 'Foxglove'. I am not wildly enthusiastic about 'Fluff' which seems to be the children's current favourite. Perhaps we shall just stick to Foxy for now.

Henry, our tabby hearthrug of a cat is prowling around today like a puma. There are people with chickens at the end of the road and a lady opposite who is afraid that someone will get bitten.

In the kitchen Anna is painstakingly mixing the rich milk formula and Foxy stands waiting outside on tiny, trembly legs. Perhaps it will all work out. I hope so. It is a wonderful thing to be seven years old and to have a baby fox to care for.

10 The Fox Grows Up

Tail-Wagger Magazine, April 1969

For the first week after the arrival of Anna's fox cub we frequently turned to our friend-and-neighbour Terry, for help and advice. She would come and squat calmly under an apple tree with the wriggly cub wrapped in an old towel, held firmly in her arms, while we fed him. He was a messy eater in the early stages due mainly to our inexperience. In fact our mealtime procession down the garden consisted of Terry in an outsize striped apron followed by me with cup of food and an old towel and Anna, with warm waiter and cotton wool for mopping up operations.

As Anna squeezed out the cotton wool and rubbed it under his chin he would close his eyes and lean towards her chuckling, obviously remembering other washings from his mother's tongue. Because of these throaty, laughing sounds he made, she decided to call him Chuckles.

When she took his drinking water to the shed he would follow so closely to heel that sometimes she would search wildly round for him, not realizing his nose was literally pressed to the back of her white sock.

In less than a week he was lapping strongly from a saucer, cleaning his paws like a cat and tiptoeing delicately to a corner of the lawn to defecate.

'We have to put ourselves in the fox's place,' said Terry, when the subject of a bed came up. 'He'd be used to a deep, dark hole and to being nuzzled and kept warm by his brothers and sisters.'

For the first few days we had made do with a small cardboard box containing a handful of straw, a toy one-eared rabbit for company and my husband's pullover draped over the top. It was knitted from rough, oiled wool and Chuckles soon learned to roll himself right up in it. We hoped that to some extent it compensated for the lack of his mother.

During one fine weekend my husband cleared out the old shed in which Chuckles' bed was housed. It had an earth floor and was quite watertight but we thought he might like a big wooden box to sleep in, placed towards the back of the shed, with the bale of straw partially covering the entrance.

Alas, the box was spurned. Instead Chuckles tunnelled a labyrinth of holes and made himself a home underneath it. He had literally gone to earth.

After about a month with us we noticed that the sides of his snout were becoming pink and bald. Was it because of his burrowing, we wondered? Up to now he was grey-brown in colour and fluffy in texture, with a white tip to his tail. Our soil is chalky and is exactly the same grey-brown colour. We thought how cleverly nature had arranged for baby foxes' protection in this way and we still wonder if cubs in other areas, where the soil is different, are themselves redder or browner than ours was.

Gradually from mid-May onwards, a wonderful transition took place. First the bald patches grew soft, white fur. Then the grey eyes became golden and characteristically slanty. Day by day, a very little at a time, the coat turned faintly reddish brown and the tail grew more bushy until at last he was a true red fox with sleek black legs and ear tips.

We took him to the vet for inoculation where he caused a minor sensation in the waiting room, although he sat aloof in my husband's arms until our name was called. The vet told us to give him plenty of roughage (whole mice, chicken heads, etc) and not to chastise him in any way as foxes are basically always wild animals and could turn fierce if frightened.

'If he makes any angry huffing noise in his throat, hold the scruff of his neck and point his head downwards,' said the vet. 'This is the submissive position in the pack and he will instinctively become passive.' We hoped it wouldn't come to that but we had learned not to reach too close at mealtimes as he was quick to nip probing fingers. This was natural enough – even the tamest of domestic animals should be left to eat their meals undisturbed.

'I shouldn't have him in the home,' added the vet. This was a relief to me because Chuckles liked to make himself a temporary home on the shelf under our coffee table, shredding several magazines in the process.

We also learned that foxes need lots of playtime so we took it in turns to leap about on the lawn. Anna loved this and so did Chuckles. He would hide behind the lupins and then dash between her legs when she looked away. On fine days I would take a deckchair down by the shed and try to read while he scurried busily about, butting me, rolling down the compost heap or playing hide and seek among the rhubarb.

Gradually, as the summer progressed, he became bigger and more adventurous. My husband spent a small fortune on chicken wire and timber for a run but Chuckles viewed it with contempt, preferring to lurk in a neighbour's thick hedge when he didn't feel like company. He was growing up now and no doubt catching the scent of other foxes on the nearby hill.

In the early autumn we went away for a holiday, leaving Terry and her family in charge of Chuckles' meals and playtimes.

When we returned two weeks later, a sad little note informed us that Chuckles had disappeared soon after we left.

'Probably thinks that we are his pack and we've deserted him,' said my husband. Anna was heartbroken. Night after night she took tempting tit-bits down to the shed and called and called.

Then, late one evening, my husband, standing at the open kitchen door, noticed two glittering eyes zig-zagging silently across the lawn. He stood quite still. Slowly a dog-like shape approached. It was Chuckles.

'Come on old fellow,' said my husband but Chuckles backed away from the house. Quietly David followed him outside and once out on the lawn Chuckles began to romp and to play hide and seek.

I was called and we decided it was such a special occasion that Anna must be awakened and told the good news.

Chuckles often came back at nightfall after that but only on his own terms. Gradually, as he reached maturity, the visits tailed off but I shall always carry a vivid picture of a delighted little girl, in pyjamas and dressing gown, prancing on the lawn in a shaft of light from the kitchen window, with a mischievous, beautiful fox dancing silently at her heels.

11 The Problems Of Captivity

My Life and I, *Good Housekeeping*, June 1969

I was wandering about with a jar of dead caterpillars when the thought struck me. Nature has arranged things admirably for butterflies. They start life in a limited way – very limited if they take part in one of my daughter's nature study projects. But if they survive the early stages they at least end their lives in an intoxicating whirl of freedom.

With us it is different. We start adult life all free and fluttery, creep into the marital cocoon and emerge to find that life has become a rather cabbagey affair.

Motherhood does have its shining moments but there are stretches when it seems to be one long search for the other Wellington boot. The trouble with captivity is that it is insidious.

When our first baby arrived I used to turn up at dinner-parties, beaded purse in one hand and carry-cot in the other. With luck I even managed to sparkle for an hour or two, before sidling of into the room full of coats and whipping out a feeding bottle.

'Me – a housebound mum?' I would say looking coolly amused, 'Never! It's all in the mind.'

Then our second baby arrived and discovered that being sick over people was *fun*. And our firstborn didn't *want* to have a nap under a pile of coats. She wanted to come downstairs and do unspeakably coy party tricks.

At this stage I stopped being amused. The obvious answer was a baby-sitter, and I suppose there *are* people to whom this is not a problem. But usually, by the time I have fed, bathed and lectured the children, heaved myself into something glittery. scooped up several dozen toys, tweaked – no, tugged – the living-room back into shape and set out a modest repast for the baby-minder, I am too tired to go out anyway.

We captive wives often lurch into each other in the High Street and swop symptoms. You can safely assume you are one of us if you get a lot of mysterious, booming headaches, keep on wearing the same old trews and sweater, find yourself babytalking to the milkman, discover that you don't like your husband and or children much, cry easily at things on television or feel nostalgic about rush-hour travel.

One friend of mine is always dashing brightly about. How does she do it?

'My dear,' she sighed, 'If I get out *annually* to a dinner dance I'm lucky. All this whizzing about I do is connected with the children. No sooner have I delivered one to the Brownies, than I must collect another from choir practice and arrange swimming lessons for the third. I am too busy to feel bleak about it but my husband gets rather edgey at times.'

The other day I visited a friend with an exuberant family of four.

'Come in,' said a resigned voice, if you can *get* in.' I squeezed through a gap in the hedge of children, moved a half-finished bowl of cornflakes from a chair and sat down. The room had started life graciously but now the fruit bowl was piled high with medium-sized toys, the floor was strewn with large toys and the ash-trays were full of small toys. In the course of conversation I asked her about her social life. She stared at me with a cold glint in her eye.

In an effort to bring cheer I said: 'Never mind – nothing is permanent. They *are* lively children but eventually they will grow up and ....'

'Yes and the thought of all those lively grandchildren *really* finishes me off.'

It occurred to me that a generation ago most families came in dozens.

'Oh, yes,' said an elderly relative. 'I came from a family of ten. But then the older children coped with the new arrivals. Mother had quite a gay social life in between confinements. My eldest sister was the bossy one. She had us all lined up at bathtime and the ones with chickenpox went to the back of the queue!'

Today is one of my *very* shut-in days. Anna's room looks as if it has been hit by whirling dervishes. Daniel has done a rather progressive drawing on the living room wall. My husband has just hammered two four-inch nails through a hot-water pipe and our television set appears to have been invaded by French-speaking shadow boxers.

Never mind, I have made arrangements to escape one day next week. I shan't actually be throwing a rope ladder over the fence but the preliminary negotiations have been nearly as complicated.

Let me see now. Hand Daniel to baby-minder A. Sprint to catch 9.10. A passes D to baby-minder B at midday. Anna goes from school to neighbour T. Husband leaves work early and gathers up D from B and A from T. It *may* work.

Anyway, I intend to enjoy my day in London. I shall squeeze blissfully into tube trains, take big, *diesely* breaths and feast my eyes on Liberty prints and Heal's furniture. But I shall probably end up buying Wellingtons for the children.

12 In Search Of Non-Conformity

My Life and I, *Good Housekeeping*, October 1969

When I was very young my favourite character was a man who stood outside his house, wearing two hats and eating privet leaves.

It wasn't a case of 'like calling to like' which is just as well, perhaps, but I do rather admire the non-conformist approach to life. I yearn to stun my fellow man with my audacity but alas, for me, it just doesn't work.

Take clothes. To hazard a swift generalization I would say that there are three ways of being well dressed. Some let Courrèges or Chanel do their worrying for them. I did once meet a girl who let me *hold* her Hartnell evening dress while she wriggled out of her Dior, but that is the closest I have come to Haute Couture.

Then there are those matt, smoky blondes who glide about in hand-made shoes, cashmere sweaters and utterly unclumpy tweeds. Taking the cue from my friends, I try on meltingly soft coats and skirts but no matter how hard I glide I still look big and militantly respectable. However, it is the third group who really intrigue me. These are the beanpoles with *character*. The girls who look ravishing in boleros made from milk bottle tops. My best friend's like that – dashing, willowy *and* a mother of four. '*Of course* you must show off your legs,' she says as I stand there gazing gloomily down at my pouffe-shaped knees. So I hitch everything up and sprawl lasciviously all over her inflatable chairs and leather sofas and feel marvellous. But then I go home to my quiet little village.

It's a funny thing, but whenever dashing girl-friends come to stay with me everyone is enchanted to see them wandering about in mini-caftans or swinging *art nouveau* bell bottoms over the sides of their sports cars. But the moment I wander outside in my genuine Hawaiian muu-muu or my real Venetian gondolier's hat people start nudging each other and wiping their eyes. (Perhaps wearing them together is where I go wrong?) Right now I want to master current trends with my own individual interpretation of same, and still look sexy.

The other day, as I rattled through my coat hangers, I realized that something immediate would have to be done about my wardrobe. There were plenty of sad old dresses suitable for housework. There were even two or three floor-length gowns awaiting further sporadic outbursts of high life. But for the great assorted limbo in between the outlook was threadbare.

'Right,' I thought. 'Where's my cheque book? It's time for chains and leather fringing.'

Oh, I was a gift to the rag trade that morning. The first assistant I approached said: 'Well these wrap-around housedresses might suit you, madam, but my coffee's poured out so would you mind waiting?'

'What about this?' I said, pointing to the sort of swinging number we mums all subconsciously yearn for. 'Could I try it on meantime?'

'Well please yourself, dear,' she said. 'But it's hardly you, is it?'

This sort of thing happens to me all the time. I have even been known to track down a responsible-looking assistant and say: 'I place myself entirely in your hands.'

In old movies this approach never fails. With cool but friendly professionalism, the sales-lady changes our heroine from tweedy clumper into sequin-studded *houri* in half-an-hour.

In my case, they either squeeze into the changing-room and tell me the story of their lives (which I *quite* enjoy as long as the oxygen supply lasts), or else they lead me firmly to the bleak end of the rack. And I don't really see myself turning up at parties in vee-necked brown crêpe with a dickie front. My idea of a party is where the ladies, wearing the latest glittering gear, flit about being witty and faintly wanton, while the husbands perk up and cast sparky looks here and there. Several of my married friends keep their parties fizzing this way without the least sign of an orgy developing.

So I comb the local boutiques for something short and shiny to wear – with peep-through portholes even – although these are pretty thin on the ground in village High Streets.

Eventually, I find or make myself a dress with so many cut-out portholes that a large, aging, mid-European professor looms out of the pulsating party gloom and says with characteristic sledge-hammer logic: 'Yes, I *vill* sleep with you. Meed me oudside in ten minids,' or else I am confronted by a tiny, hopping-mad wife screaming: 'Put my husband down *at once.*'

Eventually, I suppose, my search for non-conformity will turn me into a sort of elderly eccentric. Swathed in milk bottle tops and little purple remnants I should just about be coming into my own by the time I am past caring. I may even be nibbling privet leaves by then.

13 Hairdressing Is A Gift

My Life and I, *Good Housekeeping*, November 1969

'All my head needs is a corn dolly,' said my husband, gazing gloomily into the mirror. 'A what?' I asked.

'You know, those things thatchers plait from straw and put up on cottage roofs as a sort of signature.'

'What made you think of thatching?' I asked, but then I looked at his hair and saw what he meant. There are still an awful lot of short-back-and-sides barbers about and while my spouse does not see himself as another Jimi Hendrix, neither does he fancy the sides of his head pruned down to a field of stubble.

So he keeps on coming home newly mown, letting it grow out and then hacking little bits off when they tickle his ears.

'Couldn't you have a go at it?' he said plaintively, but the last time I tried my hand at barbering my brother had to go to a party wearing a carefully arranged muffler. 'Hairdressing is a gift,' I said, peering over his shoulder at my own wayward locks. 'And even among the practising fraternity some are more gifted that others.'

I used to have easily managed hair, but over-enthusiastic back-combing has reduced the front to frizzle. In fact there is one tuft that zooms up off my forehead like permanently escaping steam. Hopelessly I smoothed it down. Back it twanged. Just then Anna came in. 'You look like a proper mum today,' she said, giving me a passing hug. 'Right, David,' I said. 'That settles it. You and I are going to arrange a day in town. We are going down to the King's Road and we are going to place our heads in the hands of someone good and *trendy*.'

I snatched up the Sunday paper. 'It says here that Annie Russell's is the place. Let's make an appointment *now*.'

So we went. On the way up in the train I thought about all the various hairdressers I've visited in my time. Although I do occasionally come home looking like a startled chrysanthemum I have to admit that hair has come a long way since those early days of corrugated waves and snail curls, thank goodness. A browse through my photograph album reveals that we had the poodle-cut phase, the page-boy look, the long horizontal sausage and a bizarre season when I was blonde from the front and brunette from the back. At one point, long hair became standard wear and I have some really terrible pictures of myself looking like a strangely immature High Court judge. Then, suddenly, hairdressing establishments whipped all those cardboard adverts out of their windows and ripped out their partitions. Young men climbed into satin shirts and Cockney accents and we all started having a high old time sitting, peeled into open plan, like rows of attentive space heroes, our eyes darting busily about beneath our helmets. I came away from one of the first of these, in Knightsbridge, with a beautifully shaped crown and the surprising discovery that beer rinses do not leave one smelling boozy. Since then I have worked my way through a wide variety of hairdressers, ranging from young mums who do it quite well at home for pin money to enthusiastic lads who make me stand up and walk about the salon. 'It's a question of balance,' they murmur. 'The overall picture must be just right.' I have had it straightened, blistered, glued down and fluffed up. I've come home looking like everything from Lionel Bart to a toffee apple.

Occasionally I have been so pleased that I've gone to bed and slept sitting up in case I might spoil the shape. I have even come home so different that my husband has ambled into the living-room, blushed and said 'Oh, er, hello. I thought it was my wife.' (Thank you Evansky's – *how* I enjoyed that.)

There have been sexy young men who stroke my scalp and croon to me in French. Then, just as I am going all heavy-lidded and gliding out of the door, they ruin everything by calling after me: 'Madam shouldn't let it grow as long as that again because Madam has a head like a football.'

Well, today we are all set to break new ground. Back-combed and thatched we wander through Chelsea in search of the celebrated Annie Russell's.

Presently we emerge from the marigold interior transformed. My husband has super little *flicky* bits. And I have gone *smooth*. Straight away I am given the eye by a man in a pink striped shirt while my husband gets the slow stare from three little dolly birds wearing fringed hammocks.

'Let's go and buy some gear while we're here.' David's smile is expansive.

Oh my, isn't life just great!

14 On The Scent

My Life and I, *Good Housekeeping*, December 1969

There is a very strange smell around the house this morning. It isn't absolutely unpleasant, just rather jolting. I have inspected the first-aid cupboard and sniffed along the shelf of cleaning materials but without solving the mystery.

Perhaps I should counteract it by having one last good drench with the carefully saved dregs of my Schiaparelli 'Shocking'. But it *is* rather early in the day and I don't want to stun the milkman.

It's a funny thing about scent, isn't it? On days when our eyes sink without trace into their sockets and our cheeks feel like old leather saddle-bags a dash of perfume can work wonders. So it is important that I cling to the last soupçon of Schiaparelli. It is as necessary as that little swig of three-star Martell we keep in the cupboard for emergencies.

As Christmas draws near I drop heavy hints to my spouse – who finds choosing my present a great trial.

'I like anything that smells nice,' I tell my family whenever the subject crops up. 'But perhaps not bath cubes this year.' Last year someone gave me some which refused to crumble. I remember them well – like little chunks of cement they were. Breeze blocks even. Frenziedly I would stand shivering over the bath, crashing them against each other and ducking as flinty bits flew off. When I finally lowered myself into the water it was like sitting on a pebbly beach. Most unsoothing.

'Any other bath-time things would make a nice Christmas present,' I tell the children. 'And perfume would be most welcome,' I add, swinging round and staring meaningfully at my husband. 'Have to get another tin of undercoat,' he mumbles, obviously under the impression that I am nagging him about the hall paintwork again. Oh well, I shall just have to leave messages around the house. It has been known to work.

I have a newspaper cutting somewhere, which lists various scents in order of popularity. While I am searching for it, Anna dashes past and the astringent, medicinal pong becomes stronger.

'Anna!' I call. 'Are you doing experiments in your bedroom again?' She is currently uncertain whether to be a scientist or a hairdresser when she grows up – which is why her bedroom is full of sinister crystallizing substances. It is also why most of her dolls are going bald, and I am down to one hair roller.

'No, Mum,' she says blithely. 'But I've got a super surprise for you for Christmas.'

'Oh good,' I reply absently. I have found the cutting and am studying the list.

Hermes 'Caléche', it seems, leads the jet set. I wonder what 'Caléche' means? I have stumbled through France several times but haven't really mastered the language. And let me tell you it's a bit of a strain being surrounded by all those Sacha Distels and having to limit my conversation to the search for the pen of my aunt.

I turn to my French dictionary. It is yellow with age, which is perhaps why 'caléche' is listed as meaning 'barouche'. There is also some sort of obsolete reference to 'drawers or pants'. Surely Hermes wouldn't invent a new, swinging perfume and name it after a horse-drawn carriage or, for that matter, call it 'Knickers'? I really must get a new French dictionary. And I can hardly wait now to track down a bottle of 'Caléche' to see what it smells like. I feel the need of a new, swinging image, and if horsedrawn knicker-type auras are in, well so be it.

There is a lot to be said for sticking to one perfume so that it becomes one's leit-motiv. But I've gone off leit-motivs since the day I wore a big black velvet hat and someone told me I looked the spitting image of Richard Wagner.

Before marriage I did find that good old Chanel No5 worked wonders. In fact at one party a young man followed me all evening on his knees, on the strength of it. However, I couldn't very well clutter the place up with prostrate swains once I was married so I turned to safer, flowery scents for a time.

Then, like most young mums, I reached the stage where one makes do with sharing the baby talc. But gradually, as domesticity closed in, I began to feel the need to boost my morale with little secret bars of good soap and an occasional extravaganza in the way of talcum powder.

Nowadays, such are the exigencies of family life, I have ceased to go into trauma when my children sprinkle 'Blue Grass' talc down the loo as I absently dust myself with 'Sanilav'. Nor do I rave unduly when my husband cleans off the car grease with Yardley's 'Sea Jade' while I am left holding the 'Swarfega'.

But I really do cling to my drop of perfume. It is absolutely essential, when all else fails, that I leave a little trail of magical mystery – even if I'm only dashing outside in a north-east wind to empty the boiler ash.

As I sit here thinking about it, tears come to my eyes. At first I imagine nostalgia is the cause but then I am aware of Anna dropping a parcel into my lap.

'I couldn't wait until Christmas Day, Mum. You've *got* to open your present now.'

Gasping (choking even) I open the package. And there within is a great big bag of the brightest emerald green bath salts I've ever clapped streaming eyes on.

'You do *like* the smell of pine, Mum, don't you?' she asks anxiously.

15 Pets

My Life and I, *Good Housekeeping*, January 1970

There is one member of our family who hasn't so far been introduced. I am not sure I want to even think about him at the moment but anyway his name is Henry and his recent behaviour has been quite despicable. No, he isn't an unmentionable relative. Henry is our cat and the reason he is in the doghouse is because we built a bird-table.

Not that I'm madly keen about birds either, actually. The sight of them tap-dancing along our fruit tree branches, pecking next season's plums into oblivion, does not enchant me. But on the other hand I don't like to see them seizing up in bad weather and thudding down like hailstones on to the lawn. Hence the need for a bird table.

While my husband lifted it into position the children and I gathered up bread, bacon and two reluctantly spared spoonfuls of Swiss *muesli* to get things off to a banqueting start.

'We can make lists of all the birds we see,' I said, to encourage any potential ornithologists in the family. Henry, as always in wintertime, lay spreadeagled on the boiler asleep.

'Now we must all stay indoors and give the birds a chance to pass the word around,' I said. We tiptoed inside and talked about all the robins and thrushes and blue-tits we could expect any minute now. Then we looked out.

And there was Henry, firmly established on the bird-table, having eaten every last speck of bird food – even the cereal. He stayed on duty until nightfall and has remained there daily, in all weathers, ever since.

Oh well, at least he is reasonably easy to get along with most of the time. Unlike some of our past pets.

There was the time one of our tropical fish leapt out of the aquarium just as we were entertaining visitors.

'Quick everybody,' we said. 'There's a live fish somewhere in this corner.' And we all clawed wildly at bookcases and sofas, dislodging a shame-making quantity of dust in the process. But we never did find it.

There was also the day we discovered that our zebra fish was eating the baby guppies as fast as they were being born. Fishlovers had better stop reading here because I have to confess that I flushed that beastly cannibal down the loo. Which gives rise to the nightmare thought that somewhere in a subterranean sewer a mean-looking striped fish grows bigger and ever bigger.

We rather wished we'd kept it later on because the guppies proliferated so rapidly we had to buy another tank and every child who so much as passed the gate had a jam-jar full pressed upon him.

Water snails, too, throve mightily. In no time at all two became twenty-eight. People aren't so keen to be given snails, so I used to stroll nonchalantly down to the river with yoghurt cartons full, once or twice a week.

Eventually we gave the whole lot to a local school and life became less fraught for a while.

Until the arrival of Sophie. We bought her as a companion for Anna and because we rather liked the idea of a dalmatian about the place. Anna was four at the time and went around telling everybody: 'We've got a damnation.'

As Sophie grew and her true character emerged we stopped correcting Anna. She knew what she meant. Alas, poor zany Sophie was eventually run over by a lorry and for a while we just had Henry, our great, tabby tea-cosy of a cat.

At this stage Anna started school and discovered that one of the teachers was breeding hooded rats and giving them away. Rats I can do without at the best of times but the thought of them being *hooded* hardly bears thinking about. Furthermore I am not absolutely sure that my daughter didn't say they were *scarlet* hooded rats. But perhaps this was just a figment of my over-inflammable imagination. It *must* be. Surely?

Having said no to rats, along came Chuckles, our fox. And I must say, of all the assorted livestock we've nurtured – from an incredibly long-lived minnow to a garden snail called Jennifer – Chuckles has my vote as the most beautiful, amusing and intelligent animal I've ever known.

True he did rip up magazines and make a lair with them under the coffee table. True he did need a daily diet of beak and claw. True he did take to the woods the day after we forked out £3 13s 4d for distemper injections and a further £5 for building materials to extend his living-quarters. Nevertheless he enriched our lives considerably and I hope he reaches a ripe old age somewhere out there in the Chilterns. ('At least he won't be going down with distemper,' says David.)

He stayed with us from the time he was three weeks old, mud-encrusted and near death from starvation, until he reached sleek, red-gold maturity. He severed his connections with us gradually, returning in the evenings for his regular 'playtime' until winter came. There were drawbacks, of course. People used to come at all hours 'to see the fox, please'. Sometimes they just blundered in and stood silently queueing in the hall until someone led them down the garden. And I blenched a bit the day the vet said: 'You can start giving him mice with the fur on now.' I hadn't exactly been *peeling* them before this.

One family, friends of ours from a neighbouring village, really deserved full marks for cooperation at this stage. The children, dedicated foxophiles one and all, used to steal mice from their cat. Their mother would then seal them tightly in individual polythene bags and store them in her deep freeze awaiting our arrival. I enjoyed the night we went to a party at their house. As we left, our hostess waved a bag of tiny, petrified bodies and called: 'Don't forget your mice.' Which is a pretty impressive exit line by any standards.

16 Living-Room Overhaul

My Life and I, *Good Housekeeping*, February 1970

I expect we have all experienced that moment of truth when guests arrive and exclaim 'What a pretty room!' and we all look up and *everybody's* eyes focus on the gigantic cobweb hanging like a hawser from the light fitting.

Well, no one actually says our living-room is pretty, but kind visitors do sometimes murmur a word or two about the proportions before backing into the kitchen because it's cosy out there – ie, too dark to notice things like cobwebs. (On thundery, navy-blue days we have a job to find the cooker.) Sometime in the future, we tell ourselves, we are going to build a great big sun-drenched extension to the kitchen like everybody else does. Meanwhile, this year, it is the living-room's turn for an overhaul.

I wonder why it is that one can find quite fabulous ideas in magazines and in places like the Design Centre, but the moment one tries to pass this information on to one's builder he nudges his right-hand man (the one with the woolly bobble hat and the trowel) and wheezes: 'She's orf again!' Silently they both convulse themselves before returning unswervingly to their original dabbing and stippling.

Friends and relations, too, can soon fill one's home with well-meaning disasters particularly in those vulnerable days of early married life.

'What this room needs,' they say, as we step back, paint-brush in hand, to admire the play of light and shade on our simple white walls, 'is a joke done in poker-work on a slab of bark, a three-legged gilt table lamp with matching smoker's stand and/or a fire screen depicting a very bright and beautiful view of somewhere like Lake Como.' 'We'd really rather have a few simple catkins in an earthenware pitcher,' we protest weakly.

'Oh, you and your silly pride,' they say briskly. 'Just because you can't afford good stuff yet there's no need to pretend you like all this bareness.' And they go on carting in rexine-covered armchairs shaped like Odeon cinemas.

So now, at long last, after several tactful years, I intend being ruthless. Anything with splayed legs will go – except, of course, very young and very old visitors who can't help walking like that. The drunken floor standard will be replaced, perhaps by a hanging Tiffany lamp. There must at last be enough seating. (It is hard to do one's duty as a hostess when one is scrunched up in a corner on a desperately enlisted doll's stool.) Almost everything else will be arranged neatly on one wall with the aid of Tebrax.

Well, that is the theory anyway.

'The old carpet will have to be *burned*,' I say firmly. It really is so dreadful that our late dog used to come back indoors to spend pennies on it, doubtless on the assumption that it was better not to foul up the clean outdoors when one smelly stain more or less wouldn't matter in the living-room.

The history of our carpet can best be summed up by snatches of family conversation, thus …

'Photographic fix does fade out eventually – I think.'

'Who's for a cup of tea – whoops – who left that down there?'

'Well, I didn't *know* that noise meant he was going to be sick!'

'Look everybody, I made some soup – oh Lor, I'd better make some more.'

'Mummy, Daniel's *rolling* his toffee apple across the floor.'

Every now and then I say I really must have a new, properly fitted carpet. Whereupon my husband looks hunted and starts talking about moving. He is cunning about it. 'We might just get it down and then move to a *much bigger* house where it wouldn't fit,' he says.

Dazzled at the prospect of spacious living, I agree to make do a bit longer but I'm beginning to realize I am being conned. So, this very day, the old carpet is consigned to incineration and I rush out for lots of fresh white paint.

'The aim is simplicity,' I tell the family as I cart away loads of things people pinned up or put down 'temporarily' the year before last.

I suddenly realize that there is no need for me to live one more day with a leaking coal bucket and a bald hearth brush. (Picture for a moment the exquisite torture I have suffered these past several winters spraying coal dust underfoot with the former and vainly trying to clean it up with the latter.)

At last the walls are newly white, the storage shelves are up and the floor is a temporary compromise of quite pleasant rush matting.

'We will have a bold splash of colour over *there*,' I am thinking, as the first visitor arrives bearing gifts ...

I suppose eventually everything comes back into fashion, but just at this moment I'd really rather have a dash of Conran in my living-room than a pair of plaster poodles balancing fringed plastic lampshades on their heads. What do other people do, in similar situations, I wonder?

17 Saturdays

My Life and I, *Good Housekeeping*, March 1970

'Just a minute,' said this friend of ours, opening his front door a crack. 'We haven't quite finished our regular Saturday morning argument.' He retreated and the muffled rat-a-tat of conjugal warfare sounded in the distance.

'Right, you can come in now,' he said a few moments later. Silence hung in the air and his wife flung a staccato 'Hello' over her shoulder before disappearing into the kitchen to make coffee. I dearly wanted to ask if they saved everything up for weekly outbursts on purpose, or if the general tenor of Saturdays brought grievances into the open unplanned.

Because it is noticeable that, however closely knit we consider ourselves during the rest of the week, Saturdays can have a distinctly unravelling effect on our family relationships.

Monday is a bleary day. Tuesday we get into our stride. Wednesday is early closing. Thursday is a culinary challenge. Friday is lovely. By Sunday all is peace and pottering and unfinished crossword puzzles.

But Saturday is rather like wading through treacle. It is sweeping round people's feet, staggering round the shops, carburettors on the kitchen floor and living-rooms full of other people's husbands dropping in to borrow a cupful of 1-inch screws.

I try. Sometimes on a well-adjusted Friday evening I do tomorrow's sweeping and polishing. Airtight tins clamp down on home-made cakes. Weekend clothes are laid out. Comfortable, gay outfits to encourage bright, easy-going thoughts. Hair is washed and nails are trimmed. So are lawn edges if there is time. Tomorrow all will be a fiesta.

Olé, I croak, as I stumble downstairs next morning to pay the milkman. He's been up and hard at work for hours, and to make it worse he looks incredibly fit and cheerful. My husband is another early bird. His morning gesture towards peaceful co-existence is to wash up last night's cocoa mugs before climbing into his clean, bright sports shirt and crawling under the car. I can only see his turned up toes in the drive, but they look fit and cheerful.

I will make a real effort this morning. I will fill the house with *Breakfast Special* and do something exotic and herby with half a dozen eggs. Moving purposefully towards the kitchen sink my good intentions thud drearily into limbo. The sink, bleached and refreshed the night before, is now a turgid pool of cold cocoa and floating spent matches.

The children are lobbing toothpaste about upstairs, the cat is proudly laying something sinister and furry and dead at my feet, and whatever I whip up for breakfast will have to be based on the one available egg. 'Let's make an early start,' says my husband. 'I've cleaned the car.' (The drying-up cloths show evidence of this.) Now comes the centre-piece of our morning: the Saturday shopping trip. In our nearest town there is a wonderful supermarket but no attached parking facilities. Sometimes, as we cruise slowly past for the fifth or sixth time, a space appears and we tuck ourselves into the kerb. But so over-abundant and enthusiastic are our traffic wardens that there is barely time to whizz our trolley round, snatching frantically in all directions before they close in with their little notebooks. Which explains why we arrived home last week with three drums of curry and no butter.

At the open-air vegetable market parking is even more of a problem. Sometimes, in fact, it is necessary for my husband to drive endlessly round its perimeter while I hurriedly lob heads of celery in through the car's open windows.

So far the family have been more or less on my side. Food is food. But should the need arise for a dressmaking pattern or a new lipstick it is a very different matter. My ideal store would allow pushchairs on Saturdays. It would have a permanent Father Christmas/Mickey Mouse film show and/or free half-hour rides on clockwork rocking horses. There would be room to move, up-to-date buyers, air conditioning and staff who liked *people*. Not to mention a car park. I don't want to dwell on this point but recently we collected a parking ticket, drove round to the magistrates' court counting out the £2 fine, and couldn't find anywhere to park to *pay* the thing.

Home again, shopping unloaded, and now it's a race to get the potatoes on and the lunch organized before sportin' life takes over in the living-room.

Sometimes on Saturday afternoons I drag out the mower and do noisy things in the front lawn. As a gesture it fails miserably. Either the blades are set too high or too low or something drops off. Pitifully I tap on the window with a screwdriver but the smoke in there is unhealthily dense and the commentator's voice is reaching a cracked crescendo as everybody's favourite but my husband's races past the post.

As soon as I hear, 'shush, it's the football results' I know it's time to put the kippers on. I don't like kippers myself but in some mysterious way they have become an integral part of Saturday tea in our house. For this reason I always feel a bit sick on Saturday evening. But I comfort myself with the prospect of a quiet evening watching the telly.

Have you ever watched Saturday evening television? Roll on Sunday.

18 Tights

My Life and I, *Good Housekeeping*, June 1970

At the first sign of warmer weather it is my guess that many mauvish-white legs will be scurrying into back gardens and secretly exposing themselves to all available bursts of sunshine. With luck they soon weather to a creamy tan. Whereupon with relief one can cast off a major problem for a few months. A problem which can be summed up in one word: tights.

I like the *idea* of tights. In fact, once my stockings had all reached the secondary use stage, it was a moment of pure, reckless pleasure to toss all my girdles away. (I haven't come across a secondary use for girdles, but laddered stockings can, of course, be utilized in all sorts of ways, ranging from stuffing cushions to tying up rose bushes.) Henceforth it was going to be tights only for me.

Alas, I soon discovered that, in this respect as in so many others, I am not what you might call a standard size. Somewhere between the mini-people and the Mrs Michelins there should be a Warrior Maiden category.

I think I have been recommended to try just about every make of tights on the market. 'I can absolutely *guarantee* that Brand X will fit even *your* figure,' a friend says earnestly.

'I cut this out of the paper for you,' says another. 'It says the manufacturers designed their Size Triple A for *giantesses*.'

So I scurry off fervently to the shops, but it nearly always turns out that I am a giantess in the wrong places.

At one stage I thought I'd solved the problem. A biggish girl told me to try a famous make of pantie-hose. Well, I did. Have you ever stood on a main-line railway station awaiting an overdue train, while the pantie half of your hose creeps inexorably down over your hips? Let me tell you, it saps confidence. If I so much as flexed my toes my waist elastic dropped another inch. Luckily I was wearing a tent coat with two large, low-slung pockets. Diving both hands into the pockets I caught the pants just as they slithered down past the point where furtive shrugging helps. Pressing my knees together I minced towards the newly-arrived train. Commuters hastily averted pitying looks as, shoulders hunched, arms pressed to sides, legs gripped together, I somehow clambered aboard ...

Then one of those 'do-it-yourself' spasms came over me. I still had several pairs of imperishable, thickly ribbed winter stockings which happened to be extra long. So why not sew the tops of these to the legs of assorted pants?

Now I still don't know why this didn't work but it didn't. The stockings wrinkled, the joining seams split, the knickers disintegrated. There must be some built-in fully-fashioned formula to manufactured pantie-hose which my efforts lacked. In this case the stresses and strains, on garment and wearer, were terrific. Clad in my hybrid hose, I strode forth like Hamlet and once more sidled home in a state of collapse.

I *still* liked the idea of tights and the next few months were a time of expense and experiment. Grimly I staggered around in everything from foreign white ones which looked as if my legs were bandaged, to dwarf-built models with the crutch between the knees.

Discussion among friends proved conclusively that I am not alone in this. People come in a vast range of shapes and sizes. Mention the subject at any gathering and you will hear a babble of voices telling you that they have a long body but short legs/a short body but long legs/wedge-shaped legs and fat feet/fat legs and thin feet/etc, etc.

Even quite dignified ladies leap into contorted positions in their eagerness to show you how they have to fold the feet of their tights in half or arrange Sellotaped tucks above the knee.

One said she always wore her pants over the top for 'reasons of security'. Another reached just inside the neck of her shirtwaister and waggled something brown and elasticated. 'It's my tights,' she sighed. 'I'm *so* short in the body.'

But the saddest lady of all said: 'My problem is that I have a large waist, narrow hips, fat legs and tiny feet.' To do this poor soul's situation justice you should really pause here and try to visualize her figure.

For any other Rhinemaiden-shaped readers like me, who may still be searching, I have at last discovered that Wolford's No 4 really do fit tall, big-boned women, but at 16s. a pair one thinks twice about wearing them for sweeping the stairs. Anyway they get snapped up around here before they hit the counter.

So now I eagerly await each ray of spring sunshine. The deck-chair and sun-tan oil are standing by. Palely I loiter at the garden door, legs at the ready.

19 Sports Day

My Life And I, *Good Housekeeping*, July 1970

'Oh dear, it's Sports Day on Tuesday,' I sighed.

One does so want to be an ideal mum but, delighted as I am to browse around the school on Open Day and to snap up jars of bath salts on Féte Day, I do find it an effort to throw my hat in the air when they start marking out white lines on the playing field.

I just can't seem to take sport seriously. It is absolutely sweet and moving to see the Mixed Infants going for a stroll with an egg and spoon, but not so endearing when they grow up into desperate juniors who, with glittering eyes and sheet-white faces, pound to the winning post just in time. And the sight of quite podgy parents kicking off their shoes and doing themselves irreparable damage in the Mothers and Fathers Hundred Yard Dash really worries me. Oh well, I shall just have to slip my brain into neutral, arrive in good time, put on an encouraging smile and hope for the best, that day.

I find a tiny wooden chair in a nice open spot and I am just thinking to myself 'Oh good, Anna's white shirt, while no longer as dazzling as it might be, at least *blends in* with the others,' when suddenly four or five loudly talking parents come and stand right in front of me. There are all sorts of other places for them to sit or stand but I am either doomed to a view of Crimplene and grey flannel bottoms or I must stand on my chair. I do not want to stand on my chair. It looks too keen.

Sadly I find another, less favoured spot to sit and try, discreetly, to catch Anna's eye to show that I am Interested Enough To Come. After all, she may have it in her to be another Ann Packer. For that matter I wouldn't want to seem lacking in encouragement if she turns out to be The Best Three-Legged-Racer The School Has Ever Known. (Sorry about all these capital letters but just thinking about schooldays seems to bring on an attack of the Angela Brazils.)

In order to seem sportingly impartial I leap to my feet and cheer on the daughter of a local acquaintance. She is winning at the time but I don't think I improve her chances much. At the sight of my beaming face she slows down to an amble and waves.

'I *like* to see a child who isn't ruthlessly competitive,' I gush later to her slightly withdrawn-looking mother.

'Yes, but the silly thing didn't have to *stroll* past,' she bursts out crossly.

I turn my attention to another little girl who is pounding along in great fettle. This is one of those races that starts with a sprint, then into a sack for the grand finale. Alas, my chosen runner is somewhat handicapped because someone has swerved into the wrong lane and jumped into her sack. The poor child slows down and I can see that she is in great moral turmoil. Should she dart sideways into someone else's sack-stocked lane and add to the growing confusion, retire altogether, or run the rest of the way unfairly unhandicapped?

The sack stealer wins, but only to sporadic applause because he has poked his feet well down into the corners and has been running instead of hopping. (I do wish someone would lay down Queensberry rules about this sort of thing.) There are children earnestly shuffling along, some taking splendid grasshopper leaps, some with one leg out of their sack, at least two down on the ground rolling sideways and, of course, one exhibitionist who keeps on falling over dramatically.

The afternoon wears on and I wish I'd brought a cushion, but at least it doesn't rain this year. Soon I can leave. I have done my duty as a mum. Things are reaching a crescendo now. Parents are on their feet shouting. Behind me a sporty lady is leaning on my head, thumping vigorously with her handbag. The boys of Class Nine are chanting 'England – England'.

Furtively I gather up my belongings and sidle away. Anna will not mind if I am not there for the kill. She is busy jostling for ice cream ladled out by the PTA.

'Super, wasn't it?' I say, with a false smile to another scurrying mother. But oh, it's going to be so much more super to arrive home and put the kettle on for a quiet cup of tea. I expect various over-excited friends will drop by later and tell me exactly how many cups and medals and rosettes their offspring earned.

They are fairly decent about mine.

'Anna did quite well in the skipping, didn't she?' they say. 'A pity about the change of pace five yards from the line. Needs more coaching.' So *that's* what everyone's been doing behind their hedges these past weeks.

Well, I just don't see myself crouching in the Michaelmas daisies of an evening, with cap, pistol and stop watch and rousing cries of 'Play the Game!'

No, my sympathies lie with that little, slow-moving hump, still under the canvas long after the end of the obstacle race.

20 Deeply Cleansed

My Life and I, *Good Housekeeping*, August 1970

A dramatic friend of mine came over the threshold looking radiant the other day.

'What have you *done* to yourself?' I asked, peering closely at her pores.

'I am *deeply cleansed*,' she said in a dedicated voice. 'Have you any idea how much dirt lurks in the average pore? How *grimy* you really are?'

'Who's been getting at you?' I said, leading her to a chair and sitting myself down with my back to the light. Since it was my morning for sweeping under the rush matting I was no match for all that radiance. There is something splendidly indomitable about the sort of housewives who arise, bathe and anoint themselves, carefully select a crisply fresh apron, gussy up their eyelids and *then* clean out the cupboard under the stairs. I am not one of these. Nor am I much competition for this particular friend at the best of times. She is the type who says things like: 'I shall simply *have* to pop over to Rome soon – I'm running out of nail polish.'

On this particular day she had discovered the Clinique range of beauty products and so great was her enthusiasm, even her husband had apparently been swabbed down with liquid cleanser.

Shortly after this I had tea with another scientifically-minded friend and the subject of home-made cosmetics cropped up. She showed me several yoghurt cartons labelled 'Skin Food' and 'Cleansing Cream'.

'I tint them various shades with food colouring,' she said, as we stroked little pink and green blobs into the backs of our hands. 'It makes them seem more exotic somehow.'

'Is it easy to do?' I asked. She started to giggle. 'Well there was one recipe I found for clearing the complexion. The ingredients included all sorts of super things like glycerine B and even watercress. The only trouble was that, faced with the finished product, I had no idea whether to dab it on or drink it!'

Full of enthusiasm, I returned home and took stock of my current make-up situation. Spreading newspapers on the kitchen table I rounded up current handbag contents, stray bottles from bathroom and bedroom and a battered maroon beauty box which was a pleasure to receive as a twenty-first birthday present but which, like its owner, has lost a lot of bezaz since then.

My word, what a lot of old lipsticks I found that morning, not to mention bottles containing the dregs of rejuvenation down in their unreachable depths. There was just about every sort of cosmetic aid ranging from two identical jars of Elizabeth Arden Featherlight Foundation, both waiting until my skin goes Sport Light again, to a mascara brush so clogged it may well have been used at some stage for cleaning shoes.

With a bowl of soapy water, cotton wool and various poking devices, I set to for a Sorting Out Session. Bottles were upended and ingredients recklessly mixed together. I even dragged out the cat's fish saucepan and melted down all my lipsticks therein. As experiments go, it wasn't a wild success. The result was a huge, gnarled lump which only needed a wick to make an ideal Christmas table decoration. And the faint aura of rock salmon didn't help.

When further experiments with mixed nail lacquers produced one bottle of cloudy, pearlized fudge I called it a day. Later I met another, normally wholesome-looking, friend who immediately apologized for her decadent appearance. 'I'm wearing eye make-up for the first time,' she wailed. 'It's not easy is it? This is my sixth attempt.' I rather liked the overall *wickedness* her appearance suggested but I could see that it troubled her.

'I know,' I said. 'Let's trot off to a salon and get sorted out by experts.' Well I won't say where we went because we all have our off days, but any hope of gliding home like Cleopatra was rapidly dispelled as I sat, patiently staring at my reflection, cleansed down to the raw, while the entire salon staff – tall, swoopy lady, emaciated boy in white belted sweater, woman muttering 'My God, we're out of the lilac mist again', girl in fawn stetson and ringlets and finally very small dog with disdainful nostrils – who may or may not have been one of the staff – all hurried past to give their attention to something important happening behind a screen elsewhere.

Eventually an assistant slowed down and stared at me with eyes like meat skewers. (I felt like a piece of brisket anyway.) Dabbing something beige on my face she said: 'This will tone down all that high colour and just let the *brightness* shine through.' Rather like a Belisha beacon in the fog, I suppose.

Well they did help us to some extent – my companion came away with very pretty silvery eyeshadow and my skin felt as if it *fitted* for a change. But for morale-boosting atmosphere give me the Ladies Room at Victoria any day.

21 Home Economics

My Life and I, *Good Housekeeping*, January 1971

This morning I reluctantly threw away two quite large artificial roses made of leather. Yes truly, leather. Mauve leather as a matter of fact. I can't think where they came from originally, nor why I have carefully saved them for several years. By no stretch of the imagination do I see myself sewing them on the fronts of old slippers, arranging them in a vase or doing a clap-and-stamp into supper with them gritted between my teeth.

I suppose this hoarding instinct is a throw-back to those days when 'Make Do And Mend' was as much a part of our lives as 'Don't Drink And Drive' is today.

Well, I don't drive and my drinking doesn't amount to much, but I still make do and mend as if my life depended upon it. I feel guilty flinging that last little sliver of soap down the loo. (No, *please* don't tell me I should save all the little oddments in a jar of water, for washing sweaters. It all ends up too much like frog spawn.) In the interests of economy I already have to be restrained from putting spent toothpaste tubes through the mangle just in case a little dollop lurks unsqueezed. Friends are baffled to receive gifts in carefully-ironed-out wrapping paper still labelled 'To Daniel with love from Granny'. And for months I saved somebody's one remaining good shoe, just in case. It was only when the macabre significance of that 'just in case' dawned on me that I reluctantly threw it into the dustbin.

When we first moved into our present home there was evidence of many similar economies. We were delighted to discover a lean-to stacked high with home-made coal dust brickettes. I understand that the correct formula is two parts coal dust to one part cement. These were not made to the correct formula. In fact I should say they were nearer cement-and-a-dash. With gleefully frugal chuckles we lobbed them into the dying embers of the living-room fire one frosty winter's night. Disintegrating immediately, they fell straight through into the tray beneath. Sort of do-it-yourself ash.

In spite of this I still feel that the previous house-holders were kindred spirits, because in sheds and out-houses we found various tins full of men's trouser buttons, not to mention several bunches of rusty keys, a saucepan with short lengths of rope in it and a padlocked box containing gas mantles. I forced myself to discard the latter but soon found homes for everything else. Over the years I have collected rows of screw-topped coffee jars which now variously contain buttons, beads, elastic, pyjama cords, unpicked and saved zip fasteners, short lengths of anything and, finally, one mammoth jar labelled Things Found On The Floor. This one is permanently brimming with tiddlywink counters, foreign coins, marbles, bits of jigsaw, three long green metal things, and several medals which I'm pretty sure none of our family can lay claim to. The idea is that everyone can dip into this jar when the need arises. But of course they never do. They just go out and buy new jigsaws, tiddlywinks, long green metal things, etc.

If I do have a brave blitz on all the carefully hoarded odds and ends, such as the mysterious little triangular piece of black rubber I threw away last week, you may be sure that the moment the dustbin is emptied I realize there is a little piece of triangular black rubber missing from the bottom of the ironing board.

It is easy to become just a shade obsessed by the idea of home economy. A friend of mine has spent years making a careful study of bulk-buying. 'You really can save money this way,' she says, staggering in from the garage with a giant-sized can of what I sincerely hope is cooking oil. 'The secret is to decant it into smaller containers,' adds her husband, busy in a corner siphoning something off into a carefully washed HP sauce bottle.

In her house one keeps on coming across cupboards crammed full of toilet rolls bought by the gross. 'Why not use them meanwhile to insulate the roof?' I said. I still think it a moderately brilliant suggestion, but the friend became rather withdrawn at the idea.

My own obsession is to insist on keeping an open fire in the living-room so that I can use up any bits of wood found lying around in the garden. It gives me the double delight of Saving Money and Tidying Things Up. The moment comes, however, when there really isn't anything left outside to tidy up. So then I start pruning the trees. Then thinning out the trees. When I begin to waggle fence posts. speculatively, my husband draws the line and we start saving up for Welsh nuts.

'Black diamonds describes coal only too accurately,' says David, adding up the bill. My cooking also suffers from periodic outbursts of home economy. 'Oh you can fling *anything* into a risotto,' they say. So when I make one, it's coming along nicely and then I feel I *must* use up that great big blob of cauliflower cheese left over from yesterday's economy supper. So in it goes and, yuk, instant flab.

I don't think I am alone in this. There are ladies who line their cake tins with saved butter papers. There are others who can't seem to stop running up useful little aprons from old shirts. I even know one who cuts the ribbed tops off old socks and wears them round her wrists. But my favourite story concerns a late great-aunt of mine who would peel oranges carefully in sections, thread the little boat-shaped pieces of skin on to skewers, hang them up to dry and then use them to light fires. At such frugality the mind really does boggle.

22 A Walk In The Woods

My Life and I, *Good Housekeeping*, March 1971

I wonder why I like going for country rambles? They hardly ever turn out exactly as I picture them. Take Romantic Walks In Woods for example …

There was that idyllic teenage day when the blue-eyed coxswain of the boat crew took me for a day inland. I was an innocent, romantic sort of girl and as I prepared our picnic lunch I looked forward to leafy glades and perhaps a bit of hand-holding as the sun went down. (Honestly. We didn't go around wearing X Certificates on our sleeves in those days.) Anyway, there we were, all dreamy brown eyes looking into sea-washed blue eyes under a canopy of translucent green.

We chose our picnic spot by a stream and, casually, I cracked the first hard-boiled egg. Alas, I must have been a wee bit too dreamy during its preparation because out it slithered – raw, into my lap.

'Swoosh some water over it,' said my swain, with barely suppressed guffaws. I did and the albumen went mad and foamed all over my skirt. More water. More foam. As sylvan interludes go, the afternoon wasn't a great success. It put me off the coxswain but I still enjoyed woodland walks so away I went later, hand-in-hand with my future husband. I was a shade more sophisticated by now and much better at boiling eggs but still inclined to gush at the first spring flower.

'Oh look, David – did you see those violets on that bank? There must have been *hundreds* of them!' I trilled.

'There were seven,' he said. 'You do get carried away, don't you?'

On we rambled, having a ding-dong battle over those damned violets until, with a heavy sigh, he about-turned and frogmarched me back (about a hundred miles) to count the beastly things. There were twenty-eight.

Nowadays, on wintry Sunday afternoons we pile the washing-up in the sink, sort out everybody's Wellingtons and, before anyone has a chance to become faint-hearted, we are off to the woods, *en famille*, arms swinging, nostrils a-crackle.

'Today we will look for fossils,' I state. From previous excursions our living room already looks like Brighton beach.

Dutifully the children kick a few flinty stones *en route*. Once we found, along a country lane, a marvellously strange green stone. It had swirls of light and dark jade and was smooth to the touch.

'Right,' I said – it was one of my 'expanding young minds' days. 'We will take this to the museum next week and find out exactly what kind of quartz it is.'

Madly keen, I banged on the curator's door and held out our find. A dusty eagle of a man peered down at the palm of my hand and said 'Yes?'

'Please, we found this on the Berkshire Downs and we'd like it identified,' I piped. For some nervous reason I seemed to be imitating Anna's voice.

He gave me a long, strange look. 'It's basic sludge,' he said. 'Brought down from the iron-ore smelters in the Midlands. Used for road mending.'

He did a little drawing of an iron-ore smelter and explained all about the muck settling at the bottom and cooling down and going green. He was quite nice about it in a bleak sort of way. But we left fairly quickly before anyone had a chance to tell him that Mummy thought it was jade.

Undaunted, in nearly all weathers, we stride off out again. I worry that children do not seem sufficiently involved with nature these days and I just hope that some of my enthusiasm is rubbing off, although I sometimes have reason to doubt it.

There are bonus days, of course, with Daniel trotting along in the sunshine clutching three warm, lolloping buttercups, and once we saw the greatly enlarged shadow of a woodpecker, high on a tree. Often I save the life of our washing machine by discovering, in the nick of time, that the pockets of shorts are loaded down with 'interesting stones' which Dan has presumably been collecting on little garden walks of his own. And there are days, too, when Anna's bedroom looks like one vast nature project.

But young minds are notoriously fickle, so I keep on pegging away … 'Do look, children – here's a beautiful piece of speckled blue eggshell. Shall we take it home and look it up in our bird book?'

'Will you carry it, Mum?'

'And this pretty piece of fungus.'

'And this interesting old mossy branch.'

Gamely I stagger along behind. It is better really – less tiring – to limit oneself to one subject per ramble. So next time we go out I take a deep breath and try again …

'There are all kinds of ivy leaves,' I say enthusiastically. 'There are little pointy ones and big fat shiny ones. Look, I've picked a lovely assortment.' I spin round, beaming happily. The children are nowhere to be seen, but a tall, middle-aged man and his dog are drinking in my every word. Flashing them a sickly smile I wander on, swinging my leafy bundle with complete lack of nonchalance. If I ever do catch up with the children I know just what is going to happen.

'Hurry up, Mum,' they will say. 'We're missing something good on the telly.'

23 Embarrassing Moments

My Life and I, *Good Housekeeping*, June 1971

I suppose every one of us has had at least one embarrassing moment. Doubtless we've all lost a knicker or two in our time. Underwear generally can create a wide variety of hazards. There are unlimited straps that go ping and, while one may not mind the occasional drifting petticoat, bras can be a great trial. It isn't much fun when half a bosom goes thud at a party, for instance. There is a limit to how long one can go on hunching one shoulder; and standing diagonally isn't really the answer either. Perhaps even worse is the brassiere that creeps upwards under a close-fitting dress and then stops midway up one's chest. Bulging, painfully, above and below, I once smiled staunchly through just such a double-breasted evening.

Now that I suppose most of us wear tights, we no longer have to face that moment of truth when, leaping up from a casual legs-crossed sitting position, we found that the back suspender on one leg had attached itself to the front suspender on the other. Getting out of a room with one's legs locked wrap-around required more verve than I could ever muster.

Shoes, too, can be a source of embarrassment. Have you ever tried on a long, long boot in one of those serve-yourself shoe shops and then been unable to get it off? Or lost a heel and had to bob casually up and down all the way home? (You *can* try balancing things up by walking with one foot in the gutter but it looks a bit slummocky.)

Really, looking back, some moments in my life have been a complete shambles. During an interview with a Fairly Important Person, in his flat, I managed to make a reasonably graceful exit only to discover that I had backed into a bedroom. Through the closed door I could hear other visitors arriving. I stood for a long time wondering what to do. The assembled guests doubtless drew their own conclusions when eventually the bedroom door opened and a bemused-looking woman stumbled past them and made a frenzied bolt for the front door.

Uncomfortable moments fall roughly into two categories – events which happen to us and things we do to other people. I can put up with a fair amount of the former (I don't seem to have much choice) but I really do feel embarrassed if I unwittingly hurt others. The conversational hiatus one feels compelled to babble into. The silly, unthinking remark. The tactless act.

One acquaintance won't easily forget moving a gate-legged table in a shop in a moment of misguided helpfulness. We all know what happens to gate-legged tables if one isn't careful. Legs fold together. Flaps drop. So, in this case, did a small fortune in cut glass.

My own most embarrassing moment concerns a journey I was making from London to Scotland. I was to be away for some time so I packed a really huge suitcase and staggered off to the nearest bus stop. There was one other lady waiting for a bus and together we stood, for some time. Presently a car drove up and the woman driver leant out and said: 'Going to the station?' 'Oh yes, thanks,' we both said gratefully and, while my companion slipped into the front passenger seat, I opened the rear door and began, inch by inch, to slide my gigantic piece of luggage into the available space. It just fitted on the floor, leaving the back seat free for me – but of course there was nowhere for me to put my feet. So, turning round, I flung myself in backwards, landing in a horizontal and somewhat abandoned position across the seat.

I now had to close the door, but a relatively simple pivoting action of elbow and hip made it possible to claw it shut.

'Right!' I said. 'All set.'

'Tell me, Doris,' said the driver, turning to the passenger in the front seat. 'Do you know this person?'

'Why no, Agnes,' said Doris. 'I thought she must be a friend of yours.'

Together they rounded on me. 'Would you please get out of our car,' they said. So I did. But it took time.

As we get older we don't mind quite so much if we are caught off guard – although going back to a party the morning after, to reclaim one's wig, takes courage. The other morning, as we few stay-the-nighters were gathering up sticky glasses and vacuuming under the sofa, a small, dark-haired girl wandered in.

'Ah, *there* it is,' she cried, snatching up what I had taken to be a recumbent Pekingese. And lo, with not so much as a nervous titter, the small dark stranger clapped hand to head, turned into last night's blonde belle of the ball and strolled out.

If only we could develop such poise when we are young and suffer most acutely. I can remember those dreadful adolescent days of *Oh, I wish I could die/Life will never be the same again/How can I ever face my friends?* (The cause of all this mortification, by the way, was usually no more than a pimple on the chin.)

And I've just realized that it starts even before adolescence. 'Oh Mummy,' says Anna, crashing in from school and talking non-stop. 'You know those pants of mine with the pink flowers? – well, I forgot to take my PE knickers this morning and when I turned upside down on the climbing frame they all *laughed* and now they call me Flower Power!'

'Never mind,' I say soothingly. 'You'd never believe some of the embarrassing things that happened to me ...'

One does stop blushing – eventually.

24 Freedom At Last

Family Circle, October 1971

'I feel so carefree I could levitate,' I cried, handing my visitor a cup of coffee. 'But I thought mothers were supposed to feel sad on these occasions,' she said, peering at me closely for any lurking traces of sentiment.

I had just delivered Daniel for his first full day at primary school. He had done his year of 'prep' at nursery school, followed by a couple of months of mornings only at what he calls 'proper school'. At last, his fifth birthday had arrived, and he was all set to become a sniffy-nosed, shoe-scuffing, hair on end, fully fledged schoolboy.

With both my children now away all day, I was now set to become one of the leisured classes. I had everything planned. Mondays would still have to be mucking-out day. If there was one word you wouldn't apply to our family, that word is 'neat'. After two whole days of home life for all, our house looks about as lived in as it is possible to get. But by spending one complete day zooming upstairs with armfuls of strewn socks, books, sweaters and toys, and zooming down again with assorted coffee cups, apple cores and newspapers, I could restore order. Just about.

In my blurred, optimistic mind's eye I also saw Monday as wash day, vacuuming-under-beds day, cobweb-swiping day, buffing up the bathroom day, loo-bleaching day and kitchen floor wash and wax day. Other jobs, like ironing, grocery shopping and weeding the garden would have to be fitted in at my convenience, later in the week.

Roughly once a month, I thought to myself airily, I would have to spare another day for really cleaning the oven, washing paintwork, oiling door hinges and generally patching things up. But this should still leave me two or three whole weekdays to myself.

'I shall have a regular day in town,' I gloated, 'to sort of top myself up.' I had always been secretly impressed by a wife I know who keeps herself and her home beautifully well balanced and up to date by paying weekly visits to art galleries and exhibitions. She finds that this little self-imposed 'refresher course' keeps her from getting too bogged down in domesticity.

I would find time too to increase my culinary repertoire. I really enjoy creative cookery, but it is the harassed daily plod that saps initiative – that last-minute dash to get the potatoes on, that bleak moment in the pantry when one realises that the shops are shut, one's husband is due home, and the only ingredients available for supper are two wizened carrots, a tin of evaporated milk, a packet of dried lentils and some dessicated coconut.

The new relaxed me would be more like the Elizabeth Davids of this world. I would mull and marinade and simmer and sieve to my heart's content. I would do clever things with mussels and basil. Here a drizzle of melted butter, there a dash of white wine. I might even buy myself a double saucepan, at last, and a pestle and mortar, too.

Then we'd invite round all sorts of witty, worldly, colourful people I don't even know as yet, and they'd invite us back; I'd overhear them saying incredibly flattering things about me, things like 'To think that we had a woman like that living in our community and we didn't even know it. Just look at her Picasso lithograph/hand crocheted hot pants/filet de boeuf en croute/flawless complexion!'

I'd have been spending some of my spare days pampering my appearance, of course. The leathery look would be out – for the face and hands, anyway. No more gnarled knuckles and sooty streaks. My usual hectic 'floor polisher's flush' would be replaced by the creamy bloom of leisure. (Well, more or less.) I might even have an art nouveau hairdo and stroll around clasping a lily. Which just goes to show how carried away you can be – and how wrong.

Daniel has now been a fulltime schoolboy for more than a term. Those art-enriched days in town will have to wait until all the fetching and carrying to and from school is no longer necessary. There is still a desperate rush to put the potatoes on.

One of these days I shall catch up with the washing and ironing and mending and sweeping, but not today. Today I am looking through magazines for pictures of camels, knights in armour and/or the sky at night, for school projects. I am mending almost new school pullovers for the second time this week. I am helping my son collect 'interesting stones and sticks and flowers and things for the nature table, teacher says'.

No, definitely not today. Today my daughter has just rushed in and said 'Quick, Mummy, I've been invited to Gillian's party and it's the day after tomorrow and I must have a new dress and can it be cream silk and maxi with lots of smocking across the front and embroidery on the cuffs?'

'Lots of smocking *and* embroidery?' I sigh, as I reach for my tape measure.

25 Life At The Launderette

My Life and I, *Good Housekeeping*, November 1971

You wouldn't think it possible, would you, for launderettes to have character? But they vary enormously, as I've discovered lately, travelling around with my husband, my bulging plastic laundry bag in the boot of the car.

Some weeks ago our washing-machine finally reached the point of no return. Like those old maths textbook problems, more water leaked on to the floor than I could conveniently replace from the tap, thus creating endless arithmetical imponderables and a very wet kitchen.

We can't really grumble, since we bought it second-hand ages ago from a sweet old lady in a nearby village. It wasn't exactly cheap but, as David said, she was such a very frail old soul that we could hardly beat down the price. (Worth remembering if you happen to have a sweet old silver-haired relative handy and you want to sell something.)

Although public wash-houses of one sort and another have been around for a very long time, I haven't had a great deal to do with them in the past. I remember enquiring about laundry facilities earlier in our marriage.

We had just moved to a new district which, we were told, had 'no need for such places as launderettes. People here can afford their own private washing facilities.' Oh, I was glad to leave there.

And just as towns and villages vary greatly, so, too, do launderettes and the people who use them. There are the young, bed-sit brigade; retired old chaps in for a warm; mums glad to rest their legs; middle-aged ladies who need a chat. (Well if you are lonely and you don't play golf or bingo, where do you go for a chat?)

There are Good Samaritans who potter and hum and fold up absent owners' washing for them. There are elegant souls who trip in with tiny, crisp gingham bundles held fastidiously between finger and thumb. (Their washing going *in* often looks cleaner than mine does coming out.) There are vague, beaky professors leaving trails of wet socks and artful twelve-year-old boys who know all the dodges. Some are busy, steamy places presided over by jolly ladies who provide piles of magazines and who will do your washing for you if you ask them nicely. Some are pastel and unmanned, making do with lots of little machines dispensing just about everything except advice – perhaps the most needed ingredient of all, as any engineer who goes around repairing the unending damage caused by assorted users will tell you.

'You wouldn't believe the things people do,' they sigh. And the list ranges from drying somebody else's washing by mistake to 'posting' their coins down a crack between two machines and then wondering why nothing happens.

A common fault is to load one machine and put money in the one next to it. They press the handle and stand, amazed, as their washing just sits there all dormant while an empty neighbouring machine mysteriously fills up and starts to chug.

My own first novitiate gaffe was to grab someone's private detergent packet and sprinkle its contents liberally into my machine.

'I wonder why that lady is scowling at me like that?' I was thinking vaguely to myself, and then she told me.

Nowadays I am much more knowledgeable. I carry the right coins, my own measured jar of soap and a carefully marked plastic bag. Our local launderette caters to some terribly fierce elderly ladies.

'My laundry bag, *if* you don't mind,' they bray, pouncing on to my lap like tweedy lizards. But since the bag dispensing machine always supplies the same sky blue model, it is hard to tell.

I marked mine after an unseemly tug of war with a militant soul who looked not unlike a gnarled tree drawn by Arthur Rackham. We found my gloves and soap jar inside, which at least persuaded her to let go. However, she went on muttering evil spells to herself all the way up past the butchers.

But perhaps for real life drama it would be hard to beat the launderette I sometimes use, which has recently installed green stamps. The idea seems laudable enough.

'For the *Even Greater* Convenience of our Customers' it says, and it goes on to list exactly how many stamps one is allowed per wash load (6), per dry clean (20) and per soap purchase (3).

The trouble is that, instead of the stamps popping up by one's own particular machine, they all, by some magical method of remote control, roll out of a communal slot in the wall down at the far end. And nobody takes their exact due. Some people collect their stamps casually, before they leave. Others rip them off avidly the moment they appear. But few read the notice properly.

'Oh look – Green Stamps Given,' they say brightly and they look around and see about a hundred and fifty of the things ticker-taping out of the far wall. So, naturally enough, they march down and seize the lot. They only make this mistake once, however.

'Here, who's had my stamps?' thunders a little red-faced woman, staggering under the weight of a season's dry cleaning. This sparks off indignant reaction all round.

'Cor, don't it make yer sick!'

'They'd 'ave the clothes off yer back for tuppence.'

'Oh God, what *have* I done?'

'Green stamps? What green stamps?'

'I say, do you mind, six of those are mine.'

'Do you mean to say we get *green stamps*?'

Oh well, at least it breaks down a few barriers. But I seem to be the only person who finds it funny. Or I did, until some unthinking cad marched in yesterday and grabbed my six. Immediately I became absolutely livid.

'How damned unfair,' I quivered. And I don't even *collect* green stamps.

26 Party Games

My Life and I, *Good Housekeeping*, January 1972

I don't mind some party games. I can spend quite a thoughtful evening guessing what's in the matchbox and I'm terribly good at 'Bird, Beast, Flower'. But 'come to a party' can mean so many different things. At some we stand around talking, sipping, nibbling and the only game we play is keeping one eye on the door in case an absolute *dish* suddenly arrives. Well, yes, I know that for most of us the solid, dependable figure over by the soda syphon is one's spouse. But surely this need not preclude ten minutes' deeply pulsating chat about the weather with – say – Robert Redford?

At another sort of party, ladies with draped dickie fronts and mauve face powder leap up with little cries of 'Anyone for Flip the Kipper?' Honestly. I have even been to an all-female do where the lady in charge said, 'Oh goody, we've just got time for a quick game of Sardines.'

'Must dash,' I gabbled. They were a worthy group but I just didn't see myself squeezed bust to bust in the boiler room with the Hon Sec.

At the other end of the social spectrum there are parties at which people turn up and plonk down on sofas, chairs and all round the walls. Then they just sit, waiting.

I am at a loss on these occasions. Does one offer to tap dance? Or yodel? Or spin the plate? At these do's, folk wear woollies, the record player is broken and the hostess is having a super time in the kitchen with – well, if not Robert Redford, at least the pick of what is available. You can hear them out there, laughing and lobbing anchovies at each other. Meanwhile, the rest of us sit, clutching warm, empty wine glasses until, in desperation, we lean across and say brightly, 'I just love your cardigan. Did you knit it yourself?'

There are gameless parties, too, where the sexes remain rigidly divided. The ladies sit at one end and chat about the lasting qualities of various washing-up liquids, while the men cluster round the drinks table being coarse and masculine and rather splendid. Every now and then someone is detailed to round me up and return me to my rightful end, but my motto is 'mingle and be damned', so off I swirl again as soon as they put me down.

I went through a trying phase, a few years back, when I became passionately attached to self-analyzing party games and quizzes. I met myself as I really am. I discovered that I am the romantic-Robert Browning-pony-and-trap type. (In fact, I was marked down by more than one fellow guest as a full-blown cabbage rose.) I also found that I'm a rotten wife but David is an ideal husband. (I think it's just possible that he rigged that evening.)

I also met a wide circle of my friends and acquaintances as they really are. One pretty blond girl is now known, fairly generally, as 'Old Sludge' because her views on sex were revealed through a deeply psychological word association game in which sex *equalled* water *equalled* sludgy old ponds.

I used to get telephone calls at least once a week from friends, especially Americans, saying 'Hi, could you just give me a rundown on that psychological game you played with us the other night? We've been invited to those stuffy Plodhammers and I'd certainly like to unravel their ids a little.'

A similar party game listed a chosen guest's attributes in terms of flora, fauna, music, minerals, etc. But we discovered that it is unwise to play it unless one is absolutely sure of the victim's stability.

Excitable ladies have been known to stamp off home

because they've been put down as a daffodil when they've always seen themselves as a lupin.

Nowadays one hears an awful lot about wife-swapping parties. Or are they, like solid gold bath-taps, more talked about than actually gone in for?

I suppose it is just possible that some sprightly folk go around saying 'Pssst, fancy my Gladys?' Among Eskimos, of course, it is apparently a matter of custom and common courtesy. And really, with all that permafrost and sighs of 'not blubber casserole again!' they deserve whatever diversions they can manage to drum up.

The British way of life, however, is not yet so all-embracing or, if it is, then so far not one husband or wife has approached us with a furtive 'Pssst'.

And I certainly don't see myself, or my chosen mate, dropping cryptic hints or putting any strangely-worded postcards into the tobacconist's window, thanks all the same.

While I grant that exchanging a sexy glance at a party can do more for one's complexion than any amount of hormone cream, the real value of a social gathering, for me, lies not in the company nor the games they play but in the preparation.

From the moment the invitation arrives until the day itself, my life is a disciplined affair. Quite simply, my favourite current party gear is a size 14. I am a size 16. I bet no one gets through more crispbreads than I do in party season. (Eventually they taste like asbestos dinner mats.) But once I am lowered into my super black and white Biba ensemble and all zips are padlocked tight, I feel great. Breathless, but *great*.

And if I glide carefully over some festive threshold and put away more than two chicken *vol-au-vents* then I'm afraid kipper flipping would be a physical impossibility even if, unaccountably, I did ever happen to feel up to it.

These days even 'Bird, Beast, Flower' has to be played from a standing position.

27 Colour It Zing

Family Circle, April 1972

I awoke early this morning with one obsessive thought filling my mind. I simply must have a new tea caddy. A purple one. Like those pregnant ladies who develop unnatural cravings for tiny, bite-sized chunks of coal, I, too, yearn strangely. But in my case it isn't pregnancy. We are moving shortly, and you might say I am 'big with house'. All sorts of items need renovating or replacing. For several rackety, toddler-infested years I have made do with old, dented kitchen canisters – mine are still in shades of post-war cream, which just shows how much I deserve some purple ones. My kitchen cloths have developed gaping holes. (It is a nasty sensation to grasp at a dripping dinner plate, plunge through the gathered tea-cloth and find one's self drying up with the palm of one's bare hand.)

Bath towels, too, are no longer super-absorbent; some are not even slightly absorbent. In fact, our household linen generally is on the skids. My family wake up criss-crossed with seam-marks from sheets turned sides to middle and top to bottom. 'I've heard of patchwork quilts,' they say, bitterly, as they unthread themselves from their bedclothes. I admit I've left one or two replacements a trifle on the late side but, with the move in view I've hung on. 'We can all have new colour schemes when we move,' I cry. 'We really have made do for long enough.'

I am considering a soft pinkish-fawn wild rose pattern for the new kitchen walls. This may be going against current trends, but I feel the need for a pinkish rosy background more than most. Strange how our colour choice relates to personality and, perhaps, to the stage one has reached in one's life. While I collect patterns of quiet, backwater browns and pinks and beiges, Anna has her own, ten-year-old ideas.

'Mummy, what I'd really like is mauve and lime-green and orange. Sort of mixed,' she says. She then goes on to tell me, in great detail, about all the weird schemes her friends have, and how they can leave their rooms as untidy as they like. 'And at Joanna's, you can't even see the floor for toys!' she adds with a flourish.

Well, it's not going to be like that at our new house, I tell her. No, we are going to live peaceful, uncluttered lives with simple colour schemes. Good new bed linen and other replacements will be in calm, wholesome colours.

While I make a start by weeding out and replacing limp old cushions and pillows (the new pillows will settle down soon, I tell everyone, as we lurch about with stiff necks) my family looks ahead with mixed feelings at the prospect of The Good Life.

Then I take a long, hard look at the living-room settee. 'I know a marvellous man who re-covers settees,' says a friend of mine. I contact him by telephone and he says he'll be round with his swatches this evening. For some reason I expect upholsterers to be elderly and on the small side. I open the door to – well, you think of your current hero, and double it. He is exactly what would turn up if we all fed our deepest thoughts and yearnings and measurements into the computer and pressed the matchmaker button.

'You have a well-made settee,' he says, in a low, pulsating voice. 'I have?' I gasp, blushing and twisting my legs around each other. He stands tall and looks down, down, down into my eyes. He is unsmiling, commanding. His sideburns are just flecked with grey. I can't swear to it, but he may be tapping a riding crop against an elegant leather-booted leg.

'Have you anything special in mind?' he asks, flinging down his swatches. 'Well, to hell with recovering the settee for a start,' I am about to scream faintly. But then my daughter's voice breaks in.

'Mummy, could we have it redone in this?' she asks. She has found a shade of luminous cyclamen in one of the sample books. The telephone rings, and it is my mother, telling me to choose a sensible colour that won't show the dirt. The telephone rings again, and this time it is my husband telling me that he'll be home soon, and if that settee chap turns up, tell him we want something hard-wearing.

I return to everyday life with a bump, and our ravishing visitor leads me gently (deeply, pulsatingly, etc) towards the sensible-dark-brown-hard-wearing pattern range. Eventually he leaves – I'd like to say leaping astride a milk-white charger but actually he has a blue truck. 'His wife was waiting outside. Did you notice her?' says Anna, staring at me steadily.

Ah well! At this stage in my life I must just be content with new colour schemes. I get out the carrier bag full of furniture brochures and little bits of wallpaper. I close one eye and hold the strip of pinkish fawn kitchen vinyl at arms' length and concentrate very hard.

Never mind soft backwater colour schemes, for peaceful uncluttered lives, I am thinking. No, what we need is zing. Our décor shall be young and bright, and mixed up mauve and orange if we feel like it. Which is why I leapt onto a train this morning and zoomed into town. It is why I am now home again, feet propped up and kettle on for a cuppa. Draped over the chair opposite are a rainbow mixture of new drying-up cloths, several sizzling bath towels, and, would you believe, a passionate puce roll basket. Already life seems a lot more colourful, and just as wholesome.

'I think we'll have poppy red sheets for our bed,' I tell my husband. 'What do you think?' 'Powie!' he says, leaping up unasked to make tea. I can hear him whistling quite merrily as he reaches for the new purple tea caddy.

28 A Pattern For Life

Family Circle, June 1972

Some people have a flair for choosing the right clothes. Something tells them that rose pink crêpe does wonders for their aura of gentle motherhood, or that tight black satin is why all those men are following them. Early on as adults, they hit upon a style and a way of life, it seems. Effortlessly, they relate the one to the other, until the distant day when pink crêpe gives way to lavender velvet edged with grandchildren, and our black satin-clad lady gives way to arsenic and old lace. There is a pattern to their lives and I admire them for it.

Well, I am rapidly reaching an age when I am liable to give way to something, and it seems to me that I've been aimlessly drifting, so far, in my search for a suitable aura. My wardrobe shows evidence of this.

'I like to be ready for anything,' I like to tell people. But do I have to be ready for everything? Is it really still necessary for me to be standing by with jodhpurs *and* rhinestones? Not to mention the long peacock-blue evening gloves, the knee-length vest, the karate jacket?

One would imagine, with such a wealth of choice, that getting dressed would be a casual, fun-type thing. Not a bit of it. One of the reasons why I can't get up in the mornings is because I am lying there thinking 'If I wear my comfortable brown shoes to go shopping I won't be able to wear the black coat that looks nice with the white blouse, only that means I shall have to iron the white slip', etc.

In fact, it is so exhausting getting the sartorial show on the road that, when Anna skips brightly into our bedroom at crack of dawn wearing her orange sweater with her red skirt, saying 'Mummy, have you seen my mauve hair toggles?' followed by David in rust sweater, muttering 'Where's my other maroon sock?' I am so mentally overwhelmed I tend to burrow down into a pre-natal position and hope that things will sort themselves out without me for a day or two.

I tried to face up to the problem once. I had read a piece called 'Planning Your Wardrobe'. List your activities, it said, and plan accordingly. 'Housework' I put down, unhesitatingly, at the top of the list. For this, I have a shapeless old brown dress, a shapeless old brown skirt and several shapeless old sweaters. Now this, in itself, is a mystery. Did I ever really go out and *choose* that knitted, dun-coloured tubular dress? Or actually buy the ginger tweed skirt with all those pleats across the tum? Or say to myself one morning, 'That fabulous greeny-brown flecked off-the-shoulder jerkin with the knee-length sleeves and the frilled peplum is a *must* for me this spring'?

'Gardening' was my second heading. For this I simply added mud-encrusted gloves and Wellington boots to the above, plus a very, very long off-white cardigan. Before anyone rushes in and tells me that very long cardigans are in fashion I should explain that mine is longer on one side than the other.

Now, how else do I spend my days? Well, I seem to find myself out in the rain quite often. For this I am still seeking a wide-brimmed rain hat that doesn't make me look like Ned Kelly. Meanwhile I huddle in doorways and try very hard to make my telescopic umbrella do the right thing. One does feel so silly on crowded pavements when it goes all boneless and folds down over one's brow.

For evenings around the fire I have a long skirt I keep meaning to wear, and, for tennis, which I do not play, I have brand new tennis shoes (I nearly played, three summers ago). Down at the undisturbed end of the wardrobe hang a few trendy mistakes. I stopped wearing these when I heard someone describing a friend as 'mutton dressed up as lamb'. Phrases like this put one off doing anything too experimental. And anyway, once past the age of 20, ankle-length crushed velvet can soon turn one into a Madame Arcati.

After careful study of my list, my way of life and my wardrobe, I ran myself up a super floating sort of outfit, just for doing the housework. I would dive into it first thing in the morning and get the day off to a cheery start. Alas, some deep-rooted Puritan streak made me feel guilty wearing new clothes for scrubbing behind the boiler. And the floaty bits kept getting caught on door knobs.

So, to cheer myself up, I lashed out a small fortune on a rather-nicely cut cream leather coat. 'This is really me,' I thought, as I wore it for the first time. 'It's just as well you wore your plastic mac,' said my companion, 'It looks like rain.'

For gardening I found a pair of trousers that made me seem quite svelte from some angles – until I started double digging. Children do not tiptoe up and whisper that one's seams are coming adrift. No, they unhesitatingly shout 'MUMMY, YOUR KNICKERS ARE SHOWING AGAIN!'

So, really, I can't say that Planning Your Wardrobe did me much good, or that my aura has finally crystallized. Perhaps one is wiser to avoid being too rigidly categorised. Life may seem easier for those who simply forge ahead being, say, tweedy or sexy or gently maternal at all times. But we all have our Dorcas days and our Madame Pompadour days. Or we should, if we take to heart that exhausting old precept about being wife *and* mother *and* mistress.

At least, until the day comes when, as a friend mournfully puts it, 'Even if I did sidle into our bedroom wearing nothing but yashmak and tassels, my husband would merely look up from his book and say "It's your turn to make the cocoa"!'

Until then, I'll just go on muddling through.

29 The Right Kind Of Face

Family Circle, July 1972

Have you ever been approached by a stranger carrying a a microphone or clipboard and asked an out-of-the-blue question, like: 'What programmes did you watch on television last Tuesday?'

This sort of thing happens to me all the time. Just last week, passing through a couple of strange towns, I was asked to sign petitions re-instating the mayor and trying to keep the maternity hospital open. I have only to pass a pillar-box for someone to lean out of a parked car, calling: 'I say, could you pop these in the box for me?' It is almost as if they have been waiting for someone with my sort of face to come along. Apparently, I exude approachability.

I was stopped in Woolworth's once by a lady who couldn't read English, but who said that she could understand the spoken word. Would I, she asked, very kindly read out the verses in various birthday cards, so that she could make a suitable choice? So I put down my shopping bag, took a deep breath and dived into 'Roses are red …'

She was rather a sentimental lady, and pretty soon we were choking our way through 'Down The Long Years You've Been True Blue, There Never Was A Mum Like You', not to mention 'You Always Seemed To Understand, As You Dried Our Tears With A Careworn Hand'. Eventually, sobbing loudly, she stumbled off with a fairly clipped message, 'To A Favourite Uncle' and I blundered damply home, wondering if I'd made this fact absolutely clear to her.

I give of my best when I can, but it isn't always easy. How many of you, I wonder, have been asked the time by a passer-by and confidently peeled back your cuff saying, 'Yes, it's … er …' only to find that you are both staring eagerly at a blank wrist, because you aren't wearing a watch? (I do this all the time, and I haven't even got a watch, since that day Anna borrowed mine and went swimming.)

We may laugh, too, at the uninformed replies given on television by the 'man in the street', when approached and asked his views on current affairs. 'Tell me, sir', says the sports reporter, 'What do you think about Britain losing the Ashes?' 'Ashes?' he mumbles. 'Something to do with the shortage of coal, is it?'

We wonder where they've been, lately. Until it happens to us. I once spent an open day looking around a new university building with a young colleague called Norma.

'Forest green – what a wise choice for these individual study booths!' I babbled. 'And how cleverly they are linked to the main library. Ease of access. So important. Oh, and I like those proportions, don't you?' Norma, an easily impressed girl, trotted along beside me drinking in this great flood of enthusiasm.

Suddenly, a man loomed up in front of us holding a microphone. 'Would you care to give us your impressions of these new buildings?' he said. 'Oh – er – quite nice, really!' I squeaked, with a nervous giggle. 'Well, I thought you'd have more to say to him than that,' said Norma, as I scuttled away.

This experience made me determined not to be caught dry mouthed and floundering next time. Recently, our town was given new plastic milk bottles to try out, and it wasn't unusual to see teams of roving cameramen and reporters in our streets. So, since the new bottles were nasty, squashy things, I had quite a speech prepared, if anyone asked for my views. Each time I went shopping, I kept clearing my throat and licking my lips and waiting to be interviewed. In fact, the newsmen may well have wondered why the same tall, moist-lipped woman seemed to be standing radiantly at every street corner they came to. Eventually, with slightly hunted expressions, they packed up their gear and drove away. Perhaps one can look too approachable.

Meanwhile, many a passing lorry driver has lived to regret asking me 'the way to Valley Road'. 'Well, I know where it is', I tell them earnestly. 'It's just that I can't connect it up with where I'm standing now.'

Sometimes, in my eagerness to help, I send motorists off with a merry wave and a cheerful cry of 'It's over there, second left', only to have them pass me, scowling, some minutes later coming the other way, presumably armed with someone else's, completely different, set of directions.

The other day, in the supermarket, I was queueing up with my trolley when the lady in front of me gave a start and muttered, 'Oh Lor, cornflour!' Looking frantically back at the great jam of waiting mums, she caught sight of me and said: 'Would you mind my things for me? I've forgotten something.' So I leaned across and grasped her trolley. Seconds later, another laden soul trundled up behind me, gave me a nudge and said the same thing.

Like a trusty guard dog, I spread-eagled myself across all three trolleys, which contained handbags, purses and small offspring, as well as groceries. 'My day for good deeds', I said, smiling sheepishly at an amused onlooker up ahead.

'Yes, well, you've got such a dependable sort of face', she said. I *suppose* it's a good thing, really.

30 Keeping Fit

My Life and I, *Good Housekeeping*, September 1972

'Look, Mummy – quick – can you do this?' says Anna. I don't need to look. I know that my double-jointed daughter has probably got her left leg tucked behind her right ear.

Upstairs, cracking noises like pistol shots suggest that my husband is doing his press-ups again. Even Daniel is saying in a muffled voice: 'I bet you can't do this, Mum,' as he stands, doubled up and wobbling, on one leg. My family is on another Keep Fit kick.

Exercise is something I have spent the best part of my life avoiding. True, a general love of nature has me tramping around the countryside at weekends and pottering in the garden of an afternoon. But you won't find me swinging radiantly from any wall bars. Nor lashing out the housekeeping money on secret hockey sticks or shin pads.

However, just recently it has started to dawn upon me, as I look around at my contemporaries, that I ought at least keep myself limbered up or, in some places, held in – before I seize up or spread out irrevocably.

So I have bought a little book and sometimes, on a bedmaking morning, I have been down on the carpet, inhaling fluff at close range, while my astonished ball-and-sockets click away like castanets.

I know that I am not alone in this. The other day, while strolling through a new window-walled housing estate, I couldn't help noticing a bare leg sticking up from behind a sofa. When a second leg joined it and both started furious bicycling movements, I knew that yet another over-sized mum was pushing back a few frontiers.

It isn't that we don't get plenty of exercise, weightlifting our shopping home or doing arabesques round the lampshades with a feather flick and duster. It is just that, as any first game of tennis for five or ten years will show, there are a surprising number of muscles which remain mere drones in the average daily round. I soon discovered this when, rashly, I accompanied David recently to his badminton club. The people there were so nice I may even go back. One of these days.

I once enrolled at a proper Keep Fit class but it wasn't altogether a success. The girl I was paired off with seemed a shade absentminded and just as I was doing a complicated knee-grip-arm-bend-back-swing which depended *entirely* on her co-operation and support, she used to walk away. And when all the other couples were grasping each other firmly round the wrists and *heave*-ho-ing with all their might, she would see a friend and wave. And, with a forward *heave* and only half a ho, I would crash backwards on to my head. Quite often.

Furthermore, our leader was sickeningly biased in favour of two elegant, willowy, supple females who just happened to be married to two of the richest men in that particular town.

'Lovely, my dears. Well done!' she would fawn. 'Come up here so that the others can see what you're doing.'

So there was all this sinuous loveliness going on up front while we poor wobbly, wheezy, varicose job-lot thumped and trembled and fell over in heaps down at the back by the exits, unable to see or be seen.

But now, here in my nice new neighbourhood, I am game to have another try. So I have been making tentative enquiries among healthier-looking acquaintances to see if there is something moderately athletic that I can join. Just for some company, I tell myself. But also before I start getting any of those funny mauve turns.

'Have you tried square dancing?' asks a merry little lady in a gingham skirt and plimsolls. Well, I did some Scottish dancing once but the trouble is either you are frightfully good at that sort of thing and know exactly where you are supposed to be at any given moment, in which case some giggling fool mucks the whole thing up by reeling off with the wrong partner, or else you are frightfully bad at it and have to run like mad to catch up.

I was quite keen on ballroom dancing once. In fact one chap told me I had the best hip grip in the tango he'd ever experienced. But somehow all that dipping and swooping doesn't seem to go with current flinch and twitch techniques.

And another thing – even if you find yourself at a fairly traditional dinner-do, on your average dance floor these days a couple of heel turns and you're in among the diners.

So perhaps, for the time being, it would be best for me to plod on secretly at home with my exercises. It is a very gentle, reassuring sort of book I am working from.

'Start at the bottom of Chart One,' it says. 'Take your time. *Do not rush things*. When you can *easily* bring your knee up somewhere near your chest hold it there for a couple of seconds and then sit down and rest.' It goes on to say that one might like to move up the chart as and when one feels ready for the challenge.

Further on in the book, legs begin to creep around ears but I won't think about that. For the moment I will satisfy myself by getting the knee just a little bit nearer the chest. At last, lungfuls of carpet fluff later, the moment arrives … 'Hey everybody – quick!' I yell. 'Come and see what I can do!' Oh hell, I must have rushed things …

'Help. HELP!'

31 Doing The Flowers

My Life and I, *Good Housekeeping*, October 1972

There are a great many things I can't do and one of them is arranging flowers. I try. I go along to demonstrations and sit, bemused, in the fragrant, steamy atmosphere while a lady with twinkly hands does astonishingly clever things with three lilies and a stick of rhubarb.

My old Gran's godetia patch, the hedgerow search for early violets and the thrill of actually growing my own first annuals – real, live marigolds from strange green caterpillar seeds – these are happy childhood memories which help to embroider life's plainer patches. But whereas Gran could shove a few clarkia, a bit of borage and some poppy seed heads into a ginger jar and create an arrangement, when I do it they just look shoved.

Which is a pity, because I love flowers. Flowers are to me what symphony concerts, cup finals, ballet or bingo are to other people. And I really would like to be able to express my feelings by doing justice to such blossoms as come my way.

'I know you like flowers,' visitors say, and yet another bunch of gladioli is doomed to lean lopsidedly on our window-sill. Sometimes really thoughtful souls don't bring me flowers. They bring me a pinholder or some chicken wire or 'this new American gadget which is guaranteed to hold *anything* in place'. But it is no use. My gladioli just go on leaning.

So when, recently, the opportunity arose for me to attend flower arranging classes for beginners I made a last ditch stand to master the art.

'Bring a shallow container,' said the notice, 'plus a few blooms and one or two sprigs of foliage.'

Taking no chances, I packed a large shallow container, a medium shallow container and a small shallow container. I bought three bunches of ten chrysanthemums. (Whatever happened to dozens?) I strode off into the undergrowth with secateurs and staggered home with armfuls of greenery. Like Birnam Wood I came to that first meeting and sat, peering beadily through a thicket of evergreen, while the lady up front started us off with a 'vertical'. Now I will admit that I began at a disadvantage. 'Prepare your Oasis by giving it a good soak,' we'd been told in advance. This, as all proper flower arrangers will know, is a green substance into which stems may be poked at whatever angle one happens to have in mind. My husband, however, couldn't really be expected to know this. While giving me an all too rare 'hand with the dishes' the night before, he had scoured several saucepans with the piece I'd been preparing.

'This damned stuff's useless,' he said.

It was – after that. My friend and fellow learner, Dot, sliced me off a fresh piece and keenly, delicately, aesthetically, etc, I rammed home my very first main vertical, an interestingly gnarled apple branch. ('Be *bold*,' our teacher had said.) Slowly, inevitably, it did its own thing.

'You're not supposed to be doing a horizontal,' said Dot.

A quick look round the hall established that all the other ladies were on top of their Michaelmas daisies, so to speak. Here a prettily placed piece of golden rod, there a radiant uprising of dahlias.

Back in our corner, three crumbling chunks of Oasis later, I had discarded the apple tree branch, eighteen mangled chrysanthemums and my two larger containers. Now, at last, five of my remaining blooms were more or less propping each other up. A blonde lady with kind eyes had passed me two of her privet leaves and I had almost anchored down a dogwood twig. Dot, and her other friend, Irene, were still falling about, mopping their eyes.

'Best entertainment we've had in years,' they gasped. 'Certainly never thought it would be as much fun as this!'

Swiftly, it seemed, I was becoming established as the class buffoon.

By now most of the others had finished and our teacher was coming slowly round the hall Making Comments.

'Lovely; most interesting; now *that's* really good,' I could hear her saying as she drew nearer. She reached our corner.

'Now what have we here?' she said, giving my container a twirl. Silently, thirty or so pairs of eyes watched as my chrysanthemums began to move. For a split second they hovered in an interesting sunburst shape and then the whole arrangement fell out on to the table.

'What a nice, colourful plate,' she said encouragingly, and swiftly moved on.

So here we are, many chrysanthemums later, more or less eagerly awaiting our next lesson. Some come for the tuition. Others, in our corner I fear, come for the entertainment. Next week we are 'doing the triangle'.

'You will need three long stems, a candlestick and plenty of other assorted plant material,' we have been told. Plus grit, determination, secateurs, lots – really lots – of Oasis and all the only slightly dented enthusiasm I can muster.

Wish me luck.

32 Telephones

My Life and I, *Good Housekeeping*, November 1972

'Hello,' said a cheery friend on the telephone. 'What are you up to, this morning?'

'I'm changing my room round,' I said. There was a pause.

'Er – did you say you are changing your womb round?' I could almost hear her wincing. As well she might.

We cleared up that little misunderstanding but it did make me wonder about the telephone as a means of real communication.

For one thing we have the same number as the Want Ads column of a newspaper in a nearby town. And every day someone forgets to dial the appropriate exchange number first. You wouldn't believe how many times I've been dragged from the bath/the saucepan of boiling milk/the half-dug garden compost heap, only to find myself talking to querulous old souls who tell me that they want to sell their latest litter.

'You have the wrong number,' I tell them. 'Oh no I haven't,' they rap. Sometimes they are so unshakeable in their belief that I am the *Evening Post*, they even convince me, and I find myself taking down their ad on my scribbly blotter.

My husband has a rather vague attitude to telephone callers even when they do get the right number.

'Hang on a minute, I'll get him,' I tell the chap on the other end. 'David!' I yell. If he is in the garden I beckon furiously through the window and press my fist to my ear. Now I maintain that after thirteen years of marriage he should know that this little gesture means he is wanted on the telephone. But he thinks he is married to a funny woman who keeps pressing her fist to her ear.

'*Telephone!*' I yell, as he goes on digging.

'He's just coming,' I lie gallantly to the waiting chap.

At last David gathers that I am trying to attract his attention and by the time I get the window open he is coming up the path carrying a sprig of mint.

I suppose there *are* people who press their ear and shout 'Telephone' when they need mint. But not *many*, surely?

I am still wondering anxiously, too, about the old chap sent round to look at our plumbing which had sprung a leak.

'Do you mind if I just ring my wife and tell her I made it?' he quavered. Trembling over to the desk he picked up the telephone and dialled. 'Hello dear, it's me. I made it!' he said and rang off. Slowly he mounted our stairs. 'She likes to know if I've made it,' he said ambiguously.

My mother has a miniature hour-glass egg timer by her telephone which isn't a bad idea because the sand runs out every four minutes, so she knows roughly the duration and cost of each call. The trouble is that as long as the sand is running she feels it would be wasteful to stop talking. I don't mind listening in to the Four Minute Sentence when she rings *me* but I do get edgy when I ring her and I can't get a word in.

'By the way, I just rang you to ask if …' I blurt out at last, hoping to stem the flow.

'Oh dear, there goes the sand – must ring off now,' she says.

'But it's *my* sand this time,' I say, feebly, into a dead receiver. I actually have had to ring her back on occasions, diving into my own non-stop sentence the moment I hear her lift the phone.

Only once has this backfired on me. 'Ah, hallo Mum – is that you?' I cried.

'No it isn't mum. Definitely not, I should say,' said a male Pakistani voice.

It is nonplussing, too, when the line goes dead in the middle of a conversation. Should one ring back? Should one leave the receiver on in case they are ringing us back? Or have they taken umbrage at something they think we've just said and cut us off on purpose?

There is one friend who always talks when I am talking. Then we both stop and there is a long, eerie pause. At the identical moment we both rattle on again. We can't help it. We must share the same electrical impulse.

While on the subject of eerie pauses, I rang a friend on a large housing estate the other day and just as she answered someone handed me a toffee which I absentmindedly put in my mouth. 'Hallo – hallo. Who's there?' she cried, in what seemed to me a slightly hysterical voice. 'My God – it's him – quick,' she whispered.

With a great gulp I swallowed the toffee and said:
'Hallo – it's me.'

'My word,' she said, with a quivery laugh. 'You don't know how near you came to getting your eardrum shattered!'

It seems her estate was being plagued by a phantom heavy-breather. It had been suggested that everyone kept a whistle by the telephone which, if blown into the mouthpiece, should discourage further calls. But it occurs to me that perhaps the poor chap wasn't a sex maniac after all. Perhaps he just couldn't stop eating toffees.

No, one way and another, the telephone doesn't always improve our relationships with the outside world. Especially where children are concerned.

'Daddy's gone out and Mummy's lying down on the bed and she doesn't want to talk to anybody' can suggest all manner of sinister domestic crosscurrents. And I expect we've all asked our children at some time or another not to tell unidentified callers that: 'Mummy's in the lavatory. She's been there for *hours*.'

It can be equally embarrassing to be at the other end of the line.

'Hallo,' pipes a little voice.

'Is your daddy there?' we coo.

'This *is* their daddy *speaking*,' pipes the same little voice.

But I am in no position to make fun of other people's telephone *persona*. I suppose my speaking voice might be described as leaning towards the contralto. Well it might be.

In fact, on the telephone, nearly everybody calls me 'Sir.' I told a passing repair man this the other day and he looked me slowly up and down and said: 'They must be *mad*.' Which almost makes up for everything.

33 A Hint To One's Beloved

My Life and I, *Good Housekeeping,* February 1973

'My word, it's a long time since anyone sent me a Valentine,' I say early in February. I say it every year but to no avail. Well no, that's not strictly true. One year, early in marriage, I received a card. 'Here is my heart …' it said. Mistily I turned the page. '… Why don't you tear it out and eat it, you old vulture?' it went on.

'Look, I've said I'm sorry,' said my spouse an hour later, a heavily lived-through hour for all concerned. 'I honestly thought you'd laugh. Like you did when I bought you the rolling pin done up like a bunch of flowers.'

Our marriage has come a long way since then. But not quite far enough to encompass a regular stream of proper Victorian Valentines with ribbons and moss roses and lovely, treacly words.

I don't usually like sentimentally worded cards. On most occasions I'd rather receive 'Best wishes' than 'Heartfelt kisses tender and true; there never was a mum/wife/daughter like you'. But on Valentine's Day I would be only too glad of red padded satin, pressed violets, passionate yearnings and all the kisses, preferably in purple ink, that the anonymous sender can squeeze on to the card.

There are girls whose husbands go out and buy them surprise theatre tickets, fistfuls of orchids and the occasional Aston Martin. There are even girls for whom *other people's husbands* do this.

But I am not greedy. All I want is that, just once on 14th February, my doormat be littered, or better still heaped, with large white envelopes. And little lavender ones. And urgent bright yellow ones. And perhaps a few bulging airmail blue ones. I don't mind just as long as all of them are crammed with heartfelt sonnets dedicated to me.

Failing that, do let there please be just one communication, any colour you like, with the signature: 'Guess who?' That's the beauty of Valentines. Perhaps one's cousin Nelly did send it as a joke. But *perhaps*, just possibly, one's homely old profile has stirred an unknown manly breast.

I want to float through the rest of February wondering to myself who sent it. Was it the butcher? Does the fact that he broke into *Take A Pair Of Sparkling Eyes* as he weighed up my mince, have any special significance?

And what about the milkman? Does he favour all his ladies with such a direct, twinkly stare? I once had a milkman who went all pink one morning. and said he thought I was lovely. Anyone who sees me first thing in the morning and still says I'm lovely *must* be joking, I thought. So I laughed and said I could certainly use a little encouragement. Alas, I think perhaps 'encouragement' wasn't the best word to have chosen in the circumstances because he went even pinker and blurted out that any time I needed encouragement he'd be round like a shot, day or night.

In spite of the fact that (a) I don't really go in for that sort of thing, (b) I was about a foot taller than he was and (c) he was a fairly gnarled old grandfather anyway, that little doorstep encounter made me feel marvellous all day and is still a fond memory. I like to think that he'd been brooding and brooding and fermenting and fermenting for years, at the sight of me. Until at last his passion knew no bounds. Wouldn't that be *super*?

I have often thought, too, that if door-to-door salesmen were trained to say: 'Good morning madam ... er, I say, aren't you *fabulous!*' they'd sell every one of their encyclopedias, tins of furniture polish, double glazed windows and loads of firewood before they'd even finished the sentence.

I have been re-reading my old Dornford Yates collection these past few weeks and, while I no longer expect my menfolk to go down on one knee and kiss my instep, I can't help feeling that we could all do with some sort of Romantic Revival. And I could do with it more than most. Because one of the problems of being tall and – shall we say – sturdy is that I am constantly being requested by certain members of the family to:

'Give the car a bit of a heave,'

'Hold up this end until I come back,'

'Just hand me down those sacks of cement,'

'Put your shoulder to it,'

'Get your knee under it,'

'Keep her steady,'

And 'Brace yourself.'

Which is hard luck because deep down inside I am not only Romantic. I am *Frail*. Come the summer I do not want to go out into the garden and help lay paving stones for the new terrace. I want to wear swirls of pink chiffon and sit prettily in the gazebo, reading Robert Browning. I want to stare dreamily up at the nodding 'Félicité et Perpétué' rosebuds and think lovely, drowsy thoughts about all those delightfully mysterious Valentines I once received …

We all deserve at least one silent admirer. If only to help us get through the rest of the winter. So come on chaps. My doormat is all swept and ready. *Do* pop out for some purple ink and start pulsating.

34 Gathering Momentum

My Life and I, *Good Housekeeping*, May 1973

Have you noticed that one doesn't grow older gracefully? It happens in fits and starts. There is the day you stop reading Dr Spock and go out and buy a book about the menopause. Or the day you buy a new coat and someone says: 'Good heavens, you do look with it!' How long, one wonders, has one been soldiering on without it?

Or perhaps it is the day when your husband stops calling you 'Moon of my delight,' and says 'Belt up, you old faggot,' for the very first time.

Hairdressers rarely beat about the bush either. 'Such pretty hair madam must have had ...' they murmur, 'before it faded.'

I think my moment of truth came when I dropped into the chemists for some face cream. It is bad enough to have a deaf chemist's assistant (poor soul, why ever didn't she take up greengrocery or dry cleaning?) but to have to shout: '*Can I have another tube of Over-Forty Cream?*' is pushing back the veils of mystery a bit too far, even for those of us with small, blabbermouth sons who tell anybody anything anyway.

My almost teenage daughter, on the other hand, means well. 'Don't mind me saying this, Mummy,' she starts diplomatically. And I learn, from the talk they've just had at school on make-up, that not only is my eye-liner old hat but I've got to smear pinkish stuff over and under the lids to really make the scene.

Piggy-eyed but trendy I gaze bleakly into shop windows. A fifteen-year-old policeman strolls past. I dive into a boutique before he offers to help me across the road. Immediately my ears wax over – protection against the sonic boom of the latest disc which has come a long long way from Jack Jackson's Record Round-Up. My pupils meanwhile are opening at widest aperture to compensate for the boutique's midnight-blue walls, floor and ceiling. A glimmer of Lurex catches my eye through the gloom, and I'm in luck – it fits. I glide off to the next party, a shining, ageless, happy creature.

'Tell me,' says an earnest young two-inch strip of face between waterfalls of hair. 'From your long experience, how does marriage rate as an institution?'

Groping for a seat and for words to describe my institutional life, I find myself looking across at my husband. There appear to be about six terribly young women wound around him, all helping him to light his pipe. They don't seem to mind the disgusting bubbly noises it makes, nor the fact that little black, composty lumps are floating out and landing damply in all directions. I *knew* I should have discouraged him from growing that *Viva Zapata* moustache.

Later I ask some of my contemporaries how *they* feel about life and marriage now that we are – er – middlin' young.

'It's all this permissiveness that gets me down,' sighs one pent-up soul. 'When I think what I've *missed*!'

'Oh yes,' chimes in another. 'It's all very well being told that virtue is its own reward but I'm reaching the stage when I *need* a few rakish memories to get me through the day.'

'Well, I just love to take a back seat now and to watch the youngsters enjoying themselves,' says another. This little gem stuns us all into silence.

'Personally,' says a lugubrious voice from the corner, 'I've never really got over the shock of marrying Prince Charming and watching him turn back into a frog.'

'I've taken to carrying a hip flask,' admits a cheery, pinkish little woman. With various others it is good works, gardening, going blonde, *haute cuisine* and weight-watching.

For me, I think I'll start laying a few foundations to see me through into a stylish old age. It may seem a long way off at the moment, but, at the rate momentum is gathering itself lately, I shall be there waving my pension book at chiropodists and cinema managers before you can say 'Phyllosan'.

I once heard old age described as a crystallization of all that has gone before. If this is so then perhaps it isn't too soon for any of us to start weeding out our funny little ways. I certainly don't want to hear any future grandchildren saying:

'That's my granny – that one over there drinking her liniment and singing bawdy songs.' Nor: 'For heaven's sake, don't mention the word *bowels* or she'll be off again.' Nor even: 'Oh, do come off that trapeze, Gran. We all know about you and your Bio-Strath.'

No, I rather like the idea of a picturesque old age with lace at the throat and long purple tea-gowns. 'Come sit by me,' I shall say, resting a thin, freckled hand on assorted curly heads. 'I want you to have this.' And I shall slip a couple of pearl-and-emerald trinkets and a cameo or two into little chubby fists. Well, actually they may have to make do with the op-art scatter pins and my big plastic Habitat key ring, but it makes a gracious picture, all the same.

In the meantime I think I'll just squeeze back into my Lurex, fill my pores with a good blob of Over-Forty Cream and away we go for one more shimmy before it's too late!

35 On With The Dance

My Life and I, *Good Housekeeping*, August 1973

If you happened to be passing a village hall late last Saturday and you noticed a little trickle of perspiration leading from the main entrance out to the car park, that was probably me.

Now, several days later, my leg muscles are still tightly clenched and my ribs still shaking – the latter from laughter. Have you ever been to a barn dance?

'Oh do come,' said these friends of ours. 'It's all good homely fun with lashings of cider and sausage rolls and things.'

What they didn't tell us was that one has to be *fit*. Our friends play squash about four times a week, when they aren't sailing or cycling or doing off-the-cuff press-ups. So, it appeared, do barn dancers. While they all tripped-to-the-centre-one-two-three, with no more than rosy cheeks to show for their exertions, I staggered clammily up and down, praying for the music to stop or at least slow down. I nearly fainted twice.

It wouldn't have been too bad had I been able to cling to my spouse for succour but we kept on having those progressive dances. So while David, all flashing blue shirt and red neckerchief, skipped stylishly up towards the good guys, I blundered about down among the baddies. We were the ones with the hot hands, the uncontrollable giggles and the steaming temples.

'Oh, we must stand up for this one,' I heard someone say. 'It's so pretty when they weave under and over the arches.'

The idea, apparently, was to clasp one's partner's hands and make an arch. Theoretically, the next couple would then bob under it and make an arch themselves, so that we then went under theirs. Then, with lightning reflexes, we would make our frantic arch again for couple number three. And so on.

Are you with me? Well, neither was the rest of our set. For obscure personal reasons none of them wanted to make arches. They all wanted to dive *under* them. There was a very nasty moment when, head down and skipping like mad, I found myself charging straight towards a huge young police cadet, also with his head down.

'But you're our *arch*,' I screamed at him in mid-swerve. And of course the two little old ladies who were now charging towards us *were* supposed to be down there but by the time I'd grabbed my cringing partner and we'd made another arch it was too late.

Just then someone's husband galloped past wearing a fixed smile.

'Hello, where are you off to?' we called, but he couldn't seem to stop galloping and in fact spent the rest of the dance as an odd extra man somewhere down by the cloakrooms.

'Where are you, partner?' the other half of his original arch kept calling, but he seemed to be past caring. And so, towards the end of the evening, was I.

'Come on, you must join in this one,' said David. (He swims a lot and plays badminton and was still appallingly lively.) So I kept on lurching on to the floor for just one more 'doh-se-doh'. By this time I'd slowed down so much that we had to leave whole movements out in order to catch up with the others.

'What a splendid evening!' I gasped, as David helped me out to the car afterwards. But on the whole I think I'm more suited to the gentler, more rhythmic dances.

Actually, I enjoy all types of dancing but until recently there has been a longish gap in our dancing days. Now suddenly we seem to be trotting off to quite an assortment of dinner dances, local hops and dark discos. And it is immediately noticeable that things have come a long, long way from the old slow-slow-quick-quick-slow.

In fact, on current dance floors it seems perfectly possible to stand on one spot all evening merely undulating upwards from the pelvis. (In infant drama lessons this used to be known as 'being a tree'.) In the very trendiest circles it even seems to be considered smarter to do this just *off* the beat. But either way it can be soothing.

All the same, I wonder more places don't cater for those of us whose dancing style hovers somewhere mid-way between *Come Dancing* and Pan's People.

One older friend has worked out a splendid routine which sees him through any current pop sound. He clenches his fists, raises his shoulders, looks blank and marks time with his feet. Somehow he manages to make this look amazingly trendy.

I find a long skirt a great help. As long as one looks confident no one knows for sure what is going on underneath. It also solves the problem of what to wear.

'Come to our club disco – just wear any old thing,' *may* mean any old thing. Or it can mean that they are all wearing frightfully smart gear which just *looks* like any old thing. The first time I went to the expensively rough-hewn old mill with the latest sound, the swirling rainbow walls, the deeply fringed Tiffany lamps, etc., I wore something neat and dark and horribly noticeable. The second time I wore my Ossie Clark patchwork.

But for the barn dance, comfortable shoes are what matter. Roller skates even. And something to mop up the sweat. Plus some sort of advance assault course. As for me, I'll be just fine once I get my muscles unclenched.

36 Anyone For Etymology?

My Life and I, *Good Housekeeping*, September 1973

'If you don't know the meaning of a word, look it up,' my father used to say, and to this day in our house the path to the dictionary is well worn.

Not that I want to stomp about booming: 'Back to your forfars, you bosky piddock before I have at you with my daguerreotype.' (Just in case you want to, it is as well to know that you are threatening to use an early photographic process on a hairy mollusc if he doesn't return to his coarse linen cloth.)

But I would love to be able to reply to the children's: 'Mummy, what's a corollary?' with an unhesitating: 'Well dear, it's a proposition appended to one already demonstrated, as a self-evident inference from it.' If I could manage that, I might even throw in a light laugh. Or at the very least a careless toss of the head.

Reading one's dictionary for pleasure does pay off occasionally. The children haven't ever quite got over the evening when I happened to know the meanings of two words in 'Call My Bluff'.

However, my moment of glory was soon shattered by Daniel's: 'Mum, what does *the* mean?' Have you ever tried defining 'the' to a seven-year-old? I have become aware that he is developing a certain flair for the English language since he asked David why he likes doing hot-cross-word puzzles, and especially since he told us that our neighbour Jill is planting night-scented socks in front of her honeyscuttle.

But who am I to talk, having twice told the builder at our last house that what I really needed was a stainless steel stink?

One of the things my brother and I noticed early in our dictionary reading days is that certain words don't sound at all like their definitions. Take 'tyro'. To me this suggests a ruthless oppressor. Certainly not a beginner. And how about 'sanguinary'? I see a pale, languid chap – not one who enjoys bloodshed. 'Valedictory' sounds mean but it's only farewell. 'Crepuscular' too suggests all sorts of nastiness. How many, I wonder, would connect it with twilight?

Once a word establishes itself in our awareness, it seems to crop up everywhere. It leaps out at us from books, newspapers, radio programmes and conversations overheard on buses. Perhaps friends tell us that they are thinking of having a ha-ha. 'Oh, one of *those*,' we say as we slip off to look it up. Next morning on the front page of the newspaper there is a photograph of a cabinet minister gazing a thoughtfully at his ha-ha. We switch on the radio and a titled lady is telling us about her stately ha-ha. Suddenly *everybody* is going on about ha-has.

I must admit I haven't actually heard anyone say: 'My word, Millicent, it's getting quite crepuscular outside!' But there is a noticeable tendency for certain words to become trendy. (There's one for a start.) And this seems particularly true in political and television circles. For years we manage without words like cartel/unilateral/fiscal. Suddenly up they come in every news bulletin.

I suppose we all do it. Sometimes from sheer nerves. I can remember, during school days, being invited to tea with a podgy, top-drawer girl called Nina. ('I'm not *fat* – I'm *stout*,' she used to insist, showing a nice feeling for the English language herself.) Nervously I did my best to answer probing questions set by Nina's heftily regal mum. 'Tell me about your family,' she said.

'My grandfather's got *enormous* hands,' I squeaked. Mama looked politely astonished.

'And an *enormous* garden.' Her expression grew a shade more hopeful.

'But all that digging gives him *enormous* blisters.' Mama began to look rather withdrawn and shortly afterwards I left the enormous Nina and her enormous mum standing at their enormous front door, etc, etc.

Since then there have been times when I've taken a great fancy to 'pedantic', 'sardonic', 'huge', 'griddle', 'medieval' and 'swoosh'. My current is 'absolutely'. Anna's is 'fantastic'. Daniel's is 'loads'. David's is 'poignant' and my boss favours 'monies'. The last two have a certain charm but it looks as if the rest of us had better head back to the dictionary.

Not that I want the children racing in to tea saying: 'Oh by the way mum, there's a febrile satrap in the gazebo.' (Even if we do ever happen to have a feverish provincial governor in that thing down the garden.)

No, I just want to be able to avoid such little gems as these, heard recently:

'She was wearing a sort of odalisque on a chain round her neck.'

'There's nothing like turpitude for cleaning paintbrushes.'

And even: 'Well, if it's really going to be a glittery occasion I'd better wear my gold Durex.'

Let us feel able to make full, confident use of such mellifluous words as mellifluous. And clew and cleat and clerestory. And possibly even plumose. Let us get as far away as possible from sentences such as:

'Er, well, I mean, like, you know.'

Let us not grope for words. Let us *plunge* with etymological assurance.

Doubtless we'd all feel better if we could sidle up to the problem people in our lives (the idiot in the next office/the noisy neighbour across the way/that fool driving the car ahead) and hiss: 'Viscous sinapisms to you mate – all over your turgid ramekin.' Which, roughly translated, condemns him to a morbidly swollen cheese dish covered with sticky mustard plasters.

Now *that's* what I call word power!

37 Mod Con vs Old Con

My Life and I, *Good Housekeeping*, October 1973

'My word, you aren't much of a family for mod con are you?' said a switched on, fully automatic friend the other day, drifting around my kitchen and smiling tolerantly at our good old fridge, our good old hand whisk and our good old tabby cat asleep on the boiler.

'Well we do have a fairly new electric toaster,' I said, looking wildly round. I am just not a very mechanically minded person. In fact I tend to go out shopping for a steam iron and come home with a rose bush.

To impress her I waggled the Vent-Axia cord and ostentatiously fed the waste disposal unit a piece of cabbage. But since these two items were built in to the new house I can't really claim them as trophies in the kitchen gadget contest. So I suppose I should do something to update my image.

Perhaps a new vacuum cleaner might be the answer. I have to admit that, for years now, I've been writhing around the floors with an elderly, torpedo-shaped machine which certainly sounds as if it might be cleaning carpets. But lately, as more and more bits have dropped off (even the home-made string handle) and the smell of burning rubber has grown stronger, I have come to realize that my friend is right.

Not only do I not own much in the way of mod con but most of ours is becoming decidedly old fashioned con. In fact, if I can just make do for a little bit longer, much of my household equipment will become quite valuable as antiques.

My treadle sewing machine is nearly there and how I love it. It does none of those terrifying bursts of sustained electrical seaming, so useful for making parachutes, but so alarming when fiddling about with half a collar. Together we rickety-rack, rickety-rack at rocking-chair speed. No wild swerves around armholes. Just a gentle veer to the right-hand notch, steady as we go.

I like the little accompanying booklet in which a charmingly illustrated matronly lady, with dimpled hands, guides me step by step through the intricacies of bobbin replacement and adjustment of stitch. Together we ease our tensions. The booklet explains it all. There is even a chapter entitled: 'The Foot Hemmer – Felling' although I must confess that I've never yet felt quite up to reading it through to the end – or felling myself. My kitchen scales, also, are so old and picturesque that they are coming back into fashion and visitors now no longer giggle at the flat-iron and the cobbler's last that we use as bookends. They, too, are in vogue. However, neither quaintness nor antiquity can in the long run serve as very good reasons for hanging on much longer to a cooker with an ever closing door, however heat-conserving this may be.

So I start slowing down in front of gas and electricity showrooms. Isn't it strange how one can go on from year to year without giving some things a thought? Take Dalmatian dogs, or Volkswagens or pregnancy. The day comes when one is considering a new puppy/car/baby. Suddenly the world is absolutely full of spotted dogs, Beetle cars or expectant mums. This is now happening to me in the case of electrical equipment. Everywhere I look, there are windows crammed with fantastically improved cookers, not to mention stream-lined mixers, blenders, driers, freezers.

One drops into friends' homes and there in their bathrooms one suddenly notices that they use electric toothbrushes. Quite casually – without even mentioning the fact in general conversation. I visit three kitchens, one after another and they've all got washing-up machines. Another friend is just off to buy her *second* deep freeze.

Now I don't care much for those cold, pampered ladies who say smugly that *of course* they've got a chromium plated sauna or a floodlit trout-stream or whatever the last word in mod con happens to be. But these are just ordinary, comfortable, workaday chums who happen to have worn out a whole deep freeze before I've even got around to buying my first one.

I discover, too, that my family, the moment they are asked, are yearning to own all sorts of gadgets, given the slightest encouragement.

'Honestly we could eat much better if only you'd have a deep freeze,' says my spouse, excitedly. 'We could buy most of our food in *bulk*.' He is obsessed with the idea of bulk. Me, I only need a couple of chops, a pound of carrots and an Oxo cube to cater through the day. But David craves to be surrounded by gallons of HP sauce, sackfuls of frozen peas and entire oven-ready sheep. Daniel says that he could easily make do with a tiny portable television set of his own for Christmas. 'I could watch Laurel & Hardy *all the time* if I had my own set,' he tells me earnestly.

Then one morning a new vacuum cleaner comes into my life. An upright, pale blue one with assorted accoutrements for nuzzling down the backs of armchairs and even for reaching right round behind radiators. For two whole days we beat as we sweep as we clean. Non-stop. Carpets regain their lost youth. My family sit huddled in chairs with their feet off the ground. Unbelievable mounds of fluff are shaken on to the compost heap. Buttons and cobwebs and hairgrips, too.

I flop down at last, to share with Percy Thrower his 'Gardener's World'. 'Aren't these a picture?' he is saying, waving his arm over a mass of indistinct grey blobs.

'Oh do let's have a colour telly,' I burst out. 'Now I come to think of it, I've always secretly yearned for a tape recorder, too,' I add. 'And a liquidizer.'

Suddenly it is a whole new world of modern convenience. And it looks as if, at long last, I am on my way to join the converted.

38 Are You Having An Affair With Your Husband?

Woman, December 1973

Does it amaze you when girls give your husband the eye? Your comfortable pipe-smoking husband who spends his summer evenings up at the allotment and his winters heeled in around the telly. Well, don't take him too much for granted. You could be in for quite a surprise.

I was amazed, when driving through France not long ago, to find that all kinds of females waved and blew kisses at my husband whenever we happened to stop at traffic lights.

'They must be mistaking you for a French film actor or a TV personality,' I said, as a very pretty passing girl, arm-in-arm with her male escort, suddenly disentangled herself, dashed up to our car and gave David an incredibly meaningful wink through the windscreen.

'Or perhaps it's a French advertising campaign,' I added. "You know the sort of thing – if you see Monsieur Fairy Neige in your locality, a wink, a wave and a kiss may bring you a year's supply of la linen blanc-er than blanc.'

'Oh very funny,' said David, waving and grinning in all directions, as we drove off. 'I expect it is something to do with the French temperament. Or it could even be,' he added, after a modest pause, 'that I'm just naturally attractive to the opposite sex.'

When I'd stopped laughing I turned and studied him thoughtfully and, do you know, what with the red tee shirt, the holiday sun-tan and the newly cultivated brigand moustache, he *did* look wildly attractive.

Which just goes to show that we shouldn't take each other too much for granted and that there is probably room for improvement even in the happiest of marriages. If, on the other hand, married life turns out to be a lot less than perfect, then it too probably still has a great deal of unexplored potential. (And if you aren't willing to go exploring, some lonely lady somewhere will be only too glad of the chance.)

I think a day comes in most marriages, and sometimes quite early on, when the wife must say to herself: okay, so Fred's not perfect. He drinks or he gambles or he smokes too much or he plays darts too often with his mates and he's got some dirty habits I certainly didn't know about during the engagement. SO WHAT? If I'd married Steve McQueen I'd probably have a home littered with dismantled motor bikes.

Paul Newman and Joanne Woodward ascribe their long and happy marriage to doing their own thing. He likes to go off to sporting events. She prefers concerts. Mick Jagger and his wife Bianca see themselves always as lovers and never as 'an old married couple'. Throughout history there have been First Ladies of the Land sitting stoically at home being gracious while their monarchs made merry elsewhere.

So who are we to grumble about Fred's funny little ways? And come to that, why not try, just for a second, to see married life from his point of view? When was the last time *you* entered a crowded room and heard the chaps all gasp: 'Who is that gorgeous, radiant girl?'

Think back for a minute – those were the days when we were forever sprinkling perfume into our bathwater, real phlox blossoms even, and giving ourselves manicures and pedicures and Hey-Presto-Instant-Dazzle face packs.

I once had a flawlessly groomed friend who, before marriage, was forever polishing her jewellery, pressing her clothes and checking her back view in mirrors. Then she got married and now she is just a pair of wrinkled stockings and a soggy skirt dangling beneath a mountainous pile of wet nappies. No wonder her particular Fred is always dropping in at his mother's. And very lucky for her that he isn't dropping in elsewhere.

Another girl that I used to know just grunted when her kind, thoughtful and very faithful husband brought her gifts. The first time he came home, in my presence, and flung a tiny enamelled antique fob watch into her lap and she snorted: 'Huh!' I thought, oh well, perhaps when I leave she will be less constrained. But no, shortly afterwards she gave me quite a lecture on the importance of 'keeping one's husband in his place' and, a few arid married years after this, her husband's place became somebody else's bed.

So if you are sitting at home thinking: 'I'll show him, the beast ... fancy getting drunk in front of all my friends/ draining his sump oil into my mixing bowl/soaking his cylinder head in the baby's bath ...' then it might be as well to remember that someone – somewhere – will be only too glad to show him that she doesn't think he's a beast. She *loves* sweaty, uncouth men who gamble/drink and/or smoke too much and never change their socks. He can unpick his big old greasy motor bike on her little snow-white carpet any time he likes. And if he had to have plain, proper food like his mother always made, then she's more than willing to toss her spice-rack out of the window and settle for boiled cabbage. The wily sexpot.

So why not forget the faults, the disappointments, the marital black patches of the past and start having an affair with your husband? Today.

Because, sad to say if, as you read this, you are already blushing and giggling and nibbling your spouse's ear then the chances are you only got married last Saturday.

If, on the other hand, you are sitting across from a great, grey, greasy, ageing mass who habitually snoozes his time away in the best armchair then you have my sympathy. But even for him and for you, this could be a turning point.

And for the rest of us, well, if you are not having an affair with your husband, then ask yourself – who is?

39 The Imperfect Hostess

Family Circle, December 1973

I plump up everything in sight from the cushions to my husband, dare all intimate family members to touch the clean towels in the bathroom at their peril and dash in all directions with last-minute dabs of furniture cream. The house and I wear a glazed look.

'Oh Lor, look at that huge speck of dust,' I keep gasping to myself, as I flop down with a last-minute relaxer on the rocks. I think perhaps I have made the mixture a bit too relaxing, because I keep on going deaf. 'It's nerves', my mother is prone to say in a remote nasal voice, when she goes deaf under similar conditions of stress. Soon now, assorted guests will start arriving for a pre-Christmas snifter, and I really must take a few deep breaths and prepare to be the warm, welcoming hostess.

But the moment I sit back and declench myself, I notice the smudge on the banisters or the streak on the window. Windows are perhaps my greatest house-cleaning bête noire. No matter which side I am polishing on, the other side shows up in great swathes of grey smear. On my way to the banisters with a sponge, a tea splash on the hall radiator catches my eye. I have long since given up wondering about such mysteries as why tea gets splashed on hall radiators. Once one has a growing family, anything is liable to get splashed anywhere. By now deeply involved in sponging down radiators, I find a sock behind one of them. Oh good, that makes up another pair. Is your life strewn with odd socks?

I am now soaping my way along the hall skirting board and am reminded of the time we stayed with friends in their caravan. Eager to please, while they were out, I wiped the wall behind the cooker. It came up gleaming, but left a grey tide mark where I'd stopped wiping. So I cleaned a bit more wall. And a bit more. The ceiling was moulded all of a piece with the walls, The corners curved continuously. Nowhere could I decently come to a halt. I washed every inch of that van that day. I had to, once I'd started.

Reluctantly, I throw in my sponge and take a last quick stroll around the living room. This year, our Christmas decorations are based on a fairly simple snowflake theme. How I envy those who have a natural flair for decorating, then later un-decorating, their homes. Almost Midas-like transformations are achieved in half an hour with just one can of gold spray, a few twigs and some jam jars. Or they create instant Eastern splendour with nothing more exotic than dim lighting and little twirls of cooking foil. Then, when the festivities are over, they skip around with a carefree laugh and a large paper bag and, within a twinkling, their living rooms are back to Habitat or old dog-eared fawn, as the case may be.

Our own living room has acquired a tiny dash of unexpected elegance with a white drinks cabinet, our Christmas present to the house. With the drinks in the bottom and our punch bowl on the top, it looks suitably festive. The only drawback is that the shelves in between them house a motley collection of drinking vessels, most of which came to us via petrol vouchers. In fact, the purchase of petrol accounts for quite a few of our household objects. The problem is that we rarely manage to collect complete sets of anything, because so many of the coupons are come by on distant journeys. If we ever stop at that garage in Somerset again, we might manage a second sundae glass. We have two amber tumblers gathered in Cornwall, a sherry glass from Devon, three vintage car table mats from Hampshire and 14 turquoise-blue whisky tumblers from our local garage.

'I must remember to tell David to give that gilt-rimmed glass with the vine leaves painted on the side to me,' I keep thinking. It is the one we use when anyone needs a TCP gargle and unexpected astringency still lurks in its depths.

'The cat, quick, where's the cat?' I scream. He's had a funny tummy lately, and I don't want any last-minute nastiness. Nor little rodent offerings. My mother's cat – a pampered creature – is prone to stroll in and offer her guests his latest catch. 'During this past fortnight,' she sighs, 'he's turned up with one small rat, three mice, a grass snake and a newt.' 'A newt! I say, stopping in my tracks. 'Oh yes', she says. 'I get offered quite a lot of live goldfish, too, from Mrs A's pond two doors up.' 'Whatever do you do?' I ask. 'Oh, I just lob them over the fence into Mrs B's pond. It's nearer.'

So now the cat is out, the punch is stirred, the cobwebs are at bay, and a car is drawing up outside. 'Quick, they're here', we cry, straightening our shoulders and taking a last deep breath. 'Hello my dears. How lovely to see you. Whoops, mind the mistletoe!'

To hell with dust and smudges. Let's all relax and have a really super Christmas!

40 Accident Prone

My Life And I, *Good Housekeeping*, February 1974

I seem to be using up rather a lot of sticking plasters lately. It isn't that I see myself as accident-prone in a general way, but when the cereal packet says blandly: 'Insert finger under flap and move sharply to left and right,' I just know that for me it isn't going to work.

Tentatively I poke where directed and one of two things happens. Either the inserting bit is easy, I move sideways too confidently, my finger tears its own ragged route and the family is doomed to several mornings of cereal from a jagged cardboard shambles, or else I can't get started and after a great deal of prod and waggle I am the torn shambles, hence the sticking plasters. This is not the ideal way to start the day.

We once had a neighbour who leapt from her bed each morning, flicked open a freshly starched gingham cloth, gave the silver a quick polish and then skipped out into the sun-drenched morn to pick a single rose for her breakfast table. Our house isn't a bit like that. Not a *bit*.

There was one morning when I tried a tentative leap from my bed. But none of my limbs joined in and I crashed heavily to the ground. I do have a bit of a problem with my early morning limbs. And not just legs. My husband handed me a well-meant tray of tea once and we both watched as it passed right between my outstretched hands and plummeted to the carpet. But I still don't regard myself as accident-prone – just daft in the mornings.

One friend really does manage a continuous stream of accidents. We love her dearly and we worry about her but we can't help laying bets as we approach her house – will it be a squashed thumb this time – a lost purse – an exploding hot-water bottle? No, this time it turns out to be a leap from a moving vehicle: 'I sort of nose-dived,' she tells us, with an apologetic laugh. 'And I couldn't stop running. People must have thought it strange to see a woman tearing along the main road for quite some distance, with her nose a bare six inches from the ground.' Her best effort to date is the day she fell off her own trolley.

'I was changing a light bulb and I forgot I was on castors,' she said sadly. 'Before I knew it, I zoomed off into the next room.' It is fascinating enough to think that there are people who stand on their tea trolleys, but to have them whizzing from room to room as if on giant, elevated roller skates really does make one marvel.

My husband has his moments, too. Quite early in courtship I said: "Here's your coffee, dear,' as I put his coffee carefully down on a chair. 'Right ho,' he said and promptly sat on it. And I shan't easily forget the expression on a small nephew's face as David, a kindly man, advanced with a big, smiling, avuncular hello and crunched small nephew's new miniature fire engine absolutely flat into the carpet.

Another grown-up relative of my husband, not normally accident-prone, was driving dashingly through the New Forest. You know how it is – the open road, the wind-ruffled hair, the Le Mans gear changes. Suddenly a wasp flew straight down the front of his shirt.

Unless one *knew* this, it must have seemed strange when all that Graham Hill-type cool suddenly gave way to wild screams, clawings and chest beatings as his car unexpectedly zig-zagged off across the heather.

In hard-up early-married days we, too, once had a little accident in the forest.

'What's that funny smell?' I kept saying.

'Never mind that, this car's not pulling too well,' my worried spouse kept replying.

As the sweet, sickly smell grew, the car slowed down and finally stopped. When David lifted the bonnet I remembered I'd tucked my plastic mac over the engine the night before to protect it from a sudden heavy frost. As the engine warmed up the mac had dissolved.

'Anti-freeze would have been cheaper in the long run,' I said bitterly as we scraped out the glutinous remains – a collar, two patch pockets and a row of front fasteners.

Looking back, I suppose I must admit to my share of accidents. There was the day when, in a long pale blue coat, I ran for a bus and missed. Picking myself up from a sizeable muddy puddle I tried again and just managed to swing aboard. Suddenly, on the pavement, I noticed a group of people I knew. They saw me at the same moment. 'Oh look, there's Betty!' they all called, waving cheerily.

They hadn't seen me run and fall but they did think it strange, they said later, to see me hurtle past on the running board, smiling radiantly in their direction and plastered from head to foot in mud.

I suppose we've all had our moments – how many I wonder have gone away for the weekend and left a rice pudding in the Aga? Or reluctantly plugged in a terribly strong-willed, scary electric floor polisher and, at the *very second* one pressed its switch, heard a nearby car backfire?

'Why is the floor polisher lying out there on the terrace?' said David.

'Because for the children's sake, I was brave enough to *throw* it there,' I told him. And hands up all those who have forcibly turned on a tap to tackle the washing up and had the water hit the upturned bowl of a spoon? And been absolutely *drenched*. Believe me, you are not alone.

41 The Jumble Sale Cycle

Family Circle, May 1974

A large, smiling stranger stood at the front door: 'Hello! I'm collecting up any odds and ends you may have for our jumble sale.' 'You've come at just the right moment', I cried, dragging him out to the garage, where stacks of dusty magazines and comics leaned heavily against cartons of old handbags, lampshades, hearthrugs and out-grown toys.

'Super', he said, quite bravely under the circumstances, and he still managed to look cheerful as he staggered out to his shooting brake with the fifth and final armful of our spring cast-aways.

'I wonder why it is that one family's old junk is someone else's ideal home?' I was thinking as I went back indoors. The house looked strangely bare and spacious, but I knew that it wouldn't last. At the very first opportunity, I'd be down at the church hall with all the other jumble sale enthusiasts, buying up a fresh selection of old junk at bargain prices.

I love jumble sales. Some are overcrowded and smelly; some overpriced and ladylike; some are run by harassed PTA dads in school playgrounds. At a memorable Girl Guide one, held under spreading chestnut trees by the side of a village street, we bought our last vacuum cleaner. It was bequeathed by the local lady-up-at-the-manor, 'no offer over £1 refused'. So, for a pound and sixpence, we took a chance on it working, which it did quite adequately. For many a year, I beat as I swept as I cleaned, and was reminded of that sunny summer's day in the process.

There is a feeling of real adventure as we follow signs saying, 'To the Jumble Sale', down strange alleyways and up rickety scout-hut steps. Will it be packed to the door with treasure trove? Or just with other people, faded petticoats and curled-up old shoes?

'Quick, over here!' we cry, as we thread our way towards the White Elephant stall. 'Look, there's quite a nice blue and white soup tureen', we chatter excitedly, 'Oh dear! It's rather badly chipped. What a pity!'

Bemused husbands drift past, clutching padded satin coat hangers and little frilly lavender bags. A triumphant young trendy is making for the door, loaded to the gunwales with art deco. Several people are considering bartering for 'Stag at Bay', because the frame looks as if it might have possibilities, and many of the younger children present will shortly be spending a completely silent and absorbed evening reading someone else's old comics – a cheap price for silence at 2p a bundle, often reduced to ½p as the sale draws to its tattered conclusion. 'Can we go home soon?' mutter older sons and daughters, who would really love to dive in among the books and clutter, but fear the whole scene is a bit beneath their dignity. Jolly, extrovert husbands are holding old nighties across their tums and saying, 'Ooh, just what I've always wanted! But is it really me?' Thin, introvert wives are muttering: 'Put it down, Arthur. Everybody's looking.'

If the sale is taking place in or near one of the big cities, then some of the youngish customers are already wearing a fair amount of jumble. Tall, thin, bespectacled girls in old black granny gear are looking very seriously indeed at shapeless black felt granny hats. This is giving rise to a certain amount of hilarity among a nearby group of shapeless old grannies.

If the sale is in the country, the cake stall is generally worth heading for, and the laden plant counter smells freshly of moist earth. We track down a newspaper-wrapped clump of miniature campanulas – just what we need for the rockery and 'Will 5p be all right?' asks the shy, green-fingered lady in charge.

I once picked up an elderly iron cooking pot for a few pence. It looked full of character, but was really full of rust, so I stood it on a windowsill and filled it with potted plants.

'Er, I wonder if I might ask rather a big favour of you?' stammered a lady who lived nearby. 'We're having my husband's boss to dinner at the weekend, and I thought I'd try my hand at jugged hare. And, er, well actually', she said, all of a rush, 'that black pot in your window would be just what I need. You wouldn't consider lending it to me, would you? I'd take great care of it.'

I explained to her that its looks were deceiving, and that it was full of rust. 'Oh, never mind about that', she said gleefully, scuttling off with it tucked under her arm. I often wonder how things turned out at that dinner party.

Since then, we've trundled home with many an ancient bargain. But perhaps the very best jumble sale I've come across was the private one held recently by several families, including friends of ours, who share a large house in the country. Their wide range of sons and daughters decided to turn a communal basement room into their own disco, and the jumble sale was to help them raise funds for a record player. For weeks, the children stitched away at cushions and aprons, dressed Teddy bears, painted jewellery, baked cookies and collected each other's discarded toys and clothing, plus any old family heirlooms their parents could spare.

The entrance fee was tuppence, and for this you got a cup of fruit punch, 'to put you in a spending mood'. My word, how we staggered home that day – not so much from the effects of the fruit punch as beneath the weight of fivepenny Indian bedspreads, penny purple dinner mats, threepenny dolls and cars, comics galore and a fantastic stuffed thing – known in our household as the White Elephant – which is not quite a floor cushion and not quite a sag-bag, but which, whatever it is supposed to be, is just right for flopping down on to watch the television.

This spring, I don't doubt, we shall lead our White Elephant out into the garage, where he will come to rest on the latest stack of books and toys and outgrown anoraks. There will be another knock on our front door, and the whole lovely jumble sale cycle will be set in motion again.

42 Lady of Leisure

My Life And I, *Good Housekeeping*, May 1974

Three times this morning my telephone has rung. Each time I've been asked the same question:

'What does it feel like to be a lady of leisure?'

'Well ...' I keep replying thoughtfully as I peel off my rubber washing-up gloves, put down the piece of wire I've been waggling about in the vacuum cleaner nozzle and/or switch off the steam iron.

The word has got around that I've left my part-time secretarial job.

'And not a moment too soon,' I think darkly to myself as I push back a few house-cleaning frontiers. Bookshelves bulge untidily, Venetian blinds squint smudgily and even the cat looks cobwebby. So I can't honestly say that the term 'lady of leisure' strikes quite the right note.

So far, today has been about average. Early morning consciousness brings with it usual feeling of impending doom. Try to tell myself briskly that it's just familiar low am ebb but make bleary, unconvincing job of bracing myself into keen, vertical position. Loiter palely on the edge of the bed. Allow myself just one theatrical sigh. Family no longer mutter 'Wassermatter?' They accept occasional hollow groans, sighs and small screams as normal punctuations of my early mornings. With toothbrush gritted between teeth I grab ancient, demoted sponge and make futile dabs at assorted toothpaste blobs and trickles around washbasin. Think, not for first time, why ever did we choose dark blue wall tiles? Look lovely when Min-creamed. But not often

Min-creamed. Put Min and piece of old Viyella shirt at foot of stairs to remind me.

Also at foot of stairs waiting to go up: two jigsaws, blow football, wrong tie, Monopoly, one Scrabble letter, tall, wobbly Lego thing, half a pyjama, two plastic hair rollers and an interesting stone.

Enter kitchen. Cat has found piece of liver left in his bowl for surprise evening snack. Cat so pleased he has apparently arranged late night drag hunt around floor and worktops. Dried blood everywhere. Nasty start to day.

Daughter says she must have half a pound of sausage-meat, ditto best mince and two large firm tomatoes for tomorrow's Domestic Science. Son says: 'Where's my other shoe?' Son always saying things like this.

Argument now in progress over whose turn it is for Tom & Jerry joke machine, in cereal pack. Joke machines very popular but pantry full of half-full delved-into cereal packs. Allow myself smallish sigh and raised eyes.

Promise myself that today I'll get some gardening done. Always something to be divided, thinned, pruned, fed or worried over. But enormous satisfaction derived from so doing. One of life's pleasures to clump back indoors, peel off gardening gloves and gaze out of window at freshly-turned earth. While thinking this, go to window to gaze out at yesterday's newly-planted tubs. Consternation. Cat decided all that lovely crumbly John Innes No 2 potting compost some new kind of ritzy dirt box. Yesterday's efforts scattered far and wide. Cat bored with whole subject. Saunters off across main road. Brakes screech from all directions. Cat one helluva big fool. (Wonder if possibly I am dog person after all?)

Gulp down large mug of tea and feel life begin to flicker once more in veins. Wash kitchen, Min bathroom, distribute jigsaws, etc. Give usual perfunctory groan at state of children's toy shelves. Make chickenwire lids for garden tubs. Sun begins to shine slightly and 'phone starts ringing …

Dash down to shops for daughter's ingredients. Stagger back uphill and fix myself mid-day Ryvitas and cheese plus tangy Bulgarian salad I am crazy about. Listen in to Frank Muir and Denis Norden both of whom I am also crazy about. My day continues to improve as it goes along. There is a knock at the door and I answer it to a small suédy lady with a bulging clipboard.

'Good afternoon, I'm doing a survey of attitudes towards savings and investments among people over – er – thirty-five, in certain professions. Would you mind telling me what your husband does for a living?' Bemused, I tell her.

'Oh well, I won't trouble you any more. Good afternoon.'

I stand in the hallway, feeling slightly hysterical at the sheer, damned cheek of it. But it is funny. So I write it down on the blotter, to get it exactly right when I tell my husband.

Today he stamps in early, via the pantry as usual, grabbing himself a sandwich before saying 'Hello.' I wish he wouldn't *do* that. I tell him about the survey lady and he is momentarily enraged at such blatant invasion of privacy.

But we have to dash off in the car to get petrol, collect the children and visit the launderette. At the petrol station I am enchanted by a sign which says: 'Wheel Balancing While You Wait'. I wait but no cheery chap in oily overalls comes out and stands on tiptoe, balancing wheels, one above the other on nose and outstretched fingertips. Never mind, it's a lovely entertainment idea and I for one certainly hope it catches on – it could replace green stamps.

Home again, I sort out the clean laundry, the children and the ingredients for the evening meal. The man from the shop down the hill arrives with our new hall carpet clasped in his arms – we unroll it and love its deep, rich pile, especially the cat who does three very perfunctory ritual turns before curling up and sinking into its luxurious shagginess. We all trip over him thereafter.

The Avon lady calls, in a sweet woolly hat, and we choose still more luxury from her catalogue. My husband looks cross and goes and makes himself another sandwich. I leap over the cat and dash guiltily to the kitchen sink, the vegetable knife, the saucepan …

The telephone rings. More cat vaulting. 'Hello,' says grandma above the hubbub of children's telly, doorbells and hissing pans.

'How does it feel to be a lady of leisure?'

'Well actually,' I shout, 'I'm loving *nearly* every minute of it!'

43 Simmer Down Blood

Family Circle, June 1974

I was smiling peaceably, vacantly even, at the kitchen sink early this morning, when my blood started to boil. No, it wasn't the onset of the dreaded hot flushes, but the sight that met my eyes out of the kitchen window.

I suppose we all strive to take life as it comes. However, most of us have our vulnerable patches. There are those whose emotions go all wobbly at the sight of a puppy – with others it may be pop stars, kittens, royalty, weddings or Steve McQueen. With me, it's plants. So, having spent all day yesterday creating a new border, I was not overjoyed to see a little swarm of schoolboys short-cutting across the front garden and leaping about with glee among my newly-planted shrubs.

The trouble with ranch fencing is that it attracts small boys to use it as a ladder. At the most downtrodden far corner, we have recently planted a sweet briar whose thorns we had hoped would act as a deterrent. Not a bit of it. The doughty lads now cut across closer to the house. Sniff, thud, chortle, they were going this morning, right on to my still tiny Chamaecyparis 'Green Hedger'. This particular conifer has an endearing habit of bending its topmost fronds over into graceful ballet poses. Ours now seems to be bending from the waist and ankles.

At least, nowadays, we have a fence to define the boundaries. The garden at our first home was open-plan and, in those days, my blood hardly ever stopped boiling. For reasons best known to the builder, our communal garden consisted of several triangular slices, tapering from the houses to a point in the middle distance. Fencing was not permitted, so, to improve our wedge, I dug a flower bed along the baseline and planted a birch tree at the distant apex. At this stage, the phrase 'communal garden' had quite a gracious sound to it. In the mind's eye, one saw oneself having tea on cedar-dotted lawns, with other families, on little white chairs. The first time I carried tea outside I was immediately surrounded by about 20 assorted children who watched me suspiciously and in complete silence, until an older boy said menacingly, 'Wotcher doing?'

Meanwhile, their various parents were busy defining their plots with nettles, trenches, burial mounds and trip-wires. 'Why don't we all hire a tractor, plant grass seed and arrange trees and borders on a communal basis?' I cried rousingly to the family opposite. But they just went on building their burial mound and it was ages before we discovered that on their side it was studded with boulders – rather like a giant currant pudding. We felt a bit better when we knew it was meant to be a rockery, but we never did find out about the 'Family at War' two doors along, who just kept on rushing outside and digging trenches.

I think we gave up trying the day I looked out and saw the little lad next door bending back our young birch tree and using it as a catapult.

And now, here we are again, with trampled plants and boiling blood. I was just wondering how to let off steam, when another keen gardener dropped in for coffee. She listened to my tale of woe and said, 'Oh, that's nothing. We sometimes get complete strangers picnicking on our lawn.'

She lives in the gatehouse at the home of a famous pop personality, and it seems that hardly a day goes by without assorted fans turning up. Sometimes they use amazingly clever ploys to gain access to the FPP. 'Quick, can I use your loo?' they gasp, wrapping one leg around the other and hopping up and down rather like knotted pogo sticks.

'I really enjoy meeting all the different types', said my visitor cheerfully. 'Even the one who said he had arrived by transcendental meditation. He spoiled his astral image, though, by rubbing a bare foot and adding, 'But all that walking don't 'alf give yer blisters.' However, the most difficult to cope with was the chap who turned up in a white blanket, wellies and a woven shoulder bag.

'I told him there wasn't anyone at home, but he said he'd wait. Whereupon, he sat right down in the middle of a flower bed I'd only just finished planting out and started to play his guitar. Oh, I was nonplussed. 'I'll set the dog on you!' I cried, as a last resort. Well, our first guard dog, the soppy thing, took one look at the shoulder bag and thought it was full of sandwiches, because the workmen in the grounds carry their lunch in satchels.

'So, there we all were – me shouting, this fellow strumming and the dog wagging his tail like mad and swinging on the handbag. In the end, we had to get help to prise him out from among my flowers. But he remained quite unperturbed. They led him away, still playing his guitar, and, as he reached the gates, he called back over his shoulder, 'Hey – your guard dog's real freaky, man!"

And I think I've got problems!

44 What's In A Name

Family Circle, August 1974

We were driving along a familiar route the other day when a sudden diversion sign took us down a minor side road. There, at the end, nestled among a little clutch of conifers, was a tiny Hansel and Gretel house with its name on a pokerwork slab beside the door 'Owlzoot'. Now I don't know about you, but if I had a little dream house tucked away among the pines, I just don't think I could bring myself to call it Owlzoot, not even if the owls 'ooted non-stop day and night.

Since then I've been noticing house names and wondering about all those outbursts of creativity which have produced such inspiration as 'Maydit' from an otherwise intelligent family who are obviously proud of the fact that they did-it-themselves and 'The Shambles' from a cheery bunch who presumably don't mind publicly admitting defeat.

There are many such gems to be found, I discovered, although I wouldn't choose all of them myself. For instance, I don't think I'd move into a new house, even if it was at the top of a steep hill, and call it 'Bali-Hi'. Nor, come to think of it, would I choose 'The Lawns' if the only greensward I could boast of was a pocket hanky patch of moss and daisies.

Some of these names probably seemed like a rattling good joke in the wee small hours of their creation, but surely not for much more than a week or two afterwards.

I quite like the wry truth implicit in the four-bedroom-extra-study-triple-garage owner's choice of 'Pretty Penny' and the desperation of the tiny chalet dweller's 'Last Farthing'. And I just love John Steinbeck's 'The Palace Flophouse' for his bunch of down and outs in *Cannery Row*.

For the most part I'd rather see a nice neat number, even a 9372A than a 'Betkenwynron', because Dad thought it would be a pretty snappy idea to combine all our christian names. Or 'Nosnibor' because, for a real scream, we've used our surname backwards.

It's a bit sad too to see a dour old body lurking in a doorway marked 'Shanklin' or 'Ventnor' or 'Weston-Super-Mare'. Did she and her angry old mate ever really return from a radiant honeymoon and say to themselves, 'An experience like that deserves to be recorded for posterity over the front door, even if we do live in Slough'. I suppose if you already live at the seaside this could present a problem. If you live in Ventnor, it could be downright confusing to visitors to put up a sign saying 'Shanklin'. Many seaside dwellers seem to have ex-Colonial connections, hence the heavy sprinkling of coastal bungalows called 'Trinkamalee' and 'Poonah' and even 'Chotapeg'.

It would be interesting to find out how the names of the occupants relate to the names of the houses. Doubtless many a Bobby and Bunny, a Pat and Pam flashed clean colonial limbs on tennis courts of the thirties. The war produced its crop of young Winstons and Nevilles, Shirleys and Ritas, and in those days we had Aunts called Edna and Ada, Ruby and Rose. I wonder how many babies these days are christened Ruby? No, when our children grow up, the world will be full of Uncle Simons and Auntie Fionas. During this past decade we've had umpteen Marks, a sprinkling of Dominics and quite a lot of Sarahs. Not to mention recent outbursts of Tracey and Karen and Kevin and Gary.

As with houses, the joke element can creep in from time to time, with day old scraps of humanity labouring under the name of entire football teams. What happens on their wedding day when they get to the bit that says: Do you Ray

Chris Alex Trevor Larry Emlyn Kevin Peter Steve Philip Ian take this woman etc, etc? Especially if she's been named after a ladies' hockey team!

At school we had a Roma Burns and a Gayna Payne, and a girl I worked with said she once met a Lettuce Gotobed but even I find that hard to believe. However, my husband says he knew a Mr and Mrs Lord who called their son Nelson, and I'm sure we can all tell of similar flashes of jokey association.

There are some perfectly harmless names which are out because they remind us of someone ghastly. If you once knew a smelly old horror called Wilfred then it's no good, you just aren't going to be happy with an infant Wilf toddling around the living room, even if it is the traditional name for the first-born son in your husband's family.

It's tricky too, if just when you are poised at the font, your best friends choose your favourite name for their dog. Better to steer clear of Bruce, Kim, Toby and Jason if this looks like happening to you – although Spot, Fluff and Fido should be a fairly safe bet – for the dog, of course.

On the other hand, you may actually be living at 'Owlzoot' with a son called Ellington Duke and a daughter known as Fluff. You may even have a dog who answers to Chotapeg. In which case, you probably won't have enjoyed reading this very much.

45 A Real Marriage

My Life And I, *Good Housekeeping*, August 1974

When I was very young I had a clear picture of how things were going to be on my wedding day. First ingredient: a blue-eyed bridegroom. Next: myself in a white satin crinoline edged with pearls, and carrying deep red roses to match the velvet dresses of the bridesmaids. These would be a pair of merry little twins with black ringlets, green eyes and heart-shaped faces.

Well, I grew up amid a marked lack of pearl-edged crinolines and precious few merry little matched brunettes. My bridesmaids were big girls who wore lilac and my husband has hazel eyes. In real life that's the way it goes. Furthermore, our wedding group shows me lurking somewhere behind three large ladies with shopping baskets who happened to be standing outside the church at the time.

'Now let's have a picture with *everybody* in it,' cried the photographer and they must have taken him literally.

Nevertheless, I look back on my wedding day with fond affection. At this stage I still had a clear, unswerving picture in my mind of how it would be on honeymoon. You know how it is in daydreams – the Noel Coward stage setting in which our swain, twitching with barely concealed passion, strides masterfully out on to the starlit balcony where we – in cross-cut peach satin and silver eyeshadow – breathlessly await.

We found the address of a suitably picturesque hotel. Blissfully I collected together a gorgeous trousseau and just for a big joke I added, at the last minute, a voluminous red flannel nightgown. All the way down to Cornwall I creased myself with laughter – partly champagne-induced and partly at the prospect of the big red flannel joke to come later that evening.

(David had to work quite hard at reshaping my character in early married life. Certain aspects of my personality then must have been quite sickening.)

En route he dropped me at a below-street-level 'Ladies' where I shed confetti over the two dear old souls in charge of it.

'You just got married, ducks?' they cried. 'Aah, i'nt that luvly,' and they followed me up on to the pavement and gave us both a rousing cheer and a final wave. 'It's not everyone who gets a good send-off from a public convenience,' said my bridegroom as we drove away. At last we reached our country hotel where mine host, in velvet jacket, was presiding benignly over a vast topside of beef and several newly wedded couples seated along the central refectory table. A log fire blazed and to make the whole scene even more super, a film director arrived with friends for a meal and there among them was Sean Connery at the next table. I caught David's eye and smiled and he leaned towards me and whispered throbbingly in my ear:

'Why are you sweating like that? It's dripping off your chin. You're not letting that Connery chap go to your head are you?'

Alas, I continued to drip into my roast beef, the room grew blurred and, with my teeth chattering like castanets, I was eventually led away to the bridal couch.

'It's just the aftermath of all the wedding arrangements,' said David. 'Try and make an effort to brace up.'

'C-c-could you h-h-hand me my nightie,' I stuttered. 'Th-th-that one there – the w-w-warm r-red one.'

'Good God!' said David. I had a bad case of Asian 'flu. The hoteliers were very nice about it. They brought extra blankets and grapes on a silver salver and they didn't even mind when all that feverish sweating soaked through my red flannel nightdress and turned the bedclothes pink.

'What a honeymoon!' muttered David bitterly, loading his camera and trudging off out to snap seagulls. 'I do think you might try to make a bit more effort.'

Three days later he crashed alongside and they brought in extra grapes.

I suppose we were lucky really that we had to face up to reality right at the beginning of our marriage. There was none of that: 'My goddess, my queen, let me kiss your lovely fingertips' which so often swiftly degenerates into: 'Shut up hag – I'm only off to the boozer with the lads.' With a honeymoon like ours we *had* to start married life with a sense of humour.

Other brides who've been put to the test early include the wife of the chap who said: 'You won't mind, will you love, if I slip away from the reception to see the Everton replay?' Or how about: 'I know darling – let's just close our eyes and stick a pin in the map – hmm, yes, well I expect Slough is quite nice really.' And, 'Well, *of course* I know how to get to London Airport quickly. We'll just drive straight to the centre of London and ask someone.'

Yet another variation on the theme is 'Sweetheart, I've told you over and over again – I really didn't *know* our darts team would be staying at this hotel.'

Or to get things off to a really ratty start, how about two friends of mine who actually did say: 'I know – let's both give up smoking on our wedding day!' If you can weather that for starters then boy, you've really got a marriage going between you!

As for me, one of these days I'll be lurking out there on that starlit balcony, all set for our long-overdue second honeymoon. And if, by then, my mate's masterful stride is a bit doddery and my cross-cut peach satin a bit bulgy in places, well once you've started married life with a double dose of influenza just about anything else is going to seem like a blissful daydream.

46 Weekend Diggers

Family Circle, Autumn 1974

I wonder what the word allotment conjures up for you. Gnarled old granddads digging for victory during the last war? A ragged patch of derelict Brussels sprouts and straggling beanstalks? A tiny uprising of sheds amid a flutter of faded bird-scarers? That was my impression until suddenly allotments became all the rage around our way.

'Have you heard?' asked my neighbour, Jillie, excitedly. 'They've ploughed up that old allotment site across the road and individual plots are being re-allocated next Thursday evening.'

'Don't talk to me about allotments!' said another friend, Mary. In the first flush of enthusiasm in her district it seems, her husband had rushed off and dug up somebody else's plot by mistake.

'Never mind dear, I'll help you clear the weeds from the right patch,' she cried keenly. And no sooner had she cut her first helpful swathe through the undergrowth than a great big piece of nettle shot straight up her nostril. 'Did it hurt?' I gasped. Which must easily be the silliest question I've ever asked anybody. 'Well it certainly put me right off allotments,' said Mary. 'In fact I flung down my tool, plucked the nettle from my nose and stamped off home never to return.' And who can blame her, poor soul?

For the rest of us however, that particular Thursday evening was like the Gold Rush as small excited family groups milled about the hedgerow waiting to catch the eye of the man with the notebook and marker pegs. Any idea that allotments these days are exclusively the territory of patient old chaps in cloth caps was very soon dispelled.

'Hello Lucy darling!' trilled the lady with the elegant hairdo to the one in the buttercup yellow wellingtons. 'My dear, I simply can't wait to harvest my own courgettes!'

Trendy, mauve-shirted chaps in advertising kicked thoughtfully at weedy clumps; serious men with beards scowled through seed catalogues; small syndicates of home-based mums turned up with collective infants slung over their shoulders in canvas hammocks; and large extrovert families strode about in Aran sweaters amid swirls of free-range children and Labrador dogs.

'Here Dominic, here Julian,' they boomed from time to time. But neither children nor dogs came to heel.

'Well now,' said the man in charge, reaching us at last and licking his stubby gardener's pencil. 'What did you say your name was? Ah yes, you wanted a ten pole plot, didn't you? Well now, there's that one over by the lilac bush or that next one with the old shed.'

'Lilac bush,' I murmured dreamily. 'Shed,' said my husband sensibly. So for ninety pence a year we staked our claim to a good sized piece of land with a white marker peg at each corner, plus a tiny lock-up tool shed, and all only a wheelbarrow ride from our own front door.

For the first few weeks however, the only noticeable crop was string. A giant blueprint of white twine defining boundaries; brown bass stretched taut along rows of seedlings; green raffia adding a colourful note, and in the case of one dashing family, masses of pink tape, zig-zagging off into the distance.

We soon discovered that the weeds, far from disappearing, had quite enjoyed being ploughed up. Dock and nettles swung into mammoth production, an ancient legacy of rhubarb came smiling through and raspberry canes shot up keenly everywhere. A large friendly frog joined us, hopping along the rows just ahead of us as we raked and hoed.

As the summer wore on, the hungry monster lurking in our garage began to purr contentedly as I fed great armfuls of bagged carrots, blanched swede and shredded beans into its vaporous depths. An allotment and a deep freeze form a natural partnership. Gradually too, it became clear which among us had green fingers and which were gradually falling by the wayside in a tangle of bindweed and good intentions.

The idea of allotments was originally thought up in the nineteenth century 'to alleviate poverty among the labouring poor'. Nowadays as food prices rise and garden plots grow smaller, the labouring poor it seems, come from all sections of society. Some of the elegant ladies are still with us, calling across to each other with high clear voices: 'My dear, the courgettes were such a success I'm wondering if I dare have a little go at artichokes!'

A chap at the top end filled his plot with conifers and the swirly Aran family have unearthed a gnarled old granddad to do the actual digging.

As for me, it is one of the pleasures of life to take my toiling husband a thermos of mid-morning coffee at weekends (he's no gnarled granddad but he's a better digger than I am) and to gather a basketful of our own golden sweet corn and ripe tomatoes. There is a general spirit of goodwill among the weekend diggers – broad beans are praised, carrots compared, advice given and accepted from the old timers to the raw recruits. Some are talking of forming an Allotment Association as they do in many districts to enable members to buy seeds etc in bulk and to lend weight to our desire for more long-term security of tenure.

On weekdays I sometimes take my own coffee and do a spot of solo weeding. The sun shines down on my back and I chat to Froggy as he leaps along, croaking companionably, Sometimes I look up and see a passer-by eyeing me strangely as I stoop there apparently deep in conversation with a runner bean. But I don't mind.

I don't even mind when more sophisticated friends double up with laughter at the sight of me in my muddy wellies and cry: 'Been up the allottie, have you?'

As the season wears on and we come staggering home with ropes of gleaming onions and barrowloads of beet, 'up the allottie' is a good place to be. Even if one does risk the occasional nettle up one's nostril!

47 Dressmaking

My Life and I, *Good Housekeeping,* October 1974

By the pricking of our thumbs and by all the pins and little bits of thread on the carpet you can tell that Anna and I are involved in another dressmaking session.

Young teen-aged daughters shoot up like rhubarb. Their fashion requirements seem to change every few hours and what seem to me like almost new skirts/jeans/dresses are suddenly:

'Ugh, Mummy, not *that* old thing! It's practically falling to pieces. I'd look *stupid* in it and anyway it doesn't even *fit* me any more!' My own wardrobe, too, contains a selection which has become a bit old hat. And old coat. And old dress.

It is time to plan a mother-and-daughter day in town with Anna. Together we head for the pattern department at Dickins & Jones where, all around us, other mums are muttering to their daughters:

'No, not that one, dear. The collar looks tricky. And just look at all those *seams!*'

While Anna flicks through the pattern books' young trendy sections I am drinking in a Jean Muir original. (I am more than willing to drink in *any* Jean Muir original.) But would all those tiny, soft, romantic folds prove to be too much of a challenge? And is the style perhaps a fraction too young and romantic for me?

'This one would suit you,' says Anna firmly, pointing to something plain and sensible. Ah well, wasn't it the last Begum Aga Khan who said: 'Don't wear what *appeals* to you. Wear what *suits* you'?

We turn our attention to Anna's pattern choice, then on to fabrics, matching zips and other relevant haberdashery. We gasp at the current price of sewing thread; then it's home to tea, the pinning, cutting and then the waiting sewing machine.

Treadling away, my thoughts roam over past dressmaking experiences …

I first started dressmaking in my early teens out of desperation, really, because nothing in the shops seemed to fit me. (At this stage in my development, I readily concede it wasn't really the shops' fault.)

Prior to that, my only sewing experience had been at school. And you know how it is at school … The casement gardening apron with the sweaty whip-and-run seams. The whole summer term spent transferring our vital statistics to graph paper. The anything-but-vital flannelette knickers cut from the strange resultant pattern.

I suspect that it takes many of us a long, long time after schooldays to get really keen about any more needlework. However, due to my shape, I treadled on until the day came when I could actually go out of doors in things I'd made myself without causing a certain amount of undue merriment. As I grew more confident I went around saying that, with patience and practice, anybody could learn to do their own dressmaking – *and* save pounds on clothing bills.

But, alas, I have since come to realize that some poor souls need more patience and practice than others. For everyone whose bust darts end up on her bust there must be at least three or four juggling about with two left fronts and a collar which doesn't quite meet in the middle. I'm particularly reminded of a bewildered neighbour who staggered over in a pair of pyjama trousers measuring roughly four feet from waist to crotch and with legs inexplicably less than twelve inches long.

'There's something wrong here, isn't there?' she said, doubtfully, gazing down at her strangely hobbled lower half. 'I can't seem to *stride* in them.'

From this experience alone I learned that there really are people who'd be better off sticking to Marks & Spencer.

And even for those with some know-how, it's all too easy to grow overconfident and end up with one odd, shiny skirt panel because the nap is running the wrong way. Or with curved sleeves which go in like a dream but which seem, when all the easing and machining is over, to be unaccountably facing backwards.

One-way prints can be a challenge, too. At this very moment I am discovering that Anna's new dress material not only has big, definite, flower bunches which look odd upside-down, but that if I'm not very careful she's going to end up with one half of her bust heavily floral and the other half plain.

'Could you come and try this on, Anna?' I call, adjusting a gather here and clipping a seam there.

'Hm, yes,' she says. 'But I'm not too sure about these sleeves. And couldn't the neckline be a bit lower?'

'Well, I'll see what I can do,' I sigh, reaching for scissors and pincushion. What a good thing, I am thinking, that I have, over the years, learned (and earned) a dressmaking wrinkle or two. But I know better than to grow overconfident. I have only to think back to that purple-tweed incident to be reminded that we can all make some costly mistakes ...

It was a super, flecked tweed brought back personally from Donegal. I would tackle my first piece of tailoring, I decided, and make myself a coat. 'If a job's worth doing ...' I muttered and went out and bought expensive buttons, pure silk lining and a smart leather belt.

If it killed me, I thought, I would do this job really well. No short cuts. If the pattern said baste I would baste. If it said bring notches together I would bring notches together. If it said ease stitch upper curve between small o's using long stitches, disregarding interfacing and keeping seam allowances, then that is what I would do. Even if it said: 'Place small oo's at underarm seam and back lap at end of extension on cuff keeping front lap free and adjusting gathers: baste,' then, by golly, I'd have a crack at it!

And it worked. On its padded hanger the finished coat looked like something out of *Vogue*. There was just one problem though. It looked ghastly on *me*.

48 The Thirty-Nine-ish Years

Family Circle, November 1974

A friend of mine said the other day: 'I don't care what anybody says, being 40 is rotten!' 'But isn't life supposed to begin …' I began. 'Just you wait,' she muttered darkly. Which was quite flattering really, since I've been 'about 39' for slightly longer than strict accuracy allows. But then I've always believed that life is what you make it and that age is irrelevant. I go along with that wise soul who once said: 'Try to live your life so that all the people you meet wish they were your age.'

I'm bound to admit though that my embittered friend does have a point. Not that one necessarily arises on one's fortieth birthday with a face like a badly ploughed field and one's arms dragging along the ground – personally, I've always looked a bit like that first thing anyway. No, the real trouble is that, although you may feel exactly the same, other people start treating you differently. When, for instance, you say; 'Isn't it a lovely morning? to your child-bride neighbour over the fence, she listens – with respect!

That's the worst bit. To fling oneself gaily into the gabble of coffee morning conversation and have all the other mums go, 'Shush!' and actually listen. I can't tell you how many times lately a chatty, inconsequential remark of mine has wobbled away into silence because I've suddenly realised that the others present are politely drinking in my every word out of deference to my age.

I just don't feel like a wise old oracle yet, nor am I ready to start consciously *being mature.* I don't mind trimming my sails a little – it doesn't do to billow, either physically or mentally, once beyond one's teens – but I don't see why I shouldn't go on feeling young to the very end. Even when I'm very old, I shall feel cast down if well-meaning folk imply that perhaps I should take a back seat now that I'm getting a wee bit past it. Past what? Why can't the elderly go on doing anything they choose – short of trapeze work perhaps – for as long as they choose? It's their world too. So, come on Gran, pin a big rose to your hat and step out in style.

The way we dress at any age can greatly affect our whole attitude to life. Our contours may change but we can still look good if shops and manufacturers will give us the styles and the sizing. No one should have to spend their latter years shuffling around in sagging grey woollies and shapeless blancmange hats.

As for me, I'd still like to be able to try on a fabulous dress from the window of our local boutique – apricot silk perhaps with the new softer, lower neckline – without wondering why the assistant is wearing that inscrutable expression. And if by some miracle it fits me and feels good, then I want, just this once, not to bump into a down-beat contemporary who has let herself go and who can't wait to tell me that personally she hates to see mutton dressed as lamb.

I remember a rather Puritan girl saying to me once how awful it was to see women tampering with nature. Well all I can say is that by the time one reaches 40 it's nature that starts doing the tampering. Oh yes, I know there are women with gleaming iron grey hair, tanned bare complexions and beautifully etched character line around their eyes. But, alas, for many of us it's pepper and salt frizz, little red veins and a touch of the Dorian Greys if we don't keep a firm eye on the magnifying mirror.

I like the story told of Marlene Dietrich, whose friend was turning grey and letting nature take its course. 'Tell me, darling, who do you think you are helping by looking like that?' asked the mystified Marlene. Now there's a lady whose looks and philosophy I'd like to emulate. Of course she does have more going for her in the way of bone structure than most of us, but I'm sure we can all find something about our person that has stood the test of time. Even if it's only firm ear-lobes. And we can all strive to let our cheery, ageless attitude to life shine through. Above all, do let's go on doing our own thing for as long as we feel like it.

Personally, I want to plunge into the throbbing gloom of the disco at our local club and undulate spasmodically to Elton John along with all the others. I love music with a beat and so does my husband. We've always enjoyed all sorts of dancing and an occasional rave-up does us good. Or it did until two fellow members in their late twenties said: 'We must hand it to you two – you really keep up with the current scene.' The inference being that we oldies should really be sitting well back in the merciful navy blue darkness, sipping our gin and taking our yeast tablets, watching the youngsters enjoy themselves. The way things are going I have an uneasy feeling that in a swift decade or so they'll be all set to start making allowances for our 'funny little ways'.

So if any other ladies of 'about 39' are beginning to subside wistfully into the background, then let's start by telling ourselves firmly that Princess Grace of Monaco, Jackie Onassis, Audrey Hepburn and Sophia Loren are all contemporaries of ours – give or take a wrinkle. And I don't see anyone grasping them by the elbow offering to help them cross the road.

49 Popping Into Hospital

My Life and I, *Good Housekeeping*, November 1974

One has only to start up a conversation with any group of women around our way lately to learn that Maureen isn't with us today because she's gone into hospital for a scrape. Or poor old Milly's womb is on the move again. Or Pam's tubes are under observation. Or unravelling. Or being fitted up with a loop line.

And it isn't just we ordinary mortals who have our little bit o' female trouble. A beautiful, glowing girl with slumbrous eyes and peachy cheekbones was only telling me the other day that no sooner had she found *the* perfect man of her dreams than she had to pop into hospital to have a piece snipped off the end of her coccyx. Next came a crop of boils on the lower slopes. Then an operation so delicate I'm still not quite sure what it was or whether it was successful.

'My God!' said her Dreamboat as she lay once more bandaged and bottoms-up. 'We all have our problems but do yours *always* have to be *down there*?'

I, too, still blench at the distant memory of a 'down there' check-up at a large teaching hospital. I didn't mind *too* much that I lay surrounded by jostling medical students. They have to learn, I kept telling myself. I didn't mind the prodding specialist. I didn't even mind all those peering doctors and assorted nursing staff. But I *did* mind the woman in the flowery apron, leaning on her floor mop.

Our menfolk, too, have their troubles. While the older ones are busy being braced up, strapped down, held in or poked back into place, younger chaps are making their own brave decisions. Like the poor devil I heard of who chivalrously agreed to a vasectomy.

'Nothing to it!' everyone kept assuring him. 'You just pop in – quick snip – all over!'

Perhaps he chose a bad day. Because, as he tells it, while the pre-snip brigade sat around in the waiting room being noticeably nonchalant and witty and debonair, the first man was wheeled out in a dead faint. As you can imagine, the ensuing silence was deafening.

With children, of course, visits to hospital need particularly careful handling. When Anna was small, our nearest hospital was a crumbling, grim old place known locally as 'The Bastille'.

'We've only got to pop in and have your chest X-rayed,' I kept saying brightly as we approached. 'I bet it's super inside. You'll see. All flowery screens and toys and kindly nurses.'

'Card!' snapped a woman with inflamed nostrils as we followed the trail of arrows. 'In there. Strip off. I'll call you when we're ready for you.'

'In there' turned out to be a small medicine cupboard already containing an elderly lady down to her bra.

'Oh, I'm sorry, do excuse us,' I stammered.

'That's all right, dear – they're very short of cubicles here. We often have to double up.'

So we doubled up – or in our case trebled up and thrashed about together as politely as we could. I should perhaps mention that this cupboard was also the telephone kiosk. And the phone kept ringing. And people of assorted sexes kept squeezing in to answer it.

'Why aren't you undressed yet?' rapped old fiery nostrils suddenly flinging open the door and staring at me accusingly.

'Er – it's my daughter, not me,' I mumbled. 'Nonsense,' she replied. 'Look on the card. Age fifty-six!'

We did eventually convince her that our doctor had meant five years and six months and that I was a *much* younger woman, anyway. But it put us both off hospitals for a while, especially crumbling ones ruled by short-tempered dragons.

I wasn't too happy about the follow-up, either, when dozens of us sat squashed into a very narrow, hot passageway awaiting the X-ray results.

'Will Mr Ramadam please report to Ward C *immediately*,' said a slightly panicky voice over the tannoy. And the small, feverish Indian gentleman sitting right next to us leapt to his feet and stumbled off – coughing, coughing all the way.

It would only be fair to add that this particular hospital subsequently had some much-needed new buildings added and that, over the years, I've also met some very good hospital staff – and some really super ones; particularly one night nurse who was such hilarious fun that several of us used to stay awake to enjoy her jokes and antics.

'Can't understand why you lot always seem so pale and tired,' the perplexed day staff would remark.

And let us not forget that they do have to cope with a richly assorted cross-section of humanity, to say the least. Like the well-intentioned friend of mine who dashed into her local hospital to give a pint of blood. As other donors will know, they prick the thumb first for a blood sample.

'I say, do you mind if we try again?' they said, looking faintly worried as the first two jabs failed to bring forth any blood at all.

At the third attempt a *teeny* pallid dot appeared but refused to coagulate.

'I don't think we'd better take any of your blood, my dear,' they said with a wry smile. 'It looks as if you could do with some!'

Or take my own last stay in hospital when it seems I proved just a shade allergic to their brand of Mickey Finn. It wasn't every day, they said, that an unconscious patient was wheeled out of the operating theatre sitting bolt upright and singing hymns (and I didn't even know that I knew any).

Ah well, amid all the snipping and stitching and looping and scraping they deserve their occasional moments of light relief.

50 After The Party

My Life and I, *Good Housekeeping*, January 1975

'Goodbye and thank you – it's been a lovely party,' say little clusters of guests as we shake hands and squeeze shoulders and smile in the open doorway.

My husband, in the general confusion, seems to be shaking my hand and leaving with the others by mistake. At least I hope it's by mistake.

I am relieved that the food and drink have gone down well and that the mixture of guests seems to have worked.

Lovely party or no, I always enjoy the next bit when a couple of long-standing trusties rummage around for drying-up cloths and we settle down at the kitchen sink for a good long, in-depth chat about how pretty Jillie looked in her Laura Ashley print and how grown-up Anna's getting and what a marvellous person Great Aunt Dolly is in spite of all those years of gin and sin. Or perhaps because of them.

David's moment of enjoyment comes when he discovers that there is still one unopened party pack of bitter. Happily he gathers up a straggle of left-over beer drinkers and arranges a coda to the main entertainment – a finishing-off party. For the rest of us it looks as if it is going to be trifle, trifle all the way through until Monday.

I love trifle. There is something about sloshing custard over assorted odds and ends (those few elderly sponge cakes, the half tin of mandarins, that little scrape of jam left in the jar) which appeals to my 'waste not, want not' instincts.

Through the years I've hit upon some amazing variations in flavour. In fact I think I recently stumbled across the secret formula for Coca Cola. (Chocolate Swiss roll, lemon jelly and very ripe bananas, in the right proportions, taste *exactly* like Coke.)

For my last parties, however, the results have been impeccable – ever since I tried out the recipe for that *Good Housekeeping* favourite – the one with the crumbled macaroons and jammy sponge and sherry and custard and double cream and oh boy, do make it if you haven't already. This time I have to admit I overdid it, though, and in spite of second helpings all round, and some thirds and fourths, there's still lots left.

The washing up continues, enlivened by a clutter of swopped recipes and post-party gossip. Someone relates their favourite party story of the bachelor friend who bravely decided to bake and serve a pie to his guests. Being without a pie funnel he seized the spout cover from the kettle. An ideal solution! Or so it seemed until suddenly, in mid Martini, a piercing whistle was heard coming from the hidden depths of the cooker.

We discuss another friend whose parties are large, colourful and invariably marvellous. The food in this particular household is always superb – but then for this particular wealthy hostess it isn't all that difficult.

'Mmm,' cried an ecstatic guest in mid-forkful at her last do. 'Where d'you catch your salmon?'

'Harrods,' she called back blithely.

Our own parties are much less formal affairs and certainly less expensive. We quite enjoy having lots of people in for 'lunch with punch' once or twice a year. If the weather is fine, guests drift prettily about outside, and our tiny garden is greatly enhanced by the odd sausage-on-a-stick found next day sprouting from the herb bed. I'm not too sure that Caesar, the guinea-pig, enjoys these occasions. Well-meaning folk will poke party food into his cage. Twiglets, nuts and crisps he can just about cope with. But please, my dears, no more stuffed olives, dill pickles or maraschino cherries.

On the whole, though, we all feel better for an occasional culinary splurge. Even if we do find that, by the look of the hall carpet afterwards, someone must have actually *trodden* in the Stilton, we can soon dart about with a soapy sponge. Which could not be said for a friend of mine who threw a graffiti party.

'The hall needs re-decorating anyway,' she told her guests. 'So why not grab a pencil and get rid of a few inhibitions?' Which they did. With enthusiasm. In fact, next morning the hostess was amazed at some of the inhibitions they'd got rid of.

Then it dawned on her that not only would she have to call in the decorators *immediately* but she'd have to meet them face to face and discuss the new décor surrounded by some of the most explicit drawings and fruitiest phrases ever written on walls anywhere …

I am relieved, too, that after our parties we can at least all face each other next morning, unlike those we keep hearing about where by the end of the evening, Jim's wife and Muriel's husband have both mysteriously disappeared, but there's steam coming out of a cupboard upstairs. Not only do poor old Jim and Muriel have a rotten evening (unless by chance they, too, fancy each other – in which case it won't be long before little men from *The News of The World* start arriving in plain brown envelopes) but there's all that remorse and groaning and sheepishness to be got through the morning after. Not to mention weeks of scuttling up alleyways to avoid sober confrontation.

But now, with clear consciences and fairly unblemished décor, the last of the dishes and cutlery is put away. Likewise the last of the bitter. Some good soul is vacuuming the living room and an old friend who lives alone sighs and says how parties always seem to bring a house fully to life. Pantries, too, we decide. It isn't every day we get to use the chocolate strands, the crystallized violets and the little silver balls.

'Anyone for trifle?' I say, without much hope, as I juggle extra space in the fridge. I expect I shall be saying this quite often during the next few days.

51 Anyone For A Reunion?

Family Circle, February 1975

Recently I was glancing through the list of prize winners in a magazine competition and wondering vaguely whether Mrs Esmé Batson of New Malden was anyone I used to know, when it struck me that it would be fascinating to find out how one's old school chums had turned out over the years.

Not that I particularly want them all turning up on my doorstep in their mink, rags, Rolls Royces, crash helmets, emerald tiaras and handwoven caftans. But it would be interesting to hear, in one marathon gossip session, what has become of them. I expect we'd be in for some surprises.

Who would have thought for instance, that Molly Huggins, renowned in the lower fifth for her big nostrils and chapped hands, would now be smothered in sequins and tassels and fighting off Latin lovers down in Buenos Aires? Or that a golden girl like Gloria McGillicuddy who always had the best fountain pen and was every teacher's pet, should end up wearily pushing all those crying babies along the High Street? And as for Dorothy Doomswathe, I just can't imagine where such a pillar of the local chapel got her material for all those dirty books!

Sometimes scraps of real information do float our way … 'Guess what? Daphne Dimplerod finally married that ghastly chap in the beret and bicycle clips!' Or, 'You'll never believe it my dear, but June Flatbush has joined a rather intense religious sect and goes around nowadays shouting things out loud on buses!'

Of course they don't all go berserk in adult life. Some settle down and become good wives, anxious mums or a bit above themselves. But it's the ones who sink without trace that I wonder about. They can't all have emigrated or gone to the dogs.

While we're on the subject of going to the dogs, I can't help noticing among those that I do keep in touch with that the wild ones of our youth invariably didn't meet their comeuppance.

The slow and plodding may win the race in *The Tortoise and The Hare*, and in those magazine stories we used to read in which the girl had to choose between the solid dependable chap next door and the raffish easy-come, easy-go racing driver, old Ploddy won every time. But in real life quite naughty girls end up being photographed in *Vogue*. And I've met at least one daredevil who gambled his way through an entire fortune. And what happened? Someone died and left him another fortune.

It's all very well for our elders to sit around shaking their heads and saying things like: 'You mark my words – that one will come to a bad end.' The trouble is that they don't – they come to a super end surrounded by lace pillows and adoring old flames while we sit at home watching *Match of the Day* and having nostalgic thoughts about the romantic past.

Which brings us to old boyfriends – those pulse-quickening symbols of our budding teens. Are they now mowing lawns, running to seed and helping their wives with the washing up? Even that fantastic hazel-eyed lad who used to play the piano like crazy down at the local youth club, and that strange fresh air fiend who preferred canoeing to girls? Does he still paddle his lonely nut-brown way up creek and stream? Or did he finally succumb to a rosy cheeked ravisher in cords, climbing boots and an open-necked Aertex?

What of tall husky Jack, I wonder – that funny endearing boy, the one my father actually liked? While other girls blushed and waved love letters with envelopes marked SWALK, we thought it the height of wit to mark ours VLADIVOSTOK and NIJNINOVGOROD.

Then there was that sweet, if slightly immature lad who kept on telling me how much he respected me. What was he leading up to, I used to wonder? I never did find out. Our relationship wore thin when a friend invited us to a bottle party and his mother laughed and said he'd jolly well have to make do with milk or ink.

Not long ago I did catch sight of one grand passion of my teens – oh those forget-me-not blue eyes, the rich chuckly voice, the dexterous flash of his ping pong bat … He was getting on to a train with his wife – a great carping lump in a droopy coat. Poor love – he'd have done much better with me.

And what about me? Inky Bet who suffered so regularly from neuralgia that for quite a time I was known affectionately by school friends as Old Face Ache – at least I assumed it was said with affection.

Who of my childhood chums, I wonder, would imagine that I'd end up blond – and able to crochet – and married to such a lovely fella?

Alas, it is too late now for reunions. All our old haunts have long since been turned into bingo halls and supermarkets. Our old tradition-and-giggle-steeped-grammar school has gone comprehensive. As for the local boys' school where all our blazered and satchelled dream boats came swirling out, furtively stuffing their caps in their pockets – even the building seems to have disappeared!

But then you never know – perhaps one day there'll be a Grand Old Boys And Girls Reunion In The Sky. And if so, my word there'll be some gasping, nudging and some catching up to do, I can tell you!

52 Makes A Change

My Life and I, *Good Housekeeping*, February 1975

'My goodness, I wouldn't have recognized you!' said a friend of my mother's who remembers me from the days when I was a sallow brunette nail-biter and tall for my age.

I stopped biting my nails on my wedding day (which must prove *something* about marriage). I'm still tall, but the only remaining constant factors are brown eyes and a tendency to wave my arms about and talk a lot. I can't seem to help this, although if I sit on my hands it does quieten me down. Opinions vary on whether this is a good thing. Some folk squeeze my arm at parties and say: 'Never lose your vivacity my dear.' Others don't invite me to their parties. Which is quite understandable.

When we are very young we want *everybody* to like us. We want to do all the right things. We drink in advice from all quarters and stumble through our formative years believing folk who say: 'You should *always* wear pink/black/flannelette/ rhinestones/water-wings/tinfoil/old snow shoes.'

Gradually, however, we learn that you can't please them all. So it seems best in the long run to please yourself. And/or your husband if you happen to like him.

Husbands with definite views can have a noticeable effect on new brides. It only takes a few well-chosen remarks during the honeymoon, like: 'Those sandals make you look like my old music teacher', to indicate that one's image isn't all it might be.

Some men marry curvy, colourful, sexy girls. They then become enraged and say: 'Stop *flaunting* yourself like that!' and the poor dear is forced to lead a cloistered life, shuffling around in shapeless woolly hats and coats. With us, it was different. In fact, my husband quite likes men to stare and go 'Cor!' (At *me*, of course, not at *him*!) And as they don't stare much at big, sallow nail-biters I had to make a few changes right from the start. Oh, all right then. Lots and lots of changes. And I'm still working at it. Over the years I've been country tweed, Marks & Spencer, leather and beads and tie and dye. I have also changed from naturally sallow to Sport Light and from lifetime brunette to Definitely Blonde. And let me tell you, gentlemen really do seem to prefer them. (Us.)

I decided to go blonde years ago but I couldn't get my hairdresser to take me seriously. You can't really blame him. Sitting there in wet hair and nylon cover-all I did look a fairly far cry from a potential sex symbol. Not that he actually said I couldn't go blonde. He just kept laughing silently and patting my cheek.

When I finally convinced him that I really meant it I walked out of his salon all golden and gleaming, and a passing chap, with an excited cry of 'Hey there, doll', drove his van right into somebody's rosebed. That was definitely one of my good days.

Spurred on by this and one or two fascinating propositions no one ever put to me when I was a brunette (one can always say 'no' but it's *super* to be asked!) I've made other changes. I'm not quite as big as I was, although there's one thing that troubles me about dieting. Apart from actually getting started. And that is the way my slim top half gets thinner and thinner while all that hip-to-knee chub stays exactly the same.

Avidly I read slimming articles which all assure me that *eventually* the bulgy bits will disappear. So I spend weeks eating nothing but grapefruit or fish fingers or pickled gherkins – and what happens? The bulges stay put while my top whittles down to a twiglet. My old pear shape was bearable. But inverted toffee-apple-on-a-stick takes some getting used to.

To overcome this I've taken to long skirts and flappy trousers. (I'm fairly pleased with the way things are shaping up until Anna dents the *My Fair Lady* image by confiding, in a well-meaning voice, that she quite enjoys having an eccentric mother ...)

Others, less well-meaning, tell each other that I'm going through a funny phase and that it must be my age. But as people have been telling me it's my age, non-stop ever since I was eleven, I ignore this.

Then comes a real breakthrough. I manage to persuade Roy, the cheek patter, to give me a curly-wurly hairstyle, and I'm really embarking on a whole new way of life on the strength of it. After years of carefully straightening out the kinks I can at last toss and turn and dash about in the rain and still look like a cross between Shirley Temple and a slightly Afro Bedlington terrier.

True I've given one or two passers-by a fit of the giggles. True my mother did laugh nervously when she saw me and said: 'Well, *you're* certainly looking well, David". True I did stand right up close to two ladies in the powder room at Bourne & Hollingsworth while they stared at me in quite a rapt way.

And they did then say loudly: 'My word, don't you see some ghastly hairstyles about these days?' – presumably on the assumption that I was either very foreign or very deaf. But this is a small price to pay for feeling happy. (You *have* to feel happy with this hair-do. It just wouldn't go with a sad face.

So if you happen to be sitting at home at the moment, biting your nails and feeling a bit lank and yellowish – why not pluck up your courage and do something *wild*? Go *on*. I bet you'll feel all the better for it.

53 Ouch!!

My Life and I, *Good Housekeeping*, March 1975

'I really must ring the dentist for an appointment,' I say, as a tiny, icy twinge stabs me in the back tooth. 'I'll do it as soon as I've finished the washing up ... And darned these seven or eight socks ... And, my goodness, these floors need polishing ...'

And so it goes on all day, until the pricking of my conscience begins to outweigh the throbbing of my tooth. Then, but only when all the odd jobs I can think of are done, I reluctantly lift the receiver and start dialling.

Over the years we've kept to *fairly* regular check-ups and known quite an assortment of dentists. The current chap is good with teeth. But dour. So none of my family are exactly forcing my hand by clamouring for advance bookings. Anna and Daniel, who quite enjoyed visits to earlier, merrier dentists and think they are *nice* people (I made very sure no one told them any ghastly toothy tales in their infancy), are puzzled by his notable lack of humour. I tried, at first, to enliven our visits by establishing a cheery rapport.

'My uncle's dentist says our family has the Hapsburg jaw,' I said brightly before offering the contents of mine for his inspection.

'Well you haven't,' he snapped. 'It's an Angles Class III malocclusion.'

A pity, really, because we lantern-jawed types like to cling to our royal connections. And even if the Hapsburgs were a funny lot they do sound much more fun than a malocclusion. Of any class.

But no matter what sort of chap the dentist happens to be, I try hard to settle myself into a philosophical frame of mind as he pumps the chair into position. At least it's a wonderful chance to put my feet up, I tell myself firmly. It is also quite a good opportunity to tune in to his tummy rumble.

I am now ready to practice my own homespun version of yoga. I fix my thoughts on something beautiful and remote – like what I'd do if I won the pools (which *is* fairly remote because I don't actually *do* the pools) and mentally remove myself from his presence.

He can then close in with his buzz saws and mini-Hoovers and grappling irons all he wants. I don't care. I'm busy buying new houses for my nicer relatives and planning my own world cruise. I've always done this in moments of stress and can thoroughly recommend it. It sometimes rattles dentists though. 'Answer me – answer me – are you *all right*?' they are prone to shout, staring closely at my eyeballs. And there was that time just as I was rounding Cape Horn in this beautifully appointed catamaran when I was aroused by a distant cry of, 'You're *biting* me. Do you *hear* me? You're *biting* my *hand*.' But it has got me, if not the dentist, through many an appointment with minimum wear and tear.

'My God,' says David, as I return to the waiting room. 'It sounded as if he was widening the M4 in there!'

'Your husband's turn now,' says the receptionist gaily.

'Never mind, David,' I tell him philosophically (but with a certain amount of personal relief). 'At least it's better than going to see the doctor. We do at least know in this case that, whatever the diagnosis, it's bound to be confined to the *mouth*.'

He moves unenthusiastically through to the surgery and I smile cheerfully at the other waiting patients, but they just go on staring bleakly at old copies of *Horse and Hound*.

Being a raw carrot eater as a child I was well into adult life before I needed any treatment. In those days my dentist was a charming elderly man in a panama hat and alpaca jacket. He didn't seem at all like a dentist. 'Ah, my dear,' he would sigh. 'What *great* pleasure it gives me to look into a mouth like yours!' And he would hum to himself and twirl his little mirror and pat my knee. (Come to think of it, perhaps he *wasn't* a dentist!)

My first extraction came some years later when I was living in the wilds of deepest Scotland, and a visit to the surgery required a long bus ride into town.

On the return journey I noticed that the other passengers were choosing seats as far away as possible and then darting me quite frightened glances. Poor souls. I knew why when I finally saw myself in a mirror. I was ashen-faced from the experience anyway, but the trickle of dried blood running down from the corner of my mouth certainly didn't improve my appearance.

Regular bus passengers had my particular sympathy because I'd only recently travelled on that same route to see a doctor about a strange allergy I'd developed. This had brought my face up in dozens of tiny sores. Which the doctor had painted with some purple stuff …

On the whole I loved living in Scotland, but I did seem extra happening-prone up there. So if you, too, find yourself in those wilder northern reaches and you hear strange legends of a scabby vampire who used to roam the countryside by bus, don't worry. It was probably only me.

Nor am I the only strange sight you may have seen returning by bus from the dentist. A friend, hearing my story, was reminded of a dear aunt of hers who was sent home with a frozen mouth. Having forgotten her contact lenses and therefore unable to see or feel her lips, the poor lady had gamely reached for lipstick and mirror and painted in a perfect bright red mouth way down in the lower half of her chin.

Returning to the present, I gather up polish and dusters and pause to admire the fantastic shine I've just put on the woodblock flooring. It's no use, though, the twinges are gathering momentum and I'll have to make that appointment.

But I think I'll just tidy my desk first. And sharpen these pencils. And write a few overdue letters. And pop out for some new blotting paper. And – Ouch!!

Oh, all right then ...

54 Whatever Made You Choose *Him?*

Family Circle, May 1975

It is one of life's strange mysteries that really nice people choose to marry such unlikely partners. This becomes apparent when we invite our husband's old school pal to tea and a joyful reunion. 'Bring your wife. We're dying to meet her', we add. So he does and she turns out to be the sort of girl who edges away from our children, dusts the chairs before sitting down and keeps on yawning and looking at her wristwatch. Or, we go to visit a girl we once shared an office with and wait around like hat-stands while her husband wanders off into the kitchen and is plainly overheard saying: 'What on earth am I supposed to DO with them while you're getting the tea ready?'

Once, in similar circumstances, at a small housewarming party, I suggested a simple word game: Bird, Beast, Flower. 'Yes, do let's play it!' said the wife feverishly, dashing away for pencils and paper. 'Is this so-called game played objectively or subjectively?' enquired the new husband, doubtless filing me away for future reference as 'that odd friend of yours who keeps on playing games'. 'Er, I dunno. It's just played', I mumbled and we stumbled home as soon after this intellectual exchange we decently could. But not before our host had held forth at some length on his pet subject: 'The Place of Woman in the Scheme of Things.' Or, with a chap like that it could just as easily have been: 'The Social Significance of Man the Dominant Animal'. Or even: 'Why Your Views on Everything are a Load of Old Rubbish'.

Sadly, our friends drift away with their strange new partners and become pillars of society or fresh-air fiends or colourful layabouts until gradually our only point of contact is the exchange of Christmas cards.

With relatives of course, it is different. As someone once said, rather poignantly I thought: 'Our friends we can choose; our relations we are stuck with!' This becomes a crucial matter for Mums and Dads sitting at home hoping like mad that their son won't end up marrying the squeaky-voiced dumbbell, or the fearsome bossy boots he is currently taken up with. Fathers of only daughters are particularly prone to bouts of galloping adrenalin at the thought of the wordly-wise teenage cynic or the ape-like buffoon currently in the running as a future son-in-law.

For those sitting up or lying awake under similar circumstances, or for non-sleepers in general, I recommend playing 'The Family Game', in which you are free to cast all your favourite people as members of your ideal family. My selection, for example, starts off unhesitatingly with Sheila Hancock for a sister, with perhaps Ian Carmichael for an elder brother and Frank Muir as a favourite uncle. 'Now, let me see,' I mumble drowsily to myself, 'Shall I have Cilla Black or Valerie Singleton for a sister-in-law. And I really must fit Richard Baker in somewhere … as a cousin perhaps?'

The possibilities are, endless and anyone can play, even if some poor souls do wake up next morning to the ghastly reality of Alf Garnett & Co. Or perhaps to the overwhelming dazzle of Doris Day for a mother-in-law. Or the even more overwhelming prospect of becoming a mother-in-law themselves. Or perhaps like me, your children are too young yet to go a'courting, but you have single friends whom you'd like to see happily and suitably married.

Isn't it strange how all sorts of super girls who would make ideal wives and mothers sit at home alone in a world full of eligible bachelors? Not that trying to pair them off helps much. If they do ever meet, what happens? Nothing. She goes back to her knitting machine and he marries a complete ninny in platform soles who can't butter bread, let alone boil an egg.

Husbands, too, get the matchmaking bug once in a while. Suddenly they keep on telling us about a really first-rate chap they've met called Kenneth who would be the perfect mate for our friend Pam. Over the next few weeks we hear quite a lot about good old Ken and how he's so talented at do-it-yourself and how he writes poetry and wears all the latest gear. Tentatively, we start broaching the subject of chaps in general, and snappily dressed, do-it-yourself poets in particular, to Pam as she sits alone at home washing her gleaming hair yet again and embroidering all those dinner mats. And, just as she is coming round to the idea of a foursome one evening, we meet the smashing Kenneth – who turns out to be a pale, weedy chap with red-rimmed eyes, pink socks and a ginger suit.

Still, there's no accounting for tastes. You could have a terrible time keeping a dishy girl friend from meeting a scruffy type all hair oil and cycle clips, who keeps on pestering for an introduction. Then someone else brings them together and apparently all her life she's been longing for a greasy chap on a bike and they get married right away.

Real life is often much stranger than anything we could dream up for each other. So, if we can't choose ideal partners for our friends, at least we can choose and be chosen by the right one for us and hope that everyone else will share our views. My husband is particularly lucky in this respect because most of my family and friends have accepted him. I think if it comes to a choice between us, they prefer him to me.

55 Clearing The Air

My Life and I, *Good Housekeeping*, May 1975

Some people never have any rows at all. 'Never a cross word in forty-seven years,' they say, which I find hard to believe. I think it's possible that they've long since *given up* rowing. If the dear chap just goes on picking his ear with a matchstick or tossing his dirty socks behind the boiler after, say, ten years of: 'I wish you wouldn't *do* that, Cyril!' then the chances are he's not going to change his ways in any future decades.

But if they really haven't ever let the thunder clouds roll with a good old name-calling, grudge-unloading session, then either they just don't care enough about each other or one of these gloomy, broody Sunday evenings old Darby's going to be creeping up behind old Joan with a meat cleaver, you mark my words.

We all need to clear the air occasionally. And not just husbands and wives either. Sometimes (*lots* of times), one's children can get right up one's nose. Doubtless we've all discovered that it's not a bit of good bleating away at them, nag, nag, nag, morning, noon and night. They simply coat their entire brain with a protective layer of unheeding wax. So how can we best tackle the inevitable stresses and strains of what they call happy family life?

All-out shouting matches may be the answer if one lives in a fairly isolated field. But it doesn't really seem the ideal solution for those of us who live in built-up areas. I expect we've all been sitting quietly in the garden at some time or other and heard a neighbouring snatch of: 'Have you eaten *all* the biscuits, you greedy cow?' And the Battling

Bickerskills are at it again, to the distant accompaniment of door slamming and engine revving and breaking glass.

But even this seems preferable to those households where everyone keeps on smiling, smiling and sitting straight on the edge of their chairs, until eventually one of them leans forward and hisses: 'I wonder if I could have a word with you in private.' Quietly, firmly, the door closes on their rigid backs and a terribly controlled whispering goes on for a long while in another room.

There are homes, too, where no one *ever* gets around to saying what the trouble is. It's all a bit too pent up for my taste. And anyway, I could go around wearing a brave little smile until doomsday in our house without the slightest notice being taken. They already ignore loud groans, sighs and a fair amount of fist shaking. I've also tried dragging one leg along the ground, chewing my handkerchief and even lying down dramatically in front of the television. In fact, I often wonder how other folk manage to get treated for their nervous breakdowns. Mine just get: 'Sshsh – you *know* this is one of our favourite programmes!'

I am fairly philosophical about it. I have to be. I knew, right from the Woolly Rug Incident in early marriage that this was how things were going to turn out.

I am a practical soul. I like to keep busy. So when, in a moment of early marital stress, I dashed from the house never to return, I automatically grabbed my current project – a huge, almost completed, fireside rug kit. Angrily I rolled it all up and tottered off.

A neighbour, peacefully trimming his privet, looked up in amazement at the sight of this great, shaggy bundle closely followed by my grim, unsmiling face. When the first full flush of rage wore off, however, it began to dawn on me that the thing weighed a ton and that I had nowhere to go.

Then it came on to rain. I didn't really fancy a lifetime of rug-hooking in bus shelters so, sadly, the bundle and I retraced our steps; I was panting, the rug was dishevelled. The privet clipper was just packing up, but he turned and watched us, with an inscrutable expression, as we once more bobbed along past his hedge. 'Been taking it for a walk?' he said. And, well – you just can't go on being furious once you get the giggles.

Perhaps the best answer really is to harness that first flush of outraged energy and quickly polish a few floors or turn out the garage; enough fury could spring-clean the whole house for you.

And if all else fails, you could always copy a family I heard about who set aside half an hour on Friday each week for their regular family row.

'Right,' screams the wife for openers. 'I'm *fed up* with searching for my kitchen scissors ALL OVER THE HOUSE! And if *someone* doesn't clean out that guinea pig's cage, he's *going!*'

'Oh, you *wouldn't.* Honestly, Mummy, I think that's a really *grotty* thing to say.'

'What about *me*? You said I could have a pet, too. She gets *everything.*'

'It's time you children started *earning* your pocket money. Your mother and I want to see keen, willing faces …'

'I never have any fun. It's all homework and jobs and rotten early nights.'

'*Oh, shut up all of you!* Time's up.'

And presumably, after this little group therapy session, they go whistling about their jobs and their guinea pigs, Mum's scissors turn up in yet another quaint place and it's all hugs and chuckles and sweet harmony until next Friday, and another week's worth of aggro.

It might work for the rest of us, I suppose. Anyway, it seems worth a try.

'Are you all sitting comfortably, my dears? Here we go then –

'WHO FILLED MY KNITTING BAG WITH SAND??'

56 Oh For A Silent Night

Family Circle, July 1975

'Help!' I scream, clawing at the bedside lamp, 'I can hear something snuffling at my pillow! 'Oh for heaven's sake,' grumbles my husband sleepily, 'It's only my sinuses.'

Downstairs in the garage, which lies directly below our bedroom, the deep freeze is going 'jub-jub-jub-jub', punctuated sometimes by great bursts of 'judder-judder-judder-judder'.

Outside in the middle of the road, late-night cars are crashing over large metal sheets put down by the men from the gas board. For weeks now they've been digging our road up looking for something. I do hope they find it soon before the traffic starts piling up in all the many holes and trenches right outside our door. But for now they cover up their excavations with these echoing metal plates and my nights are punctuated by 'ger-bonga-bonga-bonga-clank'.

I suppose I shall just have to learn to sleep through all these strange sounds, but it isn't easy. Ah well, at least my husband is there beside me even if he does add to the nightly symphony with his noisy nose. It is far worse when he's away because then the house seems to be full of even more things that go bump in the night. Not only do they go bump. For a start, there's our dining room table which suddenly goes 'cra-a-ack' just as I'm drifting off to sleep. People keep telling me that it's something to do with the central heating cooling down and the table getting colder and contracting. Well all I can say is why doesn't it make do with a quiet little shiver like the rest of us?

Meanwhile the pipes in our bedroom start up a high-pitched gurgling. They shouldn't because the heating goes off at bedtime. Or at least it does throughout the rest of the house. But for some mysterious reason, our bedroom radiator waits until midnight and then gets hotter and hotter and noisier and noisier until, what with the gurgling on one side and the snuffling on the other, it's no wonder that my nights are filled with nervous nightmares. My husband is sweet about my nightmares. 'Poor girl,' he says when I tell him about them next morning, 'How rotten for you. You just wake me up dear if you get any more.'

So next time foul fiends start flapping noisily through my dreams, I tap my spouse on the arm and tell him so. Whereupon he leaps into the air, flails around among the bedclothes and shouts, 'WHASSAT? WHASSAMAT-TER? WHAT DO YOU WANT TO WAKE ME UP IN THE MIDDLE OF THE NIGHT FOR? CAN'T A MAN GET A DECENT NIGHT'S SLEEP AROUND HERE?' He then sinks straight back into a deep, peaceful slumber and has forgotten the entire incident by morning. Never mind, if there *had* been any foul fiends lurking about, I should think all that shouting must have frightened them back to wherever they came from!

At least his reaction is better than some. I know one poor soul whose shopkeeper husband once sat bolt-upright in bed – still fast asleep – punched her firmly in the eye and said, 'That'll be sixty-four pence please madam!'

At least my husband did try to do something about the creaking boards outside our bedroom door. 'I know just how to deal with creaky floors,' he said one keen evening. Whereupon he proceeded to drive two four-inch nails right down through the boards and, it just so happens, through the main hot water pipe as well. '*Swoosh*,' went this great fountain of boiling hot water. Oh that *was* an evening!

Pets too can add their share of nocturnal disturbances. I have one tired-looking friend whose dog has a liver complaint which requires 'walkies' at regular intervals throughout the night. 'I wouldn't mind getting up so much if he'd just pop out into the garden while I waited at the kitchen door,' she sighed, "But he's not having any of that. No, he wants company, and a nice, long, moonlit stroll across the playing fields. Sometimes he even brings his ball!'

I certainly sympathise with her because Henry, our terrible tabby cat, has long since suffered from a similar midnight madness of his own. In fact he spends most of his time these days thudding against doors and windows in an effort to be let in, and out, and in again.

Unfortunately our house isn't suitable to accommodate a cat-flap so we have had a carpenter build him a dear little draught-proof box, complete with cosy fitted carpet, just outside the French windows. The idea is that on cold nights he stays indoors with us but on warm, summer, mouse-hunting nights he can curl up snugly in his box until we let him in. Well that's the general idea. Needless to say, Henry never ever goes anywhere near his box except sometimes to jump up on top of it and from there to throw himself even higher at the windows, loudly crying to be let in immediately.

If on the other hand we try to keep him indoors overnight he wakes us up at regular intervals with his own clever impersonation of Fred Astaire doing a noisy tap dance all along the landing.

So one way and another things don't just go bump in the night down our way. No, in our house they frequently go snuffle, jub-jub, clank, gurgle, shout, creak, swoosh, thud, miaow, tappety-tap as well.

57 Magic Motoring Moments

My Life and I, *Good Housekeeping*, July 1975

With petrol the price it is, you would think that my family at last would have stopped telling me that it's about time I finally learned I to drive.

'It'll do you good – take you out of yourself,' they will keep saying. 'But I don't *want* to be taken out of myself,' I keep mumbling.

'Nonsense,' they cry bracingly. 'You're only saying that. Just think – you'll be able to nip about all over the place, once you're really mobile. You just won't *know* yourself.'

But that's just it. I *do* know myself. Past experience has convinced me that I am just not one of the Graham Hills of this world, nor ever likely to be. And, anyway, I quite enjoy walking to the shops or catching a bus or train if I get any sudden urge to 'nip about' further afield. Recently, however, the brainwashing became so insistent that, sighing heavily and with trembling hands, I dialled a small local driving school.

'You'll need a provisional licence,' said the man on the telephone. 'Nothing to it, you'll see, we'll soon have you out and away on the open road.'

He sounded quite breezy poor chap. Carefree even. Little did he know the ghastly experiences which awaited him/us/ the rest of the world. Experiences which even that classic Bob Newhart record, *The Driving Instructor* had failed to prepare us for.

When I tell you that I was so nervous I very nearly fainted in the Post Office, just filling out the provisional licence form, you will have some idea of what shape I was in by the time the driving school car pulled up outside our house …

Mindful of a learner friend of mine who said she always put on her smartest clothes and drenched herself in her most expensive perfume to give herself confidence, I, too, had taken great pains with my appearance. I had even bought myself a luxuriant chestnut wig. Looking back I can see that this may have been a subconscious need for disguise but I also thought it might make me seem young and keen and dashing. (I needn't have bothered. Long before the end of that first lesson even the wig had turned grey.)

I won't describe Lesson One in detail. Nor Lessons Two to Eight for that matter. Some memories are painful even now. Suffice it to say that the next few weeks passed in a nightmare of shuddering lurches, flinching at pedestrians and cries from the instructor to 'Stop trying to pull the damned gear stick out of its socket!'

He wasn't very nice, either, the day the door handle worked loose and fell into my shopping bag. I found it when I got home and returned it to him at the very next lesson. Which should have pleased him really as he had apparently spent a rather wet week dodging round the bonnet to release his pupils.

I was *very* apologetic the day I bent that spindly little lever jutting out of the steering column. 'It's the *trafficator* – not the gears,' he sighed as I tried several times to waggle the silly thing into neutral.

To cheer him up I told him about a girl I knew who was so tense after her first driving lesson she found that she was still gripping the steering wheel when she got back indoors. But he didn't laugh all that much.

Other far-from-magic moments included the day he saw a whole crowd of people he knew in the High Street and paused in the lesson to turn and wave at them.

Suddenly finding ourselves left to our own devices, the car and I broke into an unaccountable series of kangaroo leaps.

As we bounded over the horizon I could see all these people in the driving mirror, cheering wildly, flinging their hats in the air and hollering: 'Yahoo – ride' em cowboy!'

But even this was better than the day we passed a group of road menders. With a big, intrepid tug at the steering wheel I pulled out to avoid the row of red and white cones they had set up for some distance along the crown of the road.

You may be interested to learn that if you drive over one of these cones it goes 'ger-dung'. I know this because I could hear them going 'ger-dung-ger-dung-ger-dung' as I flattened them, every single one.

I wouldn't have minded so much if the workmen had laughed or nudged each other or even shaken their fists. But they didn't. They just leaned on their shovels, in a long solemn line, and watched in complete silence as we 'ger-dunged' away into the distance.

'Now – about your ninth lesson ...' said the instructor, in a curiously tight, breathless sort of voice, as we squealed up on to the pavement more or less outside my house. 'I'm afraid we may have to take a little break for a while. I get these asthma attacks you see ...'

I quite understood. I told him I, too, had been feeling a bit run down, lately, and could do with a break in transmission myself, ho, ho, ho.

He did his best to laugh at my little joke but I could see that it was an effort. 'I'll be getting in touch,' he said dispiritedly as he drove away. But he never has.

Just as a matter of interest, I did catch sight of him the other day, driving along the High Street. He saw me, too, but he didn't turn and wave. No, with a great shuddering of gears he turned and shot off, in a series of leaps, up a narrow alleyway. Funny that. But then, who am I to criticize other people's driving?

58 After A Fashion

Family Circle, August 1975

Oh, I am fed up. Because just as the dress designers have at last brought out soft, flowing styles that I'm sure would do wonders for me we, like surely every other family, are having an economy drive and I can't afford any new clothes at the moment. And with my luck, by the time cash starts to flow freely again (will it ever, I wonder?) fashions will have changed again, and not necessarily in my favour.

When mini skirts came in I looked down at my sag-bag knees and sighed. When platform soles sent girls rocketing up like runner beans I measured my already 5ft 8in and sighed again. But at least I didn't mind making do through all these fashions – of course it's always mum who has to make do isn't it?

As we all know, if there is ever any spare money available for clothes, young teenage daughters 'simply *must* have the latest boots/skirt/pullovers/coats, etc, because absolutely *everyone* is wearing them!' Young sons aren't so bothered about looking trendy, but they rapidly outgrow their shoes, wear out their jeans and eventually start to look like a quart-sized boy in a pint-sized anorak. Husbands too must have a reasonable turn-over of decent clothes for work although I do sometimes wonder why my husband always seems to be digging the garden in his good stuff and saving all his worn, wrinkled old gear for smarter occasions!

So that leaves mum at the back of the queue at the best of times, but it is extra hard when the shops all suddenly seem to be full of flattering feminine styles to suit all ages.

For my age group in particular, fashion seems often to have

dealt us a bit of a raw deal in the past. In fact, looking back, while I agree that the pendulum swings to and fro over a period of time, for me it always seems to have been swinging in the wrong direction. In my schooldays we skipped fetchingly around in barrel-shaped garments which looked all right on the small percentage of barrel-shaped girls but did nothing for long, thin me. The year I left – naturally – they changed the uniform to comparatively smart and flattering shirt-waisters.

This wouldn't have mattered if I could have slipped straight into the latest teenage gear, but we weren't called teenagers then. We were called Lumpy-In-Betweens. And we had clothes rationing, which meant that we saved up our coupons to buy sensible, lasting shoes and accepted whatever other hand-me-downs came our way. I particularly remember the neighbourly gift of a coat, loose fitting and pastel striped, which made me look like an adolescent camel driver.

I also remember that, whenever I was invited to a formal dance, I had to be more than usually polite to my older cousin. This was because she owned the only long dress in the family. What luxury to feel all those yards of taffeta swooshing around my ankles. Never mind that the dress was royal blue with magenta and emerald appliquéd sprays, and that I was sallow yellow!

A friend's mother took pity on me and ran me up a two-piece sunsuit from some pre-war check dust sheets. It says little for my wardrobe that this was definitely the smartest, most attractive outfit I'd owned until then.

When the New Look came in I was serving an apprenticeship in London and my wages just about covered my train fares. So, glad as I was to tuck my saggy knees out of sight, finances didn't exactly permit a headlong dash to the House of Dior. The more frugal fashion magazines told us that it was *quite all right* to lower our hemlines by inserting deep bands of contrasting material into the skirt. I still shudder at the memory of a pink daisy print with a strip of brown crêpe-de-chine let in below the knee. One of my better achievements was an enormous black velvet evening bag gathered into drawstrings at the top. When big hats became news I managed to be fashionable right away by easing out the draw-strings and wearing this great floppy object on my head.

'The fascinating thing about you Betty,' said a dashing male acquaintance, 'is that you never look the same two days running.'

I preened myself, then he added, 'Now take today for instance. You look just like The Laughing Cavalier.' So that hat became a cushion!

I would really rather not dwell on all the changes of fashion we've had since then. Suffice it to say that when bosoms were rampant I had to make do with folded handkerchiefs. As my figure blossomed, bodices flattened. At the first whisper of the sack dress I developed a willowy waistline. Later, when hipster skirts came in, I had a job finding my hips.

'Never mind, said my mother. 'At least you have pretty curly hair.' No sooner were the words out of her mouth than *everyone* suddenly started wearing their hair long and straight.

'Never mind,' said my husband more recently. 'You have the best shoulders I've ever seen.' And he's the only one who *has* ever seen them. Whatever happened to off-the-shoulder dresses?

And now, just as I am going through a slightly bulgy phase (back to the dieting any day now!) along come the flattering loose over-dresses and flaring skirts – just when our family budget doesn't run beyond urgent new shoes, school gear and anoraks for the children.

Of course future fashions *may* turn out to be just right for me. One of these days, when my hair is white and sparse, my ancient knees as slender as gnarled orange sticks and my rheumaticky old shoulders covered in woolly shawls, the pendulum will probably zoom past once again. And this time it will be the Edwardian look. You know, piled up curly hair, long graceful skirts and the barest of bare shoulders.

So you see, that's why I'm feeling so fed up!

59 Sorting Out The Rubbish

My Life and I, *Good Housekeeping*, September 1975

'Is it supposed to make noises like that?' I asked tremulously as the plumber adjusted the water flow and flicked the switch. A red light glowed and a terrible rumbling shuddered up the plug hole.

'Watch your hand, lady,' he said, gripping my wrist. 'It'll have your fingers skinned to the bone if you aren't careful!'

We both leapt back and stared respectfully down at the monster in our sink. No, we hadn't decided to keep a pet piranha fish. We were learning to live with a new waste disposal unit.

After a few preliminary skirmishes during which it growled at polythene bags, choked on plastic bottles and screamed at the odd metal object, we learned to live together amicably and I must say I wouldn't be without it now as it cheerfully gulps down all sorts of nasties like congealed bacon rinds, potato peelings and cold stew leftovers.

Although we do still sometimes have guests asking: 'Why is your cutlery such a funny shape?' as they stare in amazement at the strangely contorted assortment with which we are stirring our coffee. But I've stopped feeding it teaspoons now and my only problem these days is deciding which kitchen refuse should go down the drain and what should be saved for the compost heap.

If you, too, are a keen gardener then you will know that it's easy to become just a shade over-enthusiastic about your compost. Especially if, like me, you were brought up to 'waste not, want not'. Eagerly I dart outside with wilting carrot tops, crushed eggshells and spent tealeaves – soon, I hope, to become delicious, finger-licking humus for my flower-beds. Banana skins and apple cores are snatched from the children's lips before they can wander off and find other resting places for them. (Like under their beds.)

'A well-made compost heap should look like rich brown chocolate cake,' I read in gardening books. So I go outside and study ours but have to admit that, what with its layers of lawn mowings and cabbage stumps and guinea pig cage sweepings, it does tend to look more like a lumpy liquorice allsort.

'*Anything* goes on the compost heap,' I read on. I think perhaps other members of my family have also read this because about half-way down I can see an old bathmat. Ah well, doubtless it will all turn into something rich and nutritious eventually. However, experience has taught me to exclude potato peelings as these have a strong tendency to survive and send out shoots. New potatoes may be one of life's pleasures, but not if you have to dig them out from between paving stones or under rose bushes. So peel I feed to the waste disposal unit.

Back indoors, recycling also continues in other directions. In fact, long before we all started worrying about the reuse and conservation of world resources I was a sorter and saver of loads of old rubbish.

When the children were much younger I started a 'rainy day box' which was soon full of old cornflake packets, empty cotton reels, egg boxes etc., for them to play with. Then, as they grew and *Blue Peter* started whipping them up into bursts of white-hot enthusiasm to make Granny a useful string holder or Dad a wallpapered workshop shelf unit, they were able to rush to the box for the necessary raw materials.

The trouble with saving things is that once you start it's hard to stop. Gradually the collection grew and the empty toilet roll tubes, the bent wire coat hangers and the 'useful' pieces of cardboard began to mount up. The box bulged. Then it overflowed … Avalanches of overspill began to creep out from under the stairs and take over in the garage. Then I had what seemed like a stroke of luck.

'Don't forget,' said a rather dictatorial little note from Daniel's first school, 'that we need empty yoghurt cartons, plastic bottles, egg boxes etc, for school projects.'

Here was my chance to really stand out as a helpful parent – Yoghurt Pot Collector of the year, even. Enthusiastically I sorted through my hoard and filled up a large paper sack. Then, flushed with pride and keen motherhood, I dragged my grand offering down to the school. 'Whatever's that?' said a teacher, peering round a doorway. Beaming, I told her. 'Hm, well, we do have something of a storage problem, you know,' she said in a startled voice. So now I save those containers which might come in handy for the freezer, for potting-on seedlings or for re-filling with salads and jellies for picnics, and reluctantly throw the rest away.

But I can't quite bring myself to consign my newspaper collection to the bin. The trouble is that nobody, not even the dustman, seems to want it, sort it and bundle it how I may. Out in the garage the stack grows high – ever since Anna's netball team sent out an SOS for waste paper to raise funds and then apparently changed their minds and had a charity walk instead. Perhaps they, too, couldn't find anyone to take it.

I used to be quite keen about saving bottles and claiming a refund wherever possible. But lately I've had to ease off clanking down to the chemist's with armloads of empty PLJ bottles since I overheard one assistant nudge another and mutter: 'Oh my gawd – here she comes again!'

Never mind, I shall still continue to collect a lot of more or less precious old rubbish, telling myself that I'm just a little ahead of my time, that's all.

Incidentally, as we all grow more litter-minded and more geared to reusing our garbage it might seem that our fierce friend, the waste disposal unit, will eventually go hungry. But until someone comes up with a really brilliant use for re-cycled bacon rind and burnt toast, I for one shall go on being glad I harbour such a dear old useful monster under my sink. Long may it gurgle.

60 Pot Luck

My Life and I, *Good Housekeeping*, December 1975

I was pleased to read the other day that there's a growing trend towards informal pot-luck supper parties. For years now, particularly in these hectic pre-Christmas weeks, I have agreed at least in theory with my husband's often-repeated advice, namely, entertaining one's friends does not require a Big Formal Planning Operation. Having them in on the spur of the moment for coffee and mince-pie leftovers is, he maintains, much more fun.

It is, too, because they tend to invite you back more often and you get to meet a much greater assortment of people. In fact, once you relax and take your pleasures less formally it's surprising how informal they I can get.

'You must come and meet the Robinsons,' said a recent dropper-in. 'They're dying to get to know you and they've invited us all over to their place on Saturday. The husband, Jim, is an absolutely fascinating man. I know you'll have heaps of things in common.'

'I thought we'd have our cocoa now and then you might like to see our holiday colour slides,' said Mrs Robinson, a rather faded but brave-looking lady, as we all filed in and sat down.

'Don't take any notice of *him*,' she added, setting up the projector and pinning the screen above her husband as he lay stretched out along the sofa asleep, unbuttoned and snoring like a lawn-mower.

Poor old Jim. He may well have had his absolutely fascinating moments but all I remember of him is an evening of Majorca with his shadowy tum rising and falling in the foreground.

I was telling a friend about this and she said that she still plumped for informality every time. In fact, if she had to choose among all her assorted friends – from *Cordon Bleu* right through to Bubble and Squeak – her very favourite hostess is the one who cut into her Christmas cake and revealed, in the very first slice she handed round, a beautifully cooked yellow felt-tipped pen.

It was this same poor soul who liberally sprinkled icing sugar on her son's birthday cake. Then she lit the candles and marched into the darkened living-room saying: 'Surprise, surprise. Come on, a nice big huff and puff now ...'

So, with one mighty breath, her son dutifully blew out the candles and when they switched the lights back on the guests were all surprised to find themselves covered from head to foot in a great huffed swirl of icing sugar.

But strive as I may to emulate this somewhat devil-may-care attitude towards my guests I have to admit I do still get unnecessarily worked up when people are coming for a meal. In fact, for days before a dinner party I can't seem to help steeping – nay, marinading – myself in cookbooks. Around the kitchen, on the breakfast table, beside my bed, GH, Robert Carrier and Elizabeth David all lie propped up and bristling with bookmarks.

Perhaps I am still over-compensating for the time in early married life when, during the disembowelment of our kitchen, I was forced to do my cooking on a single gas ring. I was quite blithe about it at first.

'Come for the weekend!' I cried to assorted friends. 'You won't mind, will you – we're having to rough it a bit at the moment.'

Some took quite kindly to stews followed by fruit and cheese. But then I grew bold and started to juggle with fried chops all in one go with boiled potatoes. With salad fortifications it nearly worked. Until one daunting couple arrived and pushed their plates away.

'Can't eat hot and cold food together!' they said firmly. Later at the railway station I had barely handed them into their seats and stepped back when the husband leaned towards his wife.

'Hope I never have another weekend like that one!' he boomed, as the train began to shunt. With necks craned, various passengers stared out at me – The Hostess with The Leastest – cringing on Platform Four.

Since then I've worked hard to improve my image although I've had the occasional set-back. Like the time I discovered a fascinating little leaflet entitled *Clever Ways With Cabbage* and decided to try part of it out on two of the most sparklingly amusing couples I know.

Possibly my ways weren't clever enough or perhaps a more subtle personal alchemy was at work because sparkly chums duly arrived, clapped eyes on each other, Went Quiet and Stayed Quiet.

Have you ever noticed how you can have masses in common with both friend A and friend B but put them together and they loathe each other on sight? Equally mystifying is when A and B go off arm in arm and never speak to *you* again.

Another easy way to lose friends is via what we might call the Hostess's Upward Spiral Syndrome. This starts when you invite them over for fish and chips and Guinness. Then they invite you back for a sardine dish they discovered in the Algarve, and Mateus Rosé. So then you give them smoked salmon and rather a good white wine. So then they come up with sharks fin and saki. And *you* give *them* caviare and champers ...

But luckily, most of our friends are still with us and with the growth of informal supper parties a new relaxed atmosphere is gradually beginning to prevail.

'You'll have to take pot luck!' I shall have to get used to saying, and I think that they'll mostly agree that it's the best way to entertain. Even if for some it may be Colcannon Supreme and for others Felt Pen Surprise.

61 A Question Of Confidence

Family Circle, February 1976

Have you ever wondered why it is that you feel comfortable, likeable and perhaps even witty and wise in some company and a complete fool in others? It's all a matter of confidence, I suppose, and for most of us it is surprising how effective a little praise can be in bolstering our assurance. Or, for that matter, how deeply criticism can affect us. Sometimes it isn't actual praise or criticism we react to, but just a general assumption that we are bright or dim.

'You're the expert!' people say, and straight away you find yourself brilliantly explaining to them exactly how to turn their husbands' shirt collars or re-pot their aspidistras.

Or perhaps they introduce you by saying: 'She's a real scream!' Quick as a flash you're cracking hilarious jokes, and whenever you meet these particular people in future they're going to curl up with mirth no matter what you say.

But let somebody suggest that: 'You wouldn't understand this, dear – it's a bit above your head', and you are liable to start behaving like the empty-headed idiot they take you for.

This sort of thing happens to me a lot. 'Ah, here's Betty,' someone says. *'She'll* know the best way to make rhubarb crumble' and immediately I'm Zena Skinner, Delia Smith and Fanny Craddock all rolled into one.

The feeling of encouragement their little remark gives me can easily last all day, often with buoyant after-effects. One minute I may be shuffling along thinking: 'Oh lor, what on earth can I rustle up for dinner?' and suddenly, I am into my best apron and giving Cordon-Bleu-type demonstrations to anyone in the vicinity, even to Henry the cat if he's the only one around. In my mind's eye the television cameras are whirring …

Neatly I lay out my equipment. Efficiently I weigh and measure ounces of this and millilitres of that. 'Now we gently fold in the flour,' I tell Henry in a clear high-pitched voice, the sort that demonstrators use. He doesn't seem to mind. In fact he purrs and winds himself around my legs, presumably on the assumption that it's all for his benefit and that I'm about to experiment with Kit-e-kat popovers.

Actually, I'm what you might call a moody cook. I go along with a neighbour I once had who said: 'Give me two green peppers, a blob of mango chutney and a papaw and I'll do my best to knock you up a banquet. It's just the daily plod that gets me down.' But, with my confidence bolstered, I'm a new woman.

On the other hand, just let me overhear someone say: 'She doesn't look as if she could boil an egg, let alone make an omelette', and immediately I become a sort of culinary Tommy Cooper, bumbling about in a cloud of acrid blue smoke while all around me soufflés explode and congealed porridge forms a thick blanket over both stove and saucepan.

It is all a question of confidence, and a typical illustration of this lies in the fact that I could fry a very neat egg right up until the day I got married. No leaky yolks, no brown lace edges, no reluctance to leave the pan. Plump little gold and white darlings they were, until my new spouse uttered one sentence. 'Go careful with those eggs!' he said, and from that moment my egg frying became a shambles. I took our wedding present frying pan back and changed it three times before I realised that I was to blame for the sticky mess sheepishly scraped on to his plate each morning.

And, of course, it isn't just in the kitchen that a little praise or implied criticism can alter the course of events. As anyone with children soon learns, to stand knee-deep in building bricks, dolls, cars, teddy bears and torn comics screaming: 'Put all these toys away at once, you 'orrible kids!' doesn't have nearly the same success as: 'I'm *so* proud of the way you two pack your toys away. Now here are two nice big cardboard boxes ...'

I can well remember when I was a stringy-haired, yellowish, grumpy-looking schoolgirl, aching to feel confident about something (*anything*), being bowled over by a super new aunt who took one long, thoughtful look at me, paused, and said I looked 'interesting and rather artistic'.

A similar character-building moment came later in my teens when I overheard someone say of me at a party: 'That girl over there looks the vivacious type'. Upon hearing this, I seem to remember becoming so vivacious I had to be taken home early.

But at least moments and phrases like these give one a cornerstone to build on. And it isn't just through childhood and adolescence that we need an occasional booster to our self-confidence. We *all* need a word of praise once in a while, even if it is only for our rhubarb crumble.

62 Where Are You Now, Arthur Blenkinsop?

My Life and I, *Good Housekeeping*, March 1976

Everyone's marriage has its thread-bare patches and often it's the little insidious things like creosote on the drying-up cloths that make us realize what a terrible, terrible mistake we've made in our choice of marriage partners.

'Where are you now, Arthur Blenkinsop?' we yearn, thinking back passionately to the acne-covered dreamboat of our youth – the one we *should* have married. The way we remember it, he was last seen, head in hands, on the eve of our wedding groaning: 'Oh no, how can life go on without her?' He didn't talk a bit like that really, but a good, lush, Technicolor daydream does help to get the ironing done.

Then, once the ironing board is put away, it's back to reality and, for some, that great rumpled lump with closed eyes and open pores, sprawled all over the sofa. Perhaps we are among those who sigh and envy the wives of neat, highly active men; the sort who like to keep busy. What joy it must be, we think, to sit back and watch them oiling hinges and polishing shoes and putting up dependable shelves.

Actually I've known a couple of marriages like that and I've seen the wives grit their teeth and look painfully inscrutable when their spouses (spice?) come dancing in, screwdriver in hand, during an otherwise relaxed coffee break.

I suppose most husbands lurk somewhere between El Slob and Twinkletoes and there are moments, particularly during grim, silent car journeys, when many women start thinking exactly what they are going to say to the solicitor tomorrow/

next week/when the children grow up. But somehow or other the roses need pruning or the school Open Day looms up or a clutch of relatives arrive and they put on a smiling face.

As for me, well, I expect I'm not the only wife to notice that there are quite long spells in marriage when one finds oneself wedded to not so much a husband – more a faulty answering machine. Take the other morning. We were just finishing breakfast when the front of our house fell down.

'My God, what was that?' I cried, flinging down my toast.

'What was what?' said David, staring absently over the cornflakes packet.

'That terrible noise,' I gasped, dashing to the front door.

'Probably just the postman,' he murmured vaguely. I can quite see that his reaction to my – er – colourful nature has, over the years, become less than razor sharp, but this was ridiculous.

People were shouting and running along the road, the garden was full of concrete chunks and thick yellowish dust was swirling in through the open front door. So – at double speed – was poor Henry the cat.

As the day disintegrated into short tempers and long telephone calls, not to mention visits from worried architects and even more worried neighbours, my husband alone remained imperturbable.

'Don't worry,' he said, puffing deeply on his pipe. 'It seems much worse than it actually is. It was only some front cladding that came down and they're going to send a real old craftsman along right away to re-do it.'

Six weeks later the real old craftsman came and re-did it and, just as we all stepped back to admire his real old craftsmanship, it all fell down again.

'Cheer up,' said David, giving me a well-meant but searing embrace. (Well, how would you like to be kissed by an absent-minded pipe smoker? My left cheek is getting quite singed!) 'How about coming for a drive this evening, to a nice old country pub? It'll take your mind off things.'

So we did, and found a sweet old lounge bar full of stuffed pike. It also contained a very happily married girl I used to know quite well.

'Hello there,' I cried. 'How's your husband?'

'Rotten!' she said. And stumped out without a backward glance.

Like I said, there's a lot of it about, and even quite enviable wives have their problems. Take the mother of a friend of mine, a really charming widow who recently married a brilliant surgeon. How pleased we all were for her – until I met my friend and said: 'How's your mother?' 'Well actually,' she said, 'Mummy's in hospital. She has been, on and off, ever since the wedding.'

It seems the brilliant surgeon took one passionate, probing look at his new bride, pointed to a couple of warts and the odd bunion and said: 'That'll have to go. And *that*.' and the poor soul's been having bits cut out or snipped off ever since. I particularly liked the family's wry comment when they last took grapes to her (post-appendectomy this time) bedside: 'Really Mummy, that's the last time we'll let you marry into the medical profession!'

So you see, we're all quite liable to develop an attack of the Arthur Blenkinsops. And next time we feel it coming on perhaps the best thing to do would be to concentrate on that friend of ours with the *really* impossible husband. The one who throws his dinner on the floor and brings home his girlfriends.

Then perhaps we should pause and consider what kind of bargain our menfolk have got in the marriage stakes. Has it occurred to you that at this very moment your husband may be down in the potting shed muttering: 'Where are you now Dorothy Dimplewick?' It's a sobering thought.

63 Sportin' Life

My Life and I, *Good Housekeeping*, May 1976

'Cor, look at that Billy Bremner! Fantastic! Come on, Leeds United!' shouts my son, as I potter about on Saturday afternoons, keeping well clear of the telly.

'Shsh, it's the cricket score!' hisses my husband, on summer days, as he wanders past with a transistor.

'Come on Mum, you could easily play badminton if you'd try!' calls my daughter as feathered shuttlecocks whizz by like souped-up sea gulls.

But the sad fact is that I am a complete dud where any sort of sporting activity is concerned. And, of course, one of the troubles with being tall and – let us say – lusty looking (no, on second thoughts, let's not say that) is that everyone thinks you are sure to be frightfully athletic and good at games.

'Anyone for tennis?' they cry, bounding off, twirling their racquets and looking keenly in my direction.

'Care to join us for a spot of golf?' they ask, slinging great tartan bagfuls of assorted wood and metal into the boots of their cars.

'Ever tried any hurdling?' they puff, jogging off down to the rec' in zippy track suits. But they rarely ask me a second time. Because just as there are people who have a blank spot where foreign languages are concerned, or admit that they can't draw or sew or carry a tune in their heads, I seem to have something missing where sport is concerned. It isn't just a matter of ability, although I certainly lack that. It's also that I really don't know *why* they feel the need to chase that ball up and down. Or find it necessary to pound past the winning post first. Why can't they all pound past *together*? To music even. With their arms linked?

I have tried to discover the secret of a successful sporting life. Believe me I have tried. Especially in early adulthood when so many of the local social events tended to revolve around sports clubs of one sort or another. But fate always seems to have been against me.

This fact soon became evident at school, particularly when teams were being chosen by that unnerving method in which two leaders take it in turns to pick a player. I remember so well how it was...

'I'll have *her*,' said our games captain, tossing back great muscular pigtails and pointing to an enthusiastic soul already doing flashy press-ups on the sidelines. 'In that case I'll take the one over there,' said the other team leader indicating a tanned whippet of a girl sprinting round in circles to the whirl of a skipping rope. And so the selection process went on. First the amazons. Then the middlin' bunch. Then the lame, the halt, the wobbly and the uncoordinated. Then me. In fact, if the numbers were odd, I was often thrown in free with a girl who had pebble lenses and a recent leg fracture, in exchange for the one with wonky hips and a verruca. I still sometimes have a brave go at joining in whatever happens to be the latest activity practised (so *easily* it seems) by those around me.

In fact, upstairs right now in my wardrobe there are gleaming, hardly-worn tennis shoes, grippy-soled boating shoes, white shorts, blue shorts, ankle socks and a healthy assortment of open-pored Aertex tops. There even used to be, at one time, a pair of specially-made jodhpurs. They had to be specially made because I must be one of the few people who are actually jodhpur-shaped underneath.

However, I always felt so sorry for the poor horses who found themselves saddled with me that I've long since relegated my big, baggy breeks to other pastures.

But I still show willing to do my pitiful best in other directions.

'Come on Mum,' cry the family, tossing a frisbee up and around and back into their waiting hand. Or sending a cricket ball for six. Or expertly dribbling a football in and out among various darting and swerving opponents.

But, alas, my cricket bat misses or flies off over the horizon with the ball, my dribbling punctures the football and my frisbee sails up into elm trees or open office windows.

It is some small consolation to know that I am not absolutely alone in this.

'Come along, Daniel,' said a visiting relative who happens to be a headmaster. 'I'll show you how to fly your kite.' With studious care he clasped the spool of thread and bounded sedately off across the field, only to return a bit shamefacedly shortly afterwards, to say that he'd accidentally let go of the string and the whole thing was now tangled up in an overhead telegraph wire.

And pretty sheepish he and my husband looked, too, throwing sticks into the air for the rest of the afternoon, in their efforts to dislodge it.

My sympathies were also with the frisky Dad who, seeing the local lads scoring a few practice goals in the park, joined in and sent their ball soaring up and away and into a passing lorry.

Then there was the day my husband, keen to impress me with his fishing prowess, cast his line with a great ripple of shoulder muscle, forgot to let go, and zoomed off after it, with a dramatic plunge into the river.

But I am glad to notice that, as the years go by many keen sporting types, both male and female, gradually settle down to become armchair enthusiasts instead. So perhaps the best thing at this stage is for me to practise becoming a good spectator sportswoman.

It doesn't take all *that* much coordination or athletic expertise to sway one's head from side to side at a tennis match. Or to lean forward and Look Keen when someone scores a goal on the telly. Especially now that we've got a colour set. I may not know precisely what it is they are doing out there on the field – or even why – but at least I can now unscramble one team from the other.

So 'Come on, Billy Bremner ... Oh, WELL PLAYED!!'

64 You're Just The Person …
No I'm Not

My Life and I, *Good Housekeeping,* July 1976

One of my favourite people was once asked to make an off-the-cuff after-dinner speech to a frightfully brilliant gathering. 'Er, yes – of course,' he said, momentarily carried away with pride at being asked. Whereupon he rose to his feet, cleared his throat, paused, smiled, turned green and fainted dead away.

He still has nightmares about it and so do. My very worst dream, even in earliest childhood, was the one where I stood alone before the school assembly, blurting out: 'There are fairies at the bottom of my gar–den,' while clad entirely in San Izal toilet paper.

I seem to have outgrown the lavatorial anxiety syndrome now, I'm glad to say, but I still get a severe attack of the screaming hives just *thinking* about speaking in public. And, of course, once the word gets around that one writes a bit, folk do tend to come dashing up crying:

'Ah, Betty, you're just the person to open our school fête/ give a talk to our group/round off our annual dinner.' To which, alas, I must churlishly answer: 'Oh no I'm not.'

In fact I blush to admit that on one occasion after a great deal of: 'Oh you're only being modest. Of *course* you can make a speech,' the very direct foreign lady in charge put her arm round my shoulders afterwards and said sadly: 'You were right, my dear. Eet is not your theeng.'

I am tremendously impressed by some of my friends and acquaintances who seem absolutely chock-full of enthusiasm and *savoir faire* when it comes to projecting themselves in public, whether they be called upon to give a half-hour talk on patchwork, to propose a vote of thanks for the flower arrangements or to judge the cake baking.

Folk like this know instinctively, for instance, to wear something comfortable, becoming and loose at the throat whereas I've actually publicly choked myself in a bakingly hot new woollen dress with an elasticized neck which, due to room temperature, humidity or nervously swelling glands, suddenly gathered itself up in mid-sentence and squeezed me to a complete standstill.

And I am constantly amazed by the way these types can go on cracking carefree jokes, putting across interesting points and projecting themselves in general without seeming to mind that woman in the front row dead centre – the one with the wide-spread *directoire* knicker-clad knees and the unswerving stare.

Not to mention those two fur-coated old dears at the back who suddenly call out to each other: 'What *is* she talking about, Winifred?' 'I've no *idea*, Dorothy,' and then, after tut-tutting a bit, relapse into *fairly* well-harmonized snores. I've even, during one of my own rare public appearances, had a well-bred old soul march out, rattling like an agitated bundle of twigs, because I had used the word 'pregnant'.

So one way and another it isn't altogether surprising that in spite of stirring cries of: 'Go on, it'll do you good,' 'You'll be fine once you get started,' 'You'll feel marvellous once it's all over,' from my nearest and dearest, I return home from such affairs a keyed-up wreck and have to lie down in a darkened room for at least three days to recover. It isn't that I haven't tried. In fact, while serving in the WRNS, I even went away on a special public speaking course to overcome the problem and to learn how to put myself across with confidence.

It was a marvellous course. On Day One we poor, draggled, twitchy lot each had to jump right in with a brief chat on any subject at all that we felt reasonably knowledgeable about. There was only one other female in the class and we huddled palely together, listening to assorted nervous matelots and trying to concentrate on some none too gripping little vignettes ranging from Deck Swabbing Made Easy to How To Keep The Pressure Up In Your Boiler. My own contribution, when the dreaded moment arrived, was an extremely squeaky but fast-moving ten minutes into which I managed to cram the entire history of interior decoration.

Then on Day Two our gloriously calm, handsome instructor gave a model talk. It had a good lead-in, human interest, visual aids, audience participation, the lot. It was absolutely smashing, I understood every word of it and came away really exhilarated. Which was extremely clever of the speaker when you consider (a) me, and (b) that the talk was entitled: 'The Principles Of Jet Propulsion'. By the end of the course I was no Sheila Hancock of the after-dinner speakers' set, but I was able to hold the attention of some pretty hard-boiled engine-room artificers with a carefully paced half-hour chat on lampshade making.

Alas, I have long since forgotten most of what I once knew about lampshades, jet engines and gripping the audience. Although the quick-fire history of interior decoration did come in useful on a small boat later when the glitter-eyed chap at the helm lashed us to some sort of mid-harbour protuberance and proceeded to work the crew (of one) around to the subject of rape.

'And then furnishing got rather rococo,' I panted, scrambling up on to the cabin roof and so bemused was he, benumbed even, at the nervous turn my conversation was taking, he eventually unlashed us and silently delivered us back to port. So I suppose the public speaking course did me *some* good, after all.

65 Keyed Up

My Life and I, *Good Housekeeping*, August 1976

I recently heard a man give a talk about actors being either nervy, excitable 'high-key' types, such as Kirk Douglas, or 'low-key' such as Gary Cooper. And much as I'd love to pace steadily through life saying 'nope' to the children at well-spaced intervals, I have to admit I fall into the former category.

Especially before lengthy journeys when the family have long since learned to scuttle away out of range of me and my armfuls of lists, large dusty suitcases and little, last-minute jobs for them to do. On the whole, though, it isn't my family but newly-met strangers who cause my nerve endings to start twanging away like tuning forks. Until I am really familiar and comfortable with new people I seem to feel that it's my job to fill each shy, restful gap in the general conversation with great outbursts of nervous chatter.

This was particularly true at a party once, when I suddenly came face to face with just about the most handsome chap I'd ever seen.

'You two are just *made* for each other,' gushed our hostess, to my acute embarrassment. In my experience chaps as good looking as this one were made for the Brigitte Bardots of this world. Or at the very least for shirt commercials.

He obviously thought so, too, and for several seconds we gazed woodenly at each other. In sheer nervous desperation I then came out with one of the silliest remarks I've ever made.

'Did you know that guinea pigs were used as lawn mowers in Elizabethan times?' I asked feverishly.

'Er, no, I didn't,' he mumbled, cringing back.

There was another long, dazed silence during which it became even more evident: that we weren't meant for each other.

'We always used to have tadpoles when I was a child,' I cried.

'I used to have tadpoles,' he said, brightening up very, very slightly.

I'd like to be able to say that we then clamped arms round each other's waists and strolled off into a rosy future. But perhaps he felt, and who can blame him, that a mutual background of tadpoles wasn't quite enough.

I suppose, during some long-past, character-building moment, I'd heard someone say that animals make good ice breakers. The trouble is that we 'high-key' types never seem to get it quite right. And not only do we say all the wrong things, we frequently emit terrible, uncontrollable honks of laughter, sometimes making great, uncoordinated swooping movements while doing so. And when we're not flinging ourselves about in an exaggerated way we quite often get sudden attacks of nervous deafness or hiccups or we start winking uncontrollably. To cover all this we put on pitiful shows of jaunty cool. I seem to become especially afflicted when meeting editors.

'Goodbye and thank you for the lovely lunch,' I enthused to one, shaking hands with her and her assistant ed. 'Yes, yes, I know my way from here, don't worry, cheerio and thanks a lot,' I called, darting firmly out of the door, round a couple of corners and back face to face with them again.

'Isn't this an incredible view?' said another, speaking over my shoulder as I stood gazing out of her skyscraper window. Thinking that she meant another, even better view behind me and being desperately eager to please, I spun right round and cried: 'Oh it *is*! Yes it *is*!' only to find myself staring rapturously at a blank wall.

I am also nervously afflicted by those dreadful telephone answering machines which suddenly – deliberately – commandingly say: 'Speak *now*!' – well, I don't suppose I'm the only woman in the world to gasp, tremble and squeak: 'Oh my God, it's one of those – er – sorry – never mind!' before crashing the receiver down and blundering shakily off to tackle a little house-cleaning therapy.

Another good temporary cure seems to be to spend time in the company of someone even more keyed-up than we are. I have one particular friend who simply never stops rushing about, gossiping, gasping and waving her arms in the air. In fact on especially het-up days I've known her eyebrows to rise right up over the top of her head and disappear altogether.

A quick telephone call and over she dashes, chattering, chattering all the way. In her company there simply isn't the opportunity to do more than squeeze in a very occasional 'yep' or 'nope' before she's off on another verbal trailblazer, leaving me relaxed (limp even) and very low-key indeed.

However, carrying this theory to the extent of marrying one of the Kirk Douglases of this world may not be the ideal solution to personal problems of hypertension.

I once knew a very vivacious, active girl who married an even more vivacious, active husband. After several shared years with this chap dancing about on the balls of his feet, shadow-boxing, practising his bird calls, swiping at imaginary cobwebs and doing his 'I say, I say, I say' routine, his wife became so low-key she even began to *look* like Gary Cooper.

No, I think the best thing is to marry a nice restful sort of partner. Then tell yourself that whatever our clench-jawed, nerve-twangy, over-excitable faults may be, they're a sign of higher intelligence. They must be. Because haven't you noticed how many really clever women marry comfortable, homely-looking men? Sometimes even short, bent, really ga-ga ones.

While the handsome chaps, of course, often get the complete bimbos because only girls entirely devoid of – shall we say – nervous intelligence would be dumb enough to think themselves *worthy* of such Apollos. (Well, that's one theory anyway.)

However, before you naturally assume that my husband is short, bent, etc, I hasten to say that in fact he is tall, well-built and entirely oblivious to my nervous chatter. This can be just a shade irritating at times but at least it got us smoothly over any wildly blurted initial conversations about Elizabethan lawn mowers.

66 Oddawa

My Life and I, *Good Housekeeping*, September 1976

We nearly emigrated last year. And the year before. And the year before that. 'I'm getting fed up with nearly emigrating,' I said. 'Let's do it.'

So this year we did and home is now Canada. And, just for the moment, home is also an apartment building literally in the process of being built around us. Another floor is completed and people move in above us. Fascinating people, it seems, who play strange games on their bare golden-oak floors at dead of night. 'Per-plink' we keep hearing and after some discussion at breakfast we decide it must be tiddlywinks.

Tentatively we try pancakes with maple syrup, a popular breakfast with Canadians. 'It's not Pancake Day in England y'know,' says Dan, puzzled.

Then it's off to work in the shiny new apple green car for David and off to school in the faded new denim jeans for Daniel. No such thing as school uniform, we were told, but blue jeans *are* uniform here for at least half the population.

In great flurries of Italian, work parties crowd in upon me with paintpots and screwdrivers and proceed to do last-minute things to our walls and wiring. It is all quite jolly in spite of the fact that our only means of actual communication are nods, smiles and little bursts of opera. The foreman, who does seem to include the occasional Canadian phrase in amongst all the rich '*bella*s' and '*issimo*s', eyes my rump rather thoroughly and manages to convey that he comes from Venice. When I tell him that I once spent ten days in Lido Di Jesolo he becomes so excitable I have to go out for a walk.

I wonder what he thought I said? I must just get used to the fact that Canada is a mixture of races and even among English-speaking Canadians my Londony accent isn't always readily understood.

Loaded with great plastic cushions of milk, sweet bread-and-butter pickles (yummy) and cartons of delicious cheap fruit, I return home and approach our new gleaming white wall-telephone with some trepidation because I can be pretty sure that Long Distance will call me Sir and connect me to Oshawa when I've asked for Ottawa. They always do.

'Gee Beddy, ya hafta say *Odd*awa,' says a neat little old lady from England who seems to have found her own individual, if rather catarrhal way to break the language barrier.

Life at the moment seems to be full of well-groomed little old ladies, all with upswept specs and blue-grey waves. And all claiming me as their own special buddy. Phrases like 'at our age' and 'those younger ones' keep cropping up. Eagerly they whip out photos of 'our gang in Miami last winter'. Close inspection reveals the entire gang to be smiling and tanned and sinewed and silvery-haired. 'Hey – you'd have a ball with us,' they add.

Obviously, wearing my hair this new pewter colour is a mistake. I quite like little old ladies. I'm just not ready yet to join their ranks. Looks as if I shall have to join the other lot – the younger, untidier half in the blue jeans.

Clearing my throat carefully I try out 'Oddawa' on the operator and get put through right away. Then, shouldering my way through our swinging, ranch-style kitchen doors and *longing* to drawl at the smiling workmen: 'Okay fellas, the Milky Bars are on me' (but prudently deciding against it), I go in search of the 'Sears' catalogue and the necessary blue jeans.

As a reasonable compromise, for evening wear, I run myself up a couple of long denim skirts which are cool and useful and seem suitable for most occasions. I wear one to 'the smartest place in town' – all Tiffany lamps and really very pleasant indeed once you get over the initial shock of hearing the waiter ask: 'Anything to drink with your meal, sir and madam?' and hearing sir settle for a rum-and-coke while madam says: 'Make mine a cup of tea.'

'And why *not*?' I tell myself firmly, as I watch Café Royale being prepared quite magnificently at another table. With great sweeping arm motions, the waiter pours flaming brandy from one huge, warmed balloon glass to another to be doused, with a deft flick of the wrist, by gleaming waterfalls of rich black coffee. His performance has the attention of the entire establishment and, entranced, I await the *piéce de résistance* – the bit where he slowly, lovingly, pours the cream over the back of the silver spoon. And here it comes … with a graceful pirouette he reaches under his black tails, produces an aerosol can and – plurp, plurp – a dollop of white foam lands in each glass.

Ah well, good old Canadian know-how does also include a lot of plus factors. Splendid central heating and air conditioning and here in Peterborough, Ontario, a lovely bus service in which not only are the buses on time but the drivers *wave* and *wait* for you and set you down at your very own street corner if they possibly can. At the post office too, they are smiling and jolly, asking me how I like Canada. 'Everyone here is so helpful and friendly,' I tell them.

'But aren't folk helpful and friendly *everywhere*?' they ask, genuinely bewildered. Oh yes, I'm sure I'm going to like it here. If I can just carve a little niche for myself somewhere about midway between the tatty blue jeans and the neat blue rinses.

67 A Time For Traditions And Grandmothers

Family Circle, December 1976

One of the traditions in our family is to take the children, and anyone else staying with us, to dinner at a hotel on Christmas Eve.

We started this when Anna and Daniel were quite small because it cunningly prevents over-anxious children from palely loitering around the house, beadily hoping for early glimpses of Santa Claus. By the time we all arrive back home everyone is tired enough to sleep right round to an hour not too blearily close to the crack of dawn.

In this way we grown-ups have a pleasant break from all our own traditional culinary preparations and we avoid one stark moment of truth most parents have to face – that of being awakened at around 3am on Christmas morning by tiny excited voices piping: 'Cor, look at this train set!'

'Dad, how do these bits fit?'

'Can I use my pastry set, Mummy?'

'What's in this big tin – gosh *toffees!*'

Swiftly followed by: 'Mu-um, I feel a bit sick!'

And again later at 4am by: *Crash.* 'It wasn't *me*, Dad! Honestly, it just fell.'

Thud, scuffle, *twang*: 'Ha, ha, serves you right. I *said* we weren't supposed to ride bicycles on the stairs.'

So one of our pleasantest traditions has sprung up and we are now awakened at a slightly more civilized hour by *fairly* acceptable thuds, twangs and whispers and – because Grandma spends Christmas with us – by a nice, big early morning cup of lavishly sweetened tea. I have frequently explained to my mother that I take saccharine.

'It's all right, dear – I remembered this time,' she says, cheerfully lobbing in a sweetener *plus* two heaped spoonsful of sugar.

Then she goes downstairs for a helpful pre-breakfast potter in the kitchen, keenly drying-up any odds and ends left lying around and stacking them away in unlikely cupboards.

'I really like having Grandma to stay,' chuckles Anna, a little later, as we put the finishing touches to the mince pies. 'She's so *funny* and sort of *different*.'

'In what way?' I ask, anxious to file away any tips on ideal grandmotherhood for when my time comes.

'Well, she enjoys Christmas so much and she's super with animals, especially that time she tried to give the kiss of life to my rabbit.'

It is true that Grandma has a soft spot for animals. Who else, we ask ourselves, would feed their cat three-course banquets off a lace mat? Or arrange its box (comfortably draped, opera-type) at just the right angle for watching television? Or leave the radio on while she is out, to cheer up an elderly canary? Or give successful artificial respiration to a *goldfish*?

Her attachment to assorted pets apparently started during her childhood when her mother (bravely) allowed her to have two rabbits – a delightful story which it is also one of our Christmas traditions to hear.

'Tell us about when you were a girl and you brought home two baby rabbits on the bus …' urges Dan.

'Well …' says Grandma, and we all settle down to hear the familiar story which always ends with the same sentence: 'That day I was the Happiest Little Girl in the Whole World.'

The children love it – indeed, we all do – and clamour for more tales from the past.

So then David joins in and says he had a pet rabbit when he was a boy.

'What was it called, Dad?' we ask, falling about with mirth because we already know the answer.

'Binny Habit,' he replies.

Oh, I can just see David and me as grandparents one of these days, starting a whole new batch of family anecdotes. Already I have my own favourite vignette to tell. It occurred when we took Grandma and the children for their special Christmas Eve hotel visit last year and settled them down for a pre-dinner drink.

'What are you going to have, Daniel?' we asked, as Dan strove to look as if boozing in bars was all part of his daily life style. And I must say he rose to the challenge magnificently.

'I'll have a shandy bolognaise,' he said with all the sophisticated nonchalance that an eight year old boy can muster.

But for now it is my mother's stories the children want to hear. The tale of Mackie, for instance, the cat who was evacuated during the war. Grandma is a good storyteller, and with many a dramatic flourish we hear how poor Mackie was so upset by the move that he ran away and lived wild for six months, as a sort of early drop-out.

'Then one day, just as your Uncle Victor was coming from school, he saw these two little green eyes glinting from a haystack. We were watching out down the hill and suddenly there was his distant figure stumbling up the lane towards us carrying something black and white under his arm, shouting to us breathlessly: "I've *found* him – Mackie's come *home!*"'

Every phrase, every sentence, remains the same from year to year and we wouldn't have it any other way. Grandma's stories are a tradition and that – along with all the mince pies, the sweet tea and the shiny new train sets, is what good family Christmasses are made of.

68 Peace And Goodwill

My Life and I, *Good Housekeeping*, December 1976

I was meandering peacefully through the supermarket the other day and had just slowed down to a pensive hover when a conversation hit me midway between the glacé cherries and the ground almonds. 'Oh for God's sake; you're *impossible!* They're only *baked beans!*' screamed the furious wife, pounding her trolley with ashen knuckles.

'Damn the beans, it's the principle of the thing,' hissed her husband, thrashing furiously at her rigid back with what appeared to be a cardboard metric converter, a slide rule and a pocket adding machine.

This is not at all an unusual state of affairs when husbands and wives go shopping together, particularly during the Christmas crush. The funny thing is that left to their own devices most wives can bring home the yuletide bacon quite adequately, along with sensible bargains in butter, sugar and tea, kilograms or no kilograms.

Many husbands, on the other hand, whether they be up and coming young computer programmers or poor little old aged granddads with their pensions carefully tucked into their tobacco pouch and strict instructions from their wives, tend to go a bit barmy when sent to the shops alone.

I recently stood behind a dear old chap peering thoughtfully at a list which said:

¼ streaky
Small loaf
¼ PG
1 lb potatoes *if cheap*.

When his turn came at the check-out counter he gleefully presented the cashier with a tin of chocolate biscuits, some peaches in brandy and a box of *petits fours*. Somewhere in there between the mad lone spender and the pernickity bean calculator lie a great many shopping missions which aren't quite as successful as they might be. For instance it is a considerable culinary challenge to have the casserole/the omelette/ the meat and assorted veg standing by because one has run out of salt and to have one's partner come strolling back from the shops with an impulsive brace of kippers instead.

Or to go together to the butcher's and have the dear lad suddenly boom: 'Oh look, they've got chitterlings (and/or tripe/heart/brains/sweetbreads, etc, etc). We used to have those *all the time* when I was a boy. Couldn't *you* find out how to cook them?'

But for true drama it is the husband and wife clothes-buying syndrome that really takes the biscuit.

I shan't easily forget that day, in Marks & Spencer, when I stood not two feet away from a middle aged chap of trendy persuasion who became so enraged at the length of time his dithery wife was taking to choose a skinny rib sweater he finally bellowed: 'What the hell does it *matter*, you silly old moo – with a bust like yours they *all* look rotten!'

And if you find that hard to believe, let me assure you that once, in the adjoining fitting room of a big department store I overheard a chap say thoughtfully, after a long rustly pause: 'You know Ellen, I hate to say this but I've never been *altogether* satisfied with your nipples.'

Poor girl. I wonder if they *squinted*. Right now, during this party season especially, I wouldn't mind betting that The Case Of The Red Face Wife, in all sorts of versions, is being enacted across the country.

Husbands come in such infinite variety. And in there, among all the widely differing types ranging from the Rudolph Valentinos to the Andy Capps of this world lurk your mate and mine, I shouldn't wonder ... Fastidious fellas insisting on soft, pearly, cross-cut crêpe to complement those incredibly subtle silver flecks in their beloved's eyes/hair/ teeth.

More-taste-than-money-lads zooming their lasses into Laura Ashley.

Jolly farmers crying: 'Come on mother, let's choose summat to show off yer nice curvy bum then!'

Intense types insisting on *slashed* red satin and *heavy* black velvet.

Power-crazed Svengalis turning their cringing fair ladies into something else again.

Average no-help-at-all chaps murmuring: 'Yes, well, you always look nice dear.' And legion upon legion of hard-up, bewildered, glazed-eyed souls, slumped on tiny gilt chairs and torn between wanting to make the little woman happy and wanting to run like hell to the nearest exit.

As one friend put it: 'The really impossible part is finding a dress we both like, finding it *quickly* and finding one that makes my eyes light up because it actually fits and his eyes light up when he sees the price ticket ...'

Of course there are lucky women – and I've just been staying with one of them – whose husbands travel a lot and bring home perfect kaftans, saris, sandals, etc, from around the world. But for every one who leaps through the front doorway with a length of pure silk to match exactly his true love's eyes I bet, come Christmas morning, there are half-a-dozen presenting over-optimistic bras, unfortunately gasp-making knickers or well-meant cut-glass bottles of 'Evening By The Docks'.

I'm not sure which is worse — to be a big, overflowing flannelette nightie type trying to look pleased about flimsy size-8 baby doll pyjamas or to be the slim, glamorous, sexy sort (like you and me, of course) drumming up heartfelt enthusiasm for heavily tasselled size 8 bedsocks.

So perhaps, in spite of the possible risks and red faces involved, it might be as well for most of us, where personal Christmas shopping is concerned, to take our espoused along with us even if it does turn out to be another Mission Impossible.

69 Nothing But The Truth

My Life and I, *Good Housekeeping*, April 1977

I would like to make one thing absolutely clear. I do not write fiction. People drift up to me quite often and say: 'Oh yes, you're that woman everything seems to happen to, aren't you?' Then they wink archly and nudge me with an elbow.

'But I only write the *truth*!' I cry.

'Oh yes, sure,' they giggle knowingly. Well, maybe I rearrange the truth just enough to avoid giving offence. If you want to quote your ghastly old Uncle Charlie, it's best to make him somebody else's ghastly old Uncle Charlie. But close members of my family, who share my daily round, know that we really do drift up to button counters and overhear foreign gentlemen demanding sex. Of course it's soon established that they are mispronouncing the word 'six'. Or perhaps they really do need sex ... people's behaviour can be so *interesting*.

Take that day I popped up to London early one Monday morning for a day's shopping, hopped on a bus at Paddington and headed eagerly towards Oxford Circus. As the bus slowed down in a traffic jam I was fascinated to see a rather intense looking girl beating with her fist on the door of a sex shop crying: 'Let me in! Hoy – let me *in*!'

Now, I don't know how you would have reacted, but my mind absolutely raced through the various possibilities which could have brought this poor soul to such a pretty pass – and so early in the day, too. But when I told this little story to a friend, she said prosaically: 'Probably just one of the staff who'd been sent out for coffee before opening-up time.'

And lest you live way beyond the city commuter belt and think I'm making up the very idea of such a thing as a sex shop, let me assure you that they do exist (if not as yet in village high streets). In fact, I bravely strolled into one once and discovered it to be a pale pink place full of Sinatra background music, athletic photographs and little men in raincoats and cycle clips buying jars of cold cream labelled 'Stud' and 'Rampage'.

But then when I'm not sidling into sex shops I'm quite often listening to sad-eyed little ladies telling me that they 'Don't go in for that sort of thing' with their husbands. Nor indeed *any* sort of thing apparently – right from that day in early married life when presumably they kissed and the poor chap turned back into a frog. So maybe he's the same fella and he *needs* his faith in little pots of cold cream.

Turning back the pages of my average days, I find plenty of true life incidents to ponder on and jot down in my notebook … like the little crowd in our local market place awaiting the arrival of the organic vegetable man. There everybody stands, arranged in an orderly rectangle around the spot where he usually sets up his stall, and they are all earnestly staring at the same tiny patch of cobblestone – the *exact* spot where he normally stands. I can't help a tiny grin.

Surely they all find the situation funny? I catch a lady's eye but she quickly looks away. Unseemly merriment is apparently out of place among the organic veg brigade.

Thus my day unfolds … wandering through the town, passing a row of sweet old grey mossy almshouses – and being almost blasted across the street by the rock music pouring out of the end one … strolling down by the river and seeing, inside one of the pleasure boats, a family sitting down to a hearty meal with – plonked right in the middle of the table – a toilet roll … passing two middle-aged ladies and overhearing one of them say: 'There was this special knee-cap I wanted and they hadn't got it' … standing on a country railway platform and catching drifts of honeysuckle and meadowsweet and conversation: 'Oh, you should have come, Lavinia dear; I won a bottle of parsnip wine.'

'Well, I'm not much of a *winish* person myself.' (Crisply.)

'... and then I laughed so much I fell into the river and lost my hearing aid!' ... boarding the train and suffering that stunned, alienated feeling you get when the couple sitting opposite you are speaking in a very foreign language and darting glances at you – and laughing ... arriving home, switching on the radio and hearing a chap say, earnestly: 'Just lately we've come across some very sophisticated little dinosaurs.'

My world, like Thurber's – or for that matter your next-door neighbour's – is bound to be a little bit different. Which is strange really, considering that we all watch the same telly, shop in the same high streets and spend a lot of time pondering dreamily at much the same ironing boards and kitchen sinks.

But, in spite of this, our interpretation of situations will depend largely on what kind of people we are basically. Like that chap who travelled from his native America all round the world. 'Tell us about it. What was it like?' clamoured his friends on his return. 'Well,' he said thoughtfully, after a long pause. 'I can tell you this much. The shower didn't work properly at the Savoy!' Thus, my husband and I may take a stroll in the country together. But when we return home he quite probably will be remembering the horse manure he accidentally trod in while I'm still going on about the bluebells.

That's life. Or at any rate it's My Life, and I hope you enjoy sharing it with me for a little while each month.

70 Happy Families

My Life and I, *Good Housekeeping,* June 1977

'Our friends we can choose, but our relatives we just have to make the best of!' quoted a waspish soul recently – which unnerved me slightly because I happen to be distantly related to her.

For every Kennedyish, close-knit, sporty, let's-all-go-on-a-picnic, yes-I'd-love-to-have-all-twenty-seven-grandchildren-while-you-dear-things-go-skiing-type family, I'm pretty sure there must be dozens like that of the accountant I met recently who confided: 'I'm an only child, used to a peaceful, orderly sort of life and quite honestly when my wife's three sisters descend upon us en masse I have to go to bed and lie quite still for at least four days afterwards to recover.'

It is all very well to leap up from watching *The Waltons,* the *Forsytes* – or *The Godfather* come to that – convinced that the family's the thing, but nowadays families do come in such wild assortments. In the days of Galsworthy it was easy: Uncles were rich, aunts were straightlaced, nieces were pretty and nephews were coming along nicely. The worst skeleton in the family cupboard was likely to be a ne'er-do-well lad who signed funny cheques, or a rather intense lass who chained herself to the railings.

But nowadays it must take an awful lot of tolerance if you happen to be one of those upswept, Crimplene ladies – the sort who wear winged diamanté specs on a little black cord – and your only son weds a girl who wears what appears to be a William Morris duvet cover. Or you're an entrenched Good Lifer anxiously re-cycling everything from chicken manure to cocoa tins and your daughter goes out one morning and marries the managing director of Pollution Unlimited. Or how about the distant relative of mine who was sent overseas for 18 months and returned to find that his wife had just given birth.

'Long pregnancies *run* in our family,' she assured him firmly. But I can't say we were all absolutely convinced.

I suppose that for most of us, especially those of us who marry and thus double the *status quo*, the family includes a mixed assortment of everything from ravers to dum-dums and it is incredible really how we manage to put up with each other most of the time. In spite of the fact that if we weren't actually related to some of them we wouldn't choose them even as third reserve volunteer shovel cleaner at a blocked cess-pit party.

Indeed, perhaps it's as well, in some cases, that we only see the entire assembly at weddings, christenings and funerals. At such events the trick is to try and steer a cheery non-partisan path (but not *too* cheery of course, in the case of funerals) – from blowsy Auntie Bea to whippet-thin second cousin Winnie, even if the former *did* once discover the latter in an airing cupboard with podgy Uncle Harold and they haven't spoken since.

We all have our funny ways, we must admit, but it's particularly difficult, not to say unnerving, to be tolerant, high-minded – kindly even – to your really weird sister-in-law Gladys, only to discover that she's being tolerant, high-minded and kindly back to you. If only we could *choose* our relatives. I've often seen a face in a crowd and thought how lucky someone was to have such a pleasant-looking aunt/uncle/grandparent. I particularly remember noticing a lot of very likely-looking relations at last year's Chelsea Flower Show. With their workaway hands, tanned foreheads and sensible shoes, they'd have made a smashing mixed bunch by any standards. And if perchance one didn't see absolutely eye-to-eye with them on such subjects as cookery or cleaning or child-raising, one could at least zoom them out into the garden and lead them firmly towards the *cotoneaster horizontalis*.

Personally, I had the best possible grandmother one could wish for, with her bottle of Condy's Fluid for stings and cut knees, and her bottle of home-made potato sherry for more grown-up disorders. (If you weren't disordered when you drank it you certainly soon would be.)

I'm also blessed with a thoroughly likeable husband. In fact he's so likeable that while I *quite* understand his own mother preferring him to me, it's a bit hard to live with the lurking suspicion that *my* mother does, too!

Actually, I didn't find him all *that* likeable the day a very pretty girl dropped in about some local matter. 'Come in, come in,' he enthused, obviously in a state of instant besottment at the sight of so much radiance pouring over our threshhold. 'Here, let me pull you up a chair/table/sofa/cup of coffee,' he babbled as I faded bleakly into the wallpaper.

'We're just furnishing our new home,' she said conversationally after a great deal of husbandly blushing and crashing about and cosy re-arrangement of our living room.

'Oh are you married?' I cried hopefully.

'Good heavens no,' she said. 'I'm absolutely *anti* that sort of thing. No, as a matter of fact I live with *two* men. All this marriage business is a load of rubbish. And my mother,' she added crisply, 'says she never would have bothered if she'd known what she knows now. As for the great con game of "Happy Families"– yuk!'

Eyes ablaze, cheeks aflame, she strode off out of our lives leaving David decidedly shattered, and me with the interesting thought that while she had all the makings of a nice, racy skeleton in the family cupboard for future generations to boast about, she seemed to be doing her best to wipe out the cupboard altogether. Which does seem a bit drastic. After all, even if one's lot are a far cry from the Waltons, one can always follow the dictum of that spirited, unsinkable lady who said: 'Whenever I go to visit my relatives I always take my knitting so that the day is not entirely wasted!'

71 Moving In And Making Friends

My Life and I, *Good Housekeeping*, August 1977

'Don't worry about making new friends,' we told the children when we moved a couple of hundred miles across Ontario and plunged into the purchase of our first thoroughly mod con, deeply carpeted, Canadian 'carriage-style' home. 'Everyone over here seems very friendly and we're bound to meet lots of other folk moving on to the new estate.'

Certainly our one set of recently established neighbours seemed cheerful, outgoing people.

'Hey – come and join us for drinks on the patio,' they called as our furniture van rolled away. And neither they nor we could stop wiping our eyes with merriment when we discovered that the 'patio' was actually two tiny paving stones set in a sea of mud outside their front door, tightly encircled by folding garden chairs. Kneecap to kneecap, we raised our glasses and told each other that we were Betty and David and Judy and Bob and glad to be of mutual assistance as and when required.

'We've seen lots of families with kids looking keenly over the show houses so there should shortly be plenty of other young people around for your two,' they told us. Which was true except for one slight snag. As other new householders arrived they all seemed to have children a great deal younger than Daniel and Anna at ten and fifteen.

'Our Geoffrey simply *idolises* your Daniel,' said the newcomer on our other side. 'He's never *had* such a big boy to play with.' Which was fine for a while but a bit limiting for Dan and a bit distracting for us when Geoff, aged four, discovered he could reach our doorbell – and did, at ten-minute intervals every day, all day.

'Can Danny come out to play?' he would lisp. 'Tell him I'm busy,' Dan would mutter, deeply engrossed in Meccano or *Six Million Dollar Man*.

At which news poor Geoffrey would indicate his disappointment with loud screams of 'Whaa-aa!' all the way back to his mum until even she started ringing the bell and asking rather desperately if Daniel was free to play now?

Anna, meanwhile, had made two discoveries. One was that she was the most sought-after babysitter in the neighbourhood, being the only adolescent available of suitable age and temperament. The other was that one other teenaged girl had finally moved in just around the corner.

'Actually I don't like her much,' said Anna glumly. 'She's a bit full of herself, but as she's about the only person of my age on this whole estate I might as well make the best of it.'

I saw what Anna meant when new chum swept in while I was sitting glued to my favourite telly programme and said in a high-pitched, immediately dislikeable voice: 'Good heavens, you're not watching *that* rubbish are you?' and proceeded to click-click the channels and twiddle the dials until I didn't just want to grab her wrist, I wanted to *break* it.

Luckily, another girl – Sharon – turned up soon afterwards and became good friends with Anna, which was an enormous relief after all the shrill bouts of 'Good heavens, what on *earth* is that you're knitting/eating/crocheting etc, etc.'

Then, almost before we'd finished unpacking, along came Daniel's eleventh birthday. 'Who would you like to invite to your party, Dan?' I asked as I laid in stocks of paper plates and jelly.

'Just Jason will do – I like him. We play guns and hostages and stuff. He's a bit young but he's okay.'

Actually 'hostages' isn't my favourite game because it usually entails a third party (me) having two rifles thrust into the small of my back and being 'held' in some dark corner for incredibly long, boring stretches while we all try to figure out what comes next.

Geoffrey, we discovered, wasn't going to be home that weekend. Nor, it seemed, were any other boys available nearer to Dan's age.

'Hey I could ask Sharon over,' said Anna, adding practically, 'No point in all this cake going to waste.'

'And I've just been talking to an awfully nice chap along the road,' said my husband. 'He and his wife don't know a soul here yet and she's got a new baby so she doesn't get out much.'

'Well Sharon's parents have moved here all the way from Suffolk and they're a bit lonely and homesick too ...' said Anna, with a sympathetic throb.

'Let 'em *all* come,' I cried, in last-minute euphoria. 'Might as well pop in and ask Bob and Judy. And how about that nice newly-wed Lyn? She could bring her husband although I don't think I've actually met him yet.'

So party time arrived and at each ring of the doorbell we all rushed forward together because nearly each new arrival was a stranger to one/some/all of us. The introductions were fairly unusual.

'Er – Roger is it? Meet – er – Kevin – I think he's – um let's see now – Lyn's husband. And this is Mona over here – Oh I *do* beg your pardon – it's *Moira* – you must be married to – er – this chap.'

As eleven-year-old-boys' birthday parties go it was certainly different. Not that Daniel minded. The moment Jason arrived off they went under a bed somewhere, bristling with toy rifles and revolvers.

'Actually that was one of the best parties I've been to in a long time,' chuckled Bob a day or two later. 'Your Dan certainly knows some great grown-ups! And it's not every day a whole roomful of adults stand around a birthday cake gulping down egg sandwiches and chocolate chip cookies.'

Nevertheless, as a unique getting-to-know-your-new-neighbours party I can thoroughly recommend it to anybody.

72 The Home Rinse

My Life and I, *Good Housekeeping,* January 1978

Alas today is one of my inferior days. Well all this month actually, because the BB ego started its downhill skid the day I decided to give my hair a colour rinse.

One of the problems of moving to new surroundings is the difficulty of finding the right hairdresser. In England it was all so easy. I just placed my head in the hands of Roy, the laughing cheek-patter, and, lo and behold, I went home honey gold and curly wurly. Or pale ash and silky tendrilled. Or even tawny amber and 'My *dear* – you *are* brave!'

But what do you do, new to a foreign city, to get the message across that yes, you *know* you look like a frizzy old mum at the moment but that's why you're *here*? To get it *changed*!

It isn't easy trying to explain that while you know the tipped-forward-pudding-basin look seems to be all the go among the young smart set, it hardly does a thing for a lantern jaw. And no, I'm not ready for the dippy-wave-blue-rinse favoured by the more mature, either.

'*You* wanna look like Farrah Fawcett-Majors?' screams a bendy little lad with absolutely no hips at all.

'You say this photo was taken less than a year ago? You're *kidding* me!' scoffs another sensitive young thing.

'You *do* mean you used to be *blonde*?' says an older, more matter-of-fact soul in a big department store. 'Right – let's see what we can do for you then.' This sounds like maybe I'm on the right track at last until a couple of appointments later she says: 'Well of *course* it goes that bright yellow colour *in the sun* dear. You'll just have to keep your head covered, won't you?'

Which is why I am wandering, disconsolately daffodil, down the aisles of our friendly neighbourhood drug store when suddenly a label catches my eye. 'Light Ash Brown' it says. And there is a picture of a gorgeous girl with enviably carefree bone structure, swishing back a great swathe of the *exact* gleaming colour I have always yearned for.

Armed with ringer-timer and rubber gloves I plunge into the bathroom and start reading the small print.

Twenty minutes or so later I sidle downstairs raven black. Well no. Raven suggests some sort of sheen. My hair leans more towards unravelled soot-black knitting wool. The family actually stop watching television as this pathetic, not to say sinister, apparition floats glumly from mirror to mirror. 'Would you like a cup of tea, Mum?' says one child. Umprompted. So I know it isn't just a trick of the light.

'Here Mum, have my chair,' says the other one. Now I *know* how weird I must look. David, wide eyed and pale, seems bereft of words.

Blundering back upstairs I read the instruction through again, feverishly. It seems I should have let the daffodil grow out before starting again. Some sort of chemical clash has apparently taken place among my follicles. 'This rinse should last through approximately six shampooings,' I read.

By midnight – nine shampooings later – my head feels strangely cool and weightless. I can see my scalp, all pink and tingly and ultra-clean, gleaming away through the undergrowth. But my hair is still irretrievably matt-black. So are my hands. The gloves gave way under the pressure of my wildly clawing fingers hours ago.

Next morning in the office my bright and chatty co-worker looks up and stops talking – for the first time since I started there. 'My *dear*,' she breathes with a certain amount of awe.

'It – er – looks quite nice really,' she adds swiftly. But I can actually see a great big, desperately suppressed, shuddering wave of laughter come bursting up out of her shaking frame. Thank heavens it is mid-winter and I can clap my knitted hat back down over my brow. Right down. It doesn't suit me this way – as anyone else with a strong jawline will know – but better this than the electrified frizzy black hair that lurks beneath.

With so much attention going to my head, I forget the state of my hands until, delivering a written message to an ex-colleague on my way home from work, I see that my boss has written on the envelope: 'For delivery – by (dark stained) hand.' For two weeks I do without tea, coffee and lunch breaks in the staff canteen, or indeed any bareheaded encounters with anyone anywhere, preferring to cower at my, mercifully fairly private, desk and then dive down the back stairs at home-time.

Every night I scuttle in through our front door, straight up to the bathroom, hat off, head in basin. The family arrive home with stories about how their friend's Mum's hair went a funny shade of purple. Or how it all fell out one day and grew back chequered. So I know the good news is getting around. I keep telling myself that these stories are well meant and that things aren't as bad as that time Auntie B's hair turned green. But for me, they *are*.

When I tell you that when I absolutely *have* to make a hat-less social appearance, I even try shaking a whole tin of talcum powder into it in the hope that I will at least look *old* and *grey* and *normal*, you will see how desperately, unnaturally, exceedingly black it still is. And not just black. Repeated washings have reduced it to the consistency of a startled, mangy cat.

The world is getting used, now, to this strange, sidling creature, whose melancholy eyes peer beadily out from between jutting jaw and clamped-down woolly hat. Oh well, I tell myself repeatedly, with many a deep, despondent sigh, no doubt I shall look back on all this and laugh about it one of these days. But not yet. Definitely not yet.

73 A Smile, A Purr and A Sigh

My Life and I, *Good Housekeeping*, April 1978

It is a sad time in our family at the moment. Henry, the tabby member of our household, is quietly, and with a touching display of aloof dignity, coming to the end of his ninth life.

He has shared our life in a village and in a Thames-side town. He has crossed the Atlantic, under somewhat bleary sedation and has claimed our shaggy Canadian all-over carpeting as his own.

For nearly 14 years he has enriched our lives greatly. For Daniel, aged 11, there never has been a time when home hasn't meant a cat curled up in the best armchair, on the cosiest bedspread or in the warmest shaft of sunlight.

In younger, friskier times these comfortable snoozes have quite often taken place in my knitting basket, on many a flattened flower bed, or on David's chest while he's trying to watch telly. At one stage the favourite spot was a circular seedpan full of rare cactus seeds. I shall not easily forget that moment of acute horror when I popped my head round the door and there was this *enormous*, hairy *mound* growing, apparently, from the teeny seeds I'd carefully pressed into the soil the night before.

'Fancy bringing a cat all the way to Canada!' said some folk when we arrived here. 'Well I think you should have him put down right away,' said others, when the vet told us the diagnosis (poor Henry has leukaemia). 'He's not in pain – in fact he has remarkable stamina for an old cat – but I'm afraid he's probably only got a couple of months left.'

But we do not regret our decision. He is one of our family. And so with medication, little pieces of raw liver and kidney and tempting bowls of cream, we do our best to make his last days comfortable, as slowly he tucks his forepaws under his chest, sinks down on a spot close to his water bowl and dreams his own quiet dreams.

Does he, we wonder, remember that distant happy day in Anna's young life when the grocer's wife leant across the counter and said: 'I suppose you wouldn't be able to give a home to this little kitten, would you? He was left, with his brother, on our doorstep. Lots of people were keen to take the ginger one but no one wants this little tabby chap and I can't keep him, because of my dogs.'

'Oh Mummy, *could* we?' breathed Anna, her soul in her eyes.

'Well I don't know – I'll have to see – we'll ask Dad – I only came in for a pound of cheese,' I mumbled.

'... Oh *please* Daddy, couldn't we? He's sweet!'

'Oh Lor, I don't know. Ask your mother.'

And so, on a sunny summer morning, we came back from the shops carrying a basketful of tabby fur with white bib, paws and whiskers and smokey grey, soon-to-be-green eyes. A game little bundle which straight away jumped in his saucer of milk, ran up the curtains and disappeared out of the window.

'We'll call him Henry,' we said. 'It's a nice, sensible, sedate sort of name and perhaps he'll grow into it as he gets older.'

'Henry,' we called, 'Hen, Hen, He-en ...'

... With a mighty Evel Kneivel leap, our sensible, sedate Hen came crashing down out of the Blenheim apple tree, right into the big old rain butt by the back door. By sheer good fortune we'd been having a lengthy dry spell because there he sat, looking as detached as it's possible to look in several inches of muddy sediment. I'm quite sure he'd have tried a nonchalant whistle too if he could have pulled it off.

'And is this your cat?' said a kindly lady visitor, sitting down and sipping tea in our living room. 'I love cats,' she beamed, patting her lap invitingly. Whereupon Henry, eager to please, sprang into the air, zoomed across her knees, shot out a paw to save himself and ended up hanging, by one claw, from her nylon tights. The Fred Astaire phase was slightly easier to live with but not much. I didn't mind the Busby Berkeley routine in the day-time.

'I got *rhythm – crash – crash*,' he would go, twirling his way along assorted shelves of glass ornaments.

It was the *'Wee small hours of the morning'* bit I could have done without, as he did his nightly tap dance in the bath.

But there were occasions when we overslept and were glad of his anxious tappings to get the day under way.

And other happy family moments to remember: those lawnmower purrings on lie-abed weekend mornings when he genuinely *knew* he didn't have to sound the time-for-work alarm. *'Hey, hey, the gang's all here'*, he would chortle, rolling among the bed-clothes in great arcs of ecstasy.

One day, not long ago, I found some notes I'd started to make on a typical day in his life. 'Conned three breakfasts off assorted members of the family,' I'd written, 'closely followed by four mid-morning snacks. Curled up in the middle of the jigsaw we were doing and refused to budge. Ate rest of potted palm and suddenly seized doormat in mouth and ran upstairs. After two lunches, took a quick stroll out to the tulip tubs and squatted inscrutably over the right-hand one.' At this point I must have flung my pencil down in disgust – not to say rage. (We had no tulips *at all* that year.)

But then I remember the day we accidentally left him locked in the house with nowhere to make his – er – ablutions, and how, with marvellous feline finesse, he chose a spot as close as he could to the bath plug hole.

I remember the always welcoming gleam of his immaculate white shirt front, running towards us as we turned our car into the drive at night.

Even now he wears his best bib and tucker at all times and a tickle behind the ears still produces the rusty echoes of a lawnmower purr. But we know that the moment is close when he will have to make his last journey. Until that time he doubtless has his memories. He will certainly leave us ours of many a smile, a purr and the occasional exasperated sigh. He will also leave a sad place in our hearts.

74 Bounding Through Life

My Life and I, *Good Housekeeping,* May 1978

One of the problems of bounding spontaneously through life, I have long since discovered, is that people do tend to react to me quite strongly. I'd like to say that my life is therefore littered with heavily breathing Valentinos bowled over by my outgoing temperament. My radiance even. (I'd *love* to be able to say that.) But, alas, the strong feelings I seem to arouse rarely work out in my favour.

If I were asked for a quick, off-the-cuff description of my personality I. suppose that I'd have to say that I see myself as your *fairly* average Mrs Miniver – with a strong dash of Auntie Mame. Which definitely doesn't suit all tastes.

'Tell me,' hisses a suspicious lady to my husband, well within my earshot, 'Why does she wave her arms about like that?'

'You don't *really* mean that you'd rather dance to those Rolling Stones than to Englebert! You are just *joking* aren't you?' murmurs a worried, ever-so-matronly contemporary during a current coffee break.

'Did you wear those black tights on purpose, dear?' whispers my mother. 'Or couldn't you find any normal-looking ones?' All of which might lead one to suppose that I soon see the error of my ways and go sedately swirling through the rest of my days, pale-legged and with hands clamped carefully to sides. The heck with that. Somewhere in this world, I tell myself firmly, there must be whole shoals of people eagerly searching for tall, arm-waving, black-legged girls who really move it to the beat.

And the trouble is that there *are*. But not, alas, equally outgoing, non-processed souls with whom one can laugh and leap and push back a frontier or two. No, it seems that great swoopy types like me stir a whole cross-section of folk we didn't have in mind at all …

Take Ernie, our landlord from way back. He was definitely stirred. Pale, skeletal, hairless Ernie whose departed wife's fur coat was left hanging in our closet during our year's tenancy.

'She's gone now. It would really suit you,' yearned Ernie, catching me many a time alone as he sidled in with his master key to 'check things over'.

'I just wonder *where* she's gone,' I complained to David, who didn't seem to notice any sinister undertones. Until that day when I finally plucked up the courage to ask where the locked door at the end of our hallway led to.

'I'll show you,' rasped our Ern, drawing out a whole bunch of master keys. Bounding bravely forward I found, to my horror, that not only was I leaning out of a doorway that led absolutely nowhere except to a sickening drop of several floors to an overgrown garden plot below, but that Ernie, while explaining that he 'meant to put a fire escape in eventually', was thoroughly goosing me from behind with a relentless, bony hand.

'Well, good grief David, I wasn't going to move *forward* and I couldn't move *backward*. I had to hold still!' I cried later, as we started packing and looking for new digs.

Then there was the truly awful old chap in the pink socks I worked with for a while, who gripped my knee and chortled: 'By crikey, as soon as I saw the kind of girl you are I knew I'd clicked!'

(Really! *Where*?' I murmured, but he didn't seem to notice.) Oh yes, the world is full of folk just waiting, it seems, for outgoing BB types to bound into their lives. And not just chaps either.

There was the not very happily married couple I knew slightly, felt a bit sorry for and invited to a party along with heaps of assorted friends, acquaintances and downright strangers. It turned out to be quite a good party. Everybody meshed. By that magical stroke of luck all hostesses pray for, it had lift-off. Swept up in the general euphoria our couple stopped bickering just long enough to decide to make us their Instant Best Friends.

'See you around,' we said blithely, as they left. And we did. All the time. Morning, noon and night. When it seemed that our Christmases, our New Years, our birthdays and our anniversaries were all rapidly becoming a part of their own Master Marriage Therapy Plan we began to make excuses.

'What's the matter?' they said, turning up anyway and scowling. 'What have we done to offend you?'

On the credit side there is the elegant lady who came up to me at the big social event, patted my hand and said: 'You don't know me but I've been watching you and I just want to say – don't ever lose that vivacity!'

Which was very nice and very flattering. How was she to know that, at the very same gathering, the old BB pzaz attracted: (1) a man with red eyes who seemed confident I was – in his words – 'available for sex', (2) a budding psychiatrist who whipped out a notebook and started questioning me closely on my attitude to hot baths, thunderstorms and water in general and (3) an implacable soul who said I was just the sort of person she was looking for to make pot holders for her bazaar. Bounding through life isn't all fizz and frolic. But it certainly is eventful.

75 A Cure For The Blues

My Life and I, *Good Housekeeping*, June 1978

I was reading the telephone directory the other day. Well we all have our flat days – days when our minds feel like old grey sag-bags and our indoor plants stare reproachfully at us from dry, neglected pots. On such days the sun is wasting its time up there above the dark grey cloud barrier.

Actually, on days like this, if the sun does happen to be shining it just shows up how smudgy our windows are getting. Well, anyway, on just such a morning, there I was staring bleakly at the phone book and half-noticing that I could, if I wanted to, easily ring up and find out the correct time, the latest cricket score, recipe, bedtime story etc, when a brilliant thought struck me.

What we housewives need is a new service called: 'Dial-A-Compliment'.

Then on days when our shoulders feel like old bent wire coathangers and our legs hang heavy from our hips we could pick up the phone and a Robert Redfordish sort of voice would instantly, keenly, awarely cry:

'Hey – I've been *waiting* and *waiting* for you to ring because I think you're absolutely *smashing!*'

Or perhaps to make the whole thing seem a bit more personal, he would first ask: 'What number are you ringing from?' and then when we told him he'd cry: 'Oh yes – you're that lady/girl/little darling with the gorgeously wicked gleam in her eye. And the truly delectable earlobes!'

No matter that we happen to be huddled over the telephone with eyes like dried gravy and earlobes like spent balloons. I guarantee we'd perk up and start looking and feeling better right away.

But until the telephone company catches on to my scheme we'll just have to turn our thoughts to other ways for curing the blues … It's not a bit of good anybody telling us to Beat The Blues By Going On A Diet. If we felt up to doing that we wouldn't *be* blue. Starting a diet, like giving up smoking, requires a confident, buoyant sort of mood to get Day One under way.

On drear days we must set our sights much lower. We might re-pot the house plants perhaps. Or clean the silver. But even these require a certain amount of get-up-and-go. As one glum chum recently put it: 'When I'm having one of these sorts of days I can sit for hours staring at a cobweb without being able to do a thing about it.' As a matter of fact, just writing that last sentence reminded me that I've been staring out at a rather dank-looking stringy thing hanging down outside the window for several weeks now. So hold on a minute while I dart away for my new, very fancy, peacock blue feather flick …

… There, that's better. Oh dear, except that it looks as if I shall spend the next few weeks staring out at a gaudy, left-behind feather, now wedged and fluttering in the eaves. But that does bring me to one aspect of blues-curing we might consider on our slightly more radiant days. A psychiatrist once told a very sad woman I knew that, yes, he'd be glad to have a go at cheering her up but that, first of all, she must go home and get her house in order.

Gloomily she trailed home and dragged out the vacuum cleaner, wax polish, ironing board and mending basket, and for three days grimly followed his instructions, non-stop. Whereupon, as the clever chap obviously suspected in her case, she found herself surrounded by gleaming furniture, pressed clothes and darned socks – and feeling so cheerful she decided she didn't really need psychiatric treatment after all.

I shouldn't think *many* psychiatrists are quite so altruistic in their approach but I pass it on here for all those women who may happen to be reading this while slumped despondently in tatty tights, droopy trews or dusty armchairs.

I especially pass it on to all those worn out young mothers like the one I visited recently who had let things go so far that, following a rolling pencil, I plunged my hand down the back of her sofa and came up with a very old, cold and flabby fried egg.

The whole key to successful cheering-up operations seems to be in managing to reach a turning point; that critical moment when we stop glaring at the piece of dried bacon rind under the kitchen table and actually drag ourselves up and over to dustpan and brush. So let's all make our broom cupboard, shelf, box or wherever we stow our cleaning materials, a really happy place to drag ourselves over to.

Hence my peacock blue feather flick. Hence too, my new orange dusters, my new pink rubber gloves and my new purple-flowered ironing board cover. Well yes, I agree my cleaning cupboard is a shade on the jazzy side but at least it is *cheerful.* Although, just in case pride in all this sparkling new gear should begin to flag, it would be nice, wouldn't it, to be able to summon a few words of inspiration and encouragement from the outside world?

So I still think there's a very good argument in favour of the telephone company taking up my 'Dial-A-Compliment' idea. Then, as our orange dusters begin to fade and we feel another of those hard up, cast down, worn out, thoroughly misunderstood days coming on, we could at least bask in the cheery illusion that somewhere out there somebody fancied us, if only for our earlobes.

76 Finding A Job

My Life and I, *Good Housekeeping,* July 1978

One of the important things to bear in mind upon arrival in Canada, we kept being told, is that you must be willing and adaptable. It's no good expecting, for example, that the ideal job awaits you right away. You've got to be prepared to have a go at anything. You'll soon find your feet if your attitude is right.

And so, keenly, willingly, adaptably, I began to read the Sits Vac. The best thing to do, I decided, was to apply for just about everything. Well not quite everything. I didn't feel quite adaptable enough for 'Lusty farmer seeking well-built, companionable female help under thirty'.

But, since one of the nice things about Canada is that all local telephone calls are free, I armed myself with pencil and newspaper, took a deep breath, picked up the phone and started working my way down the column.

By mid-morning I had an appointment at a mysterious CIA-type offshoot of the US army, a 'Come on over' from a large department store and a 'Glad to see you any time' from a temporary manpower agency.

The army place was very smart, with richly purple carpets and potted palms. The only thing makeshift was the table on which I had to fill out my application form. It wobbled wildly, especially when the girl opposite hit a tricky question on her form, groaned loudly and flung her head down in her hands.

Pacing myself between these outbursts I managed Section I without too much difficulty. By section MXVIII, however, I began to join in the groans and head flings. I simply didn't *know* my maternal great-grandmother's place of birth. I did feel fairly confident that she hadn't taken part in any sort of Communist uprising and that, ethnically speaking, all our lot are Anglo-Saxon but I did worry a tiny bit about that uncle of mine who once had a holiday in Czechoslovakia – and *liked* it.

At the department store I discovered a door marked *Staff Enquiries*, flung back my shoulders and strode in. Two ladies behind typewriters were describing how ill they felt.

'Well I've got this searing sort of pain that runs right down here and along here and back up here,' one was saying. 'Well I can't raise my arms like this without my wrists going all funny like this,' the other was replying.

'I've come about a job,' I said, catching Funny Wrists' eye and feeling uncomfortably healthy and out of place. 'I've had heaps of experience at selling, including ...'

'Yes, well never mind dear. Between you and me it doesn't make a scrap of difference. Just fill out your name and address and this medical section here and we'll be in touch.'

Gamely I listed chickenpox, measles, influenza and a few assorted funny turns which seemed to please them. I noticed them studying it, heads together, as I left.

'Try this typewriter,' said the flinty lady at the temp agency, 'and as soon as you're sitting comfortably I'll start timing you. Here's your test card. OK?'

'Fine,' I said, nervously wriggling down into my seat and eyeing, with growing horror, the machine before me. I learned my typing the hunt and peck way and, although moderately fast once I get steamed up, I had so far been used to manual typewriters. And here I was, face to face with the biggest, widest, most jet-propelled electric model I'd ever seen ...

'Are you ready?' called the supervisor, stop-watch in hand. It was the moment before take-off. '*Go!*' she cried and, reaching out a sweaty finger, I pinged bravely at a likely-looking button. It certainly pinged all right. In fact the paper shot straight up out of the machine, zoomed out of the doorway and was heading steadfastly out of the building altogether when I finally caught up with it.

'Er sorry,' I gabbled to old Flinty Eye as I raced back to the typing room. For some deeply apologetic reason I conducted all this paper chasing bent double at the waist, but even the sight of a nervous female Groucho Marx impersonator failed to add a spark of merriment to the proceedings.

Wordlessly she whipped my finished effort from the machine and began to count. 'Hm, nineteen words in five minutes,' she said, inscrutably. 'Well, I suppose you'd better complete the interview. Come through into my Office.'

And that was the last I ever heard from the agency, or the department store, or the CIA. Which didn't really matter because shortly afterwards, I heard I'd got my present job with a magazine for the Canadian Scout Movement.

'There is a certain amount of typing involved,' said the editor. 'Do you have any approved typing qualifications?'

'Well actually, I'm fast hunt and peck,' I gabbled. Now I don't know whether the strangeness of my English accent, falling on Canadian ears, gave the impression that 'Fast, Hunt & Peck' was some kind of Better Business Bureau of the typing world, but his expression brightened and I got the job.

And I've *still* got it, thank goodness, after a lovely, hectic, fascinating, colourful six months in the assistant editor's chair. During which my great-grandmother's ethnic origins haven't cropped up once. Nor my lack of really interesting medical history. I've even come to a happy arrangement with my great big clever IBM typewriter. I will shampoo its little golfball head once a week and be more gentle with its p's and q's if it will stop making those *moaning* noises and adding its own private little hyphens all over the place.

Willing I certainly was to have a go at anything Canada might have to offer. But happy I definitely am to have found my ideal job at last.

77 Not Smoking

My Life and I, *Good Housekeeping*, August 1978

'Thank you for not smoking,' says the sign propped up on our refrigerator and I take deep, happy breaths of the nice, non-fuggy atmosphere that prevails in our house these days. Our family are on a giving-up-smoking kick and it looks as if, this time, they really mean it.

'Who finished the peanuts? Have we got any potato crisps? Oh help, I can't seem to stop eating!' says Anna, rifling through the kitchen cupboards.

'You'd better hide my pipes. Have we got any beer left? What's for dinner?' says David, pacing up and down while gnawing quite violently at a banana.

'The hardest time is now I've started work at my new job,' says Anna's boyfriend Rick, too, folding himself down into a chair and gazing yearningly at an empty ashtray.

I know just how they all feel. I too used to smoke my daily packet of twenty and woe betide any unfeeling *nerd* who casually reached for my last one. Especially on a rainy night after the shops were closed. I really *needed* all twenty. No more, no less. At delicately spaced intervals from the mid-morning coffee break, gathering momentum until that last satisfying drag-of-the-day at bedtime.

Other poor, hooked souls I used to compare notes with all seemed to have their own personal pattern for puffing.

'Can't start the day without my fag first thing,' wheezed a desiccated soul with dark brown vocal chords.

'My dear, it's that moment after a luxurious dinner when they pour the liqueurs ...' sighed a languorous lovely, toying with gold lighter and ivory holder.

'Absolutely rely on a quick drag in moments of stress,' chattered a hyper type with a twitch of the shoulder-blades.

And it wasn't a bit of use anybody nagging them to alter their lifestyle. Like the philosopher said: Things happen to us when the moment is right for them to happen to us. And for many a long year my moment failed to arrive.

I'd like to look back on my teens and twenties as a time of delicately flowering womanhood. Of tremulous moments reading Elizabeth Barrett Browning in the gazebo. Of peach blush cheeks and velvet glances across crowded rooms.

I have to be honest, though. A great deal of my time in those sensitive, formative years was spent seeing how many roll-your-owns you could get from a packet of Digger Shag. (Boy, you should have *seen* how thin I could roll them just before payday.) I even tried inhaling tightly rolled tubes of smouldering blotting paper during one period of extreme financial crisis. It wasn't what you'd call a wild success, but was slightly less hazardous than my experiment with tea leaves and toilet paper. (Don't bother to try it. It goes off like a sparkler.)

And if I wasn't busy teasing one thread of baccy into a carefully licked paper tube the breadth of a toothpick, I was probably frantically doing other not terribly romantic things, like pumicing my orangey-brown index finger or learning how to invisibly mend a nice new red Jaeger coat with an even newer brown burn-hole right at nipple point. Or gazing blearily into early morning bathroom mirrors, wondering what it must feel like to actually *taste* things and not to have permanent catarrh. Not to mention a skinned lip from tugging at a too firmly attached Woodbine the night before. One of the true trials of being sophisticated and nonchalant with the opposite sex was not screaming aloud or letting one's eyes water when one tore great layers of skin away, along with one's fag end.

'Still smoking are you? You silly cuckoo!' my dear old Gran used to say. 'Don't know how you can afford it, the price they are,' said well-meaning friends. (Well-dressed friends they were too, with nary a darned nipple among the lot of them.)

'I'm not too happy about being married to a girl who smokes shag,' grumbled David. Which wasn't altogether fair because he was only too glad to smoke it himself when he ran out of Players Number Three.

'We both ought to give it up,' I croaked one morning, as we stopped the car in a New Forest layby. And that was our moment of truth. Because we both looked up from banging ash off our laps and noticed that outside the car windows the world was really beautiful. The sun shone down on sparkling treetops which cast their vivid shadows across ploughed corduroy fields. Two gleaming technicolour pheasants strutted along beside a green and scarlet and purple bramble hedge ... And there we were, like two wheezy kippers in our smoky box on wheels, scrabbling around for little cardboard packets with just two left – and, oh lor, we'll have to find a machine soon –and who's got the matches – and *boy*, that's some cough you've got there!

So we gave up smoking cigarettes that very day. Whereupon David, rather sneakily I thought, started buying cigars by the handful. And inhaling them until they crackled. But he did eventually go such a funny colour that he slowed down a bit and switched to pipe-smoking.

And now here I am, not smug exactly, but certainly catarrh-free and with taste buds back in action. Feeling terribly understanding and proud of my family as they pace about groaning and munching and clawing at the fruit bowl. So hang in there folks. I know it's rough at first, but you can do it. Look at me – I'm even off the wine gums these days.

78 Dressing For The Occasion

My Life and I, *Good Housekeeping*, December 1978

Last year I was a knockout at the Christmas Ball. By some unfathomable stroke of magic, while on my way to buy the Sunday roast, I saw this fabulous Jean Varon swirl of chiffon in the window of our local boutique. Bravely I confronted the inscrutably laconic girl in charge. Yes, she would get it out of the window. (Incredible.) Yes, it was in my size. (Unbelievable.) Yes, I could just about afford it. (The heck with roast beef. Meat loaf can be *fun*.) And best of all, yes, it *suited* me. In fact the metamorphosis from Worried Sallow Shopper to Instant Glowing Raver even stopped the boutique people in their tracks.

So off to our gala staff bash I pranced and, for once, I did not instantly clap eyes on some groan-makingly gorgeous lovely – all ivory satin and high cheekbones and December-in-Nassau tan. The sort that instantly makes one's own light go out. No, for just about the only time in my entire history of partygoing, my hair had bounce, my dress felt great and even my cheek contours were doing their best, with a little help from Estée Lauder.

Oh, would that it had always been thus. But, alas, the story of my life includes some truly awful moments of sartorial uncertainty.

Heading the list of mistakes I have made is definitely the day a very dashing acquaintance invited me over to meet her new fiancé. Interpreting this as an engagement party and since this girl lived in frightfully smart surroundings – she was one of those souls who feel comfortable with an all-white living room – I suppose I felt I owed it to the occasion to dress up. Enormous can-can petticoats were in at the time, as were circular skirts, cinch belts and pin-tucked blouses with vast sleeves gathered at the cuff. And so, with a red rose pinned at the throat and (oh how I blush even now) silver sandals, off I billowed – to discover girl and chap waiting in their hiking gear for a day in the country. And we went. To the glazed astonishment, I might say, of several sheep and more than one hedger and ditcher.

Other similar incidents spring all too readily to mind, including the day David came home and said his boss was throwing a Christmas party at his house and we were invited. 'His wife is fantastically smart,' he added. So into my smartest party dress I clambered. Turquoise blue and silver Lurex with three great big frills around the hem. (I may never go shopping in Newbury again.) Then, in one of those wild moments of over-think we uncertain types are prone to, I said to myself hey, how about that rhinestone set someone once bought me for my birthday? They looked so pretty, the necklace, the bracelet, the pendant ear-rings, all twinkling away in their padded case and I hardly ever found just the right occasion to wear them. (Does anybody?) Boy, did I shine that evening. And oh, why hadn't David explained. that the boss's wife really was fantastically smart. I mean *really*. In the elegant, understated, *Elle* sense. There was she, in a plain, plain, *quiet* sort of dress and no accessories at all. And there was I giving an extremely good imitation of an illuminated Christmas tree. To make matters even worse, one wild glance over her (subtle, beautifully cut, etc) shoulder, revealed that every other wife had turned up in laced brogues, shirtwaisters and knitted cardies.

They may still be wondering about the strange, glittering creature who, with a strangled cry of 'Merry Christmas everyone', scuttled straight upstairs to the bathroom, clawing wildly at neck, wrist and earlobes and came down later, slightly more subdued but nonchalantly wiping her nose on a knotted lace hankie bulging with rhinestones. I think now that it might have been even wiser to have ripped off some of the Lurex frills, too, but with my luck the whole dress would doubtless have unravelled before that long, long evening finally drew to a close. It goes without saying that for the very next party I played safe in white blouse and black skirt. But of course this time everyone else was in rave gear and I looked like a waitress.

It's only the heartening tale of one of the smart set who confessed to me recently that, clad in trendy jumpsuit, she'd actually missed half the party trying to get out of the damned thing to spend a penny in an extremely small loo, that makes me realise even the best among us have problems.

My own immediate problem, as you will readily gather, is how to top last year's success at this year's imminent staff dance without actually wearing the same dress two years running. In fact I'm off to comb the boutiques now, cheque book in hand and with an eager gleam in my eye. I've even practised deep breathing exercises and a few furtive press-ups to get myself in trim for the search.

Will my luck hold out, I wonder? Alas, with my track record I have to admit it seems unlikely.

It's all a matter of inner confidence really, I suppose. If I take a deep breath and swoosh out on to the dance floor with my shoulders flung well back and my cheeks sucked well in, I *might* just get away with *anything*. And it's time the rhinestones had another airing.

79 The Husbands We Deserve

My Life And I, *Good Housekeeping,* February 1979

I read in a magazine the other day that we mostly all get the sort of husband who is best for us. There are times when we may find this hard to believe but, according to the article we do tend, subconsciously, to make the right choice.

However, I'm sure that, as St Valentine's Day approaches, many a wife/girlfriend/lover starts casting a speculative eye at her chosen mate and mentally labelling him. And I suppose that, for most of us, the labels go something like this:

(a) Mr Right. The Ideal Romantic – sure to send a big fat padded red satin heart-shaped card. Which arrives on the right day. With a skilfully devious postmark (Addis Ababa, perhaps?) and a lovely, totally disguised, *yearning* sort of message in purple ink.

(b) Oh Well, I Could Have Done Worse. The Fairly Romantic – unstamped card found on mat with 'Guess Who?' in husband's unmistakable handwriting.

(c) That Slob! The Somewhat Unromantic – 'Saint *Who*'s Day?'

If you've been married as long as I have (I can't *believe* how long it's been … well some days I can), then you more or less know what to expect. But in the event of any sad hiatuses, not to say hysterical outbursts, come February 14th let's all pause a moment and really try to hang on to that thought about getting the husbands we deserve and really, subconsciously, *need*.

Thus if, like me, you too see yourself as a somewhat high-spirited filly, it's probably a jolly good thing if your chosen mate is a solid, dependable type with capable hands firmly on the reins. Even if he doesn't exactly thunder home first each year in the Valentine Stakes.

Actually, I do think my own particular Steady Pacer should get a special rosette for the *two* super-swoony cards he sent me last year. Directed to my place of work. And purposely not marked 'Personal'. So that I'm *still* getting narrow, speculative glances from the female staff in the mailroom. Not that he's always been a Five Star Romantic. But ever since, here on this very page, I wrote a little piece about not doing very well on St Valentine's Day – and so many of you really great readers rose to the challenge and *smothered* my doormat (Oh, that *was* a wondrous February) – he's had an uneasy feeling that some of them might have been for real. And he's been *so* nice to me ever since (not to say downright wary).

As well he might be, since one of that particular bumper bundle, a lavender beauty postmarked Oslo, was from the suave, grey-eyed and dark-lashed, much-travelled husband of a good friend of mine. At least, I *think* it was. And wow, did he go on at length about my – well my just about *everything* – from the trembling joy of my quivering right eyebrow to the passionate curve of my sensual left instep. To put it mildly. So much so, in fact, that I'm still wondering if the friend put him up to it, just for fun. Although I can't very well *ask* her. And anyway, why spoil one of the more dazzling moments in the life of Betty B?

However, prior to all this, there have been Valentine's Days, doubtless for all of us, when nary a card has come thudding our way. Not even husbandly ones which our beloveds pretend, with total lack of conviction, not to have sent. Days when we just know we'd have done better to have married tall, exciting, blue-eyed Justin Fotheringay. So mightn't it be a good idea to consider how things might really have turned out if we had?

Could we have staunchly weathered life with Justin after he threw away all those Youth Club table tennis trophies and started wearing the sequined kaftan? Or, for that matter, gone on watching him decade after decade, close cropped and grey flannelled, ping-ponging across the living room?

Would our pulses still have raced for Kenny the Sidesman of Satan, when he traded his black leather jacket and gleaming silver Velocette for a custard-coloured Ford Popular and a job at the pie factory? Or maybe he didn't. So who needs Eastbourne Rave-Ups when there's all that ironing to be done? Not to mention all those oily motor-cycle parts lying to soak in the sink.

Should we have stuck it out with pale, poetry-steeped Theodore even when his moods grew blacker and blacker along with his vile, smelly old raincoat? Some girls, I know, really need to be married to the Theodores of this world. I once had a friend like this and when her chosen chap did finally start selling his poems and buying new raincoats, she left him for a heavily over-weight literary failure lying around in a basement somewhere, totally surrounded by empty beer bottles. And the *moment* all the puffiness went down and the first book got accepted, she was off combing the garrets for other likely, and preferably starving, artists in need of care and attention.

So maybe we do all get the mate who best suits our needs after all. Come Valentine's Day, some of us may yearn for the Poetic or the Rich or the Romantic. Others may say they need lots of wit or travel or philosophical conversation. But perhaps it is true that what we really are best off with are the fumble-fisted, kindly, patient, not-very-discerning-but-doing-their-best old darlings most of us have already got.

80 Looking Back

My Life and I, *Good Housekeeping*, March 1979

'Hey, guess what?' said David, thudding into bed and removing my book at bedtime. I'd just reached the chapter where Frodo meets Bilbo again, at Rivendell, so Tolkien enthusiasts will understand that I only tolerate late-night interruptions of a very serious nature. David certainly knows this, since he spent all last year buried deep in Middle Earth and shushing my every word.

'Whatever is it?' I mumbled crossly. 'And it'd better be good.'

'It is – or at least I think so. Rick has just asked me, formally, if he and Anna can get engaged.'

'Goodness me,' I said, as much bowled over by the old-fashioned courtesy of 'asking the father' as by the news itself. Which didn't altogether come as a surprise, once the initial adjustment was made to the fact that my daughter – so recently, it seems, a tiny, owlish stare from a fluffy pink blanket – is now a highly perceptive and remarkably likeable (if untidy) University student with her own refreshing individuality.

But I do still sometimes ask myself whatever happened to all those fast moving years between the day we introduced her to the Dr Seuss books and the day she introduced us to *The Lord of the Rings*?

I haven't got any older and nor has David. So when did that chubby-legged toddler in the miniscule Liberty print dresses start skilfully running up Laura Ashley skirts and tops for herself?

And learning to smoke – silly chump.

And demonstrating to me how Rick's sister does her super lasagne. It was only *yesterday* I was giving Anna and her small school friends those little lessons on rock cakes. In their own individual mixing bowls. With *real* ingredients, just like Mummy's. And now my kid makes a much better Yorkshire pudding than I could ever do!

I expect all parents experience that jolting moment of truth when the children, so recently on the receiving end of watchful guidance, advice and generally superior intellect, suddenly turn around and give *us* a telling lecture on the economic state of the Third World. Not to mention earnest advice on where we're going wrong in our interior decoration/general philosophy/and/or use of eye liner.

It's a strange feeling, too, to overhear them going on about 'the good old days when we lived here or there' – brief stopping places we only registered lightly in passing but which they apparently see as cornerstones in their young lives. Daniel at twelve (Ye Gods, it's his birthday next week when he too will be a teenager!) still tells everyone about 'the worst moment of his life' when, with the best possible intentions, we fitted up a two-way baby alarm system by his nursery door and trotted off to our next door neighbour's to connect the other end. 'Daniel – Daniel – can you hear me?' I warbled through the microphone from the neighbour's house.

'Eeee-aaah-eeek!!' came the chilling reply.

'What's the matter – whatever is it?' we panted, hurling ourselves back through our own front door.

Only to find poor, chubby little Dan, turned ashen pale and clinging to his cot bars screaming 'Mummy, Mummy, Grandma's in dat box up dere!'

So cherubic, so rosy, so curly and cuddly was our Daniel in his early days that I really find it hard to look back through our family albums and note the passing of time. Did my ears deceive me or did I *really* hear our little lad recently say solemnly, from the back seat of the car, 'J just can't seem to help whistling at air hostesses!'

I think perhaps I became aware of this particular turning point in his life when I took him to lunch with a very pretty member of the *Good Housekeeping* staff and told him, in my fussy mum-ish way, to take his elbows off the table. Whereupon he requested me, very firmly, to please be quiet – and I looked up surprised and caught him *winking* at her! Luckily, at the moment, sport still seems to have a firm edge on his enthusiasm, plus Scouting, swimming and tracking us down to try out new card games.

But then, it was only yesterday that Anna too, was badgering Dad to play ball and shaking with excitement at the birthday arrival of her first doll's pram. (Oh, how proudly, but how slowly, we trundled round our village shops that year!) Then came the magic, for an eight-year-old, of raising a baby fox cub from near-starvation to vibrant mischievous manhood. And the sadness when he left us and took to the wilds. All this plus the richly unfolding pageant of good school teachers and not so good. The well chosen friends and the oh dears. The later anxiety of a bad car accident – and the taken aback feeling when the solicitor dealing with the resultant damages case starting writing directly to her instead of to us since she'd 'reached the age of majority and could handle her own affairs'. And now the nice, blue-eyed fiancé twinkling away at us all from his semi-permanent seat on our sofa. So much to have happened so quickly …

'My goodness me,' I repeated, sinking back on the pillows and unthreading my specs from my current tangled Afro. (That's a hairstyle, by the way, not some extra chap who has suddenly crept into my lifestyle.) And yes, I do admit to furtively-worn reading glasses these days. I wouldn't be wearing them quite so furtively, actually, if I hadn't made the mistake of choosing wire granny frames. Which look simply fantastic on everyone else but make me look exactly like a wire granny.

And that's something I'm definitely not ready for yet awhile. Although at the rate our little pink bundles reach womanhood, I suppose that's another mental adjustment I'll be making much sooner than I think.

81 Red In The Face

My Life and I, *Good Housekeeping*, July 1979

Recently my husband experienced the most excruciating moment of his entire life. 'See you in the supermarket,' we cried blithely to each other as we parked the car and went our separate ways. So I wasn't surprised to look up from the cereal aisle and see David coming through the swing doors. What did surprise me, however, was that, at the very instant he flung them open, the entire plate glass window – acres of it – smashed dramatically, and deafeningly, from top to bottom.

'It wasn't me! It really wasn't!' gasped poor, red-faced David, doing his pitiful best to look nonchalant and detached as several dozen startled pairs of eyes snapped in his direction.

It did eventually come to light that someone had witnessed another chap, loading groceries into his car, who had launched his trolley a shade too violently back towards the doorway. And it had swerved smack bang through the window just as David made his spectacular entrance.

And while I'm about it, I may as well tell you his other most red-faced moment – at least in retrospect. Poor love, he still squirms at the memory of the day he volunteered to take part in an interdenominational religious survey taking place on a big new estate.

All went well until a little nut-brown lady came to answer the door and cried: 'I am sick – I am sick!'

'Oh dear, I'm sorry to hear that,' smiled David. 'I'll come back another time.'

'I am sick – I am seeek!' screamed the poor little lady.

'Er, do you want me to fetch a neighbour or a doctor or

anything?" said David, backing away worriedly down the garden path.

'No, no, I am seeeeeek!' shrieked the woman, and it wasn't until he got back and rather agitatedly reported all this to the chap in charge that it was gently explained to him. She was Sikh.

Doubtless we all have our own private memories of high embarrassment. I know I have – right from that early childhood moment when I stayed in a terribly elegant antique-filled cottage near the sea with a fearfully top drawer chum and her starchy family. Carefully stacking my day's haul of pretty curly shells in my room, I awoke to find that each shell had apparently been the home of a small crab or other small, scrabbly and/or slimy sea creature and that my bed, my carpet, my curtains even, were now absolutely alive with the wretched things. Scooping them up in my seaside pail and zooming as many of them as possible out on to the croquet lawn didn't really go down all that well, either.

Or, to bring the BB blushes a bit more up to date, I once sold an article to *The Observer*. And I suspect the reason I only ever did sell them just the one was that, shortly after its publication, I went to visit their editorial offices. And as I rushed up to town in my smart new leather coat and black tights I fell and tore the latter to ribbons. I knew, therefore, that I wasn't looking exactly at my best upon arrival. What I didn't know was that they have leather chairs. Have you ever sat down in a leather chair wearing a leather coat? You get terrible screaming noises if you wriggle at all. What I also didn't know was that my face was quite heavily grazed and bleeding down one side. I wondered why no one seemed to want to catch my eye that day and why everyone sprang to their feet shortly after my arrival and dashed off to 'this rather important meeting'.

But then, as regular readers will know, my life is absolutely littered with this sort of thing. So here, to balance things up a bit, are a few gems gleaned from other folk in similar moments of excruciation …

One robust chum of mine, for example, still chortles at the time her husband, on his way for a medical check-up, snatched up an empty whisky fifth to use as a specimen bottle, filled it appropriately, left it on the car seat while he popped off somewhere, and returned to find the bottle stolen!

Or how about the elegant, bird-like soul who confessed to me that she still blushes at the memory of dashing in to buy armfuls of booze for a party while her husband found a parking spot outside the shop. And of hurrying out, leaping into the car and crying: 'Okay darling, let's go!' only to discover she had leapt into the wrong car, absolutely weighed down with liquor, and was apparently propositioning a quite pleased looking stranger.

Along similar lines is that terrible classic tale (which I'm not too sure I should mention at all, actually) of the couple who hired a caravan on a trailer camp for their holidays. 'I'll just go and find out about laundry facilities while you settle in,' said the wife, toddling off to get the lie of the land. Which she did, quite efficiently, until on the way back she began to realise that all the trailers looked much the same. However, she finally retraced her steps and, full of relief, flung open their van door to find her husband, stark naked, in the process of pulling his shirt over his head.

'Caught you!!' she cried archly, lunging forward and giving him a frightfully intimate tweak. Whereupon the poor chap flung his shirt aside and revealed himself to be a totally strange and totally furious man in the totally wrong caravan.

But perhaps best of all is the true tale of an old chum of mine who moved into the corner house on a new estate.

Clambering out of her ritzy new bath, she swanned gracefully and stark nakedly across her nice new landing towards her spacious, sunny new bedroom. Only to discover an entire family of complete strangers coming up the stairs.

'Oh Lor, we thought this was the Show House!' they gasped.

I'd be inclined to say that it was.

82 I Would Take A Lover But …

My Life and I, *Good Housekeeping*, September 1979

'David – have you been cleaning your pipe with my Afro pick again?' I call, as I retrieve a bent, smelly, nicotine-stained object from the back of the sofa. (I'm describing my comb incidentally, not my husband.)

I think I could reasonably describe myself as a happily married woman. But there are times when I've been known to fling myself down in pre-natal positions. Like that day I tracked down a really smart new washing up bowl in a particularly zingy shade of apple green. And before I could even get it to the kitchen sink, David decided to give the car an oil change. And needed a nice big, deep receptacle to catch the dirty oil …

That was the day a friend of his dropped by to help. A loutish lad but well meaning. 'We need a bit of rag to get a grip on this nut,' called my husband from deep within the bowels of the engine.

'Here, will this do?' said eager chum, passing him my best Heals drying-up cloth. The one with the pretty pink and purple flower border. And the now permanent black grease marks.

Small incidents really, although over the years they do tend to accumulate. But fortunately I don't, even in moments of deep certainty that I'm travelling through life on the wrong bus, ever quite reach the stage of ending it all by gulping down every damned thing in the entire medicine cabinet – *that'll* show him! Actually, since our cabinet mostly contains nose drops, suppositories and yeast tablets, it is probably as well for all concerned that I don't settle for this particular alternative to married life.

But there are moments when many a woman might be forgiven for broodingly deciding to divorce the rotter/go home to mother/ go on an eating binge/jump up and down on his stereo equipment/take up smoking again/take a lover and/or drink that entire bottle of cherry brandy left over from last Christmas.

I must say, if I had to make a choice from the above selection, I'd definitely settle for the lover. Someone who'd *really* appreciate the true, inner, sensitive, vibrant, talented, sexy, radiant, essential Betty B. At least, I think I would.

I've never quite got over a play I once saw on telly in which this long-married lady and this middle-aged smoothy clap sparky eyes on each other at a party and rush to the nearest bed … And spend Act I, Scene II blundering around in total darkness. Because they're both afraid that if they turn on the lights they'll die laughing at each other's spindly legs, appendectomy scar, varicose veins, droopy tum, wobbly thighs, etc, etc. And even in total darkness you've got to be frightfully passionate not to mind all those wheezy, clicky, creaky, rumbly noises folk can't seem to help developing as the years go by. Not to mention funny little ways.

Would some new chap, I wonder, still pant heavily and lunge for my ear lobe once he realised that I simply have to chomp away at a nice crisp apple every night upon retiring? And read at least one soothing chapter of my book at bedtime? Would his hot breath still sear my nightie as pages rustled and apple cores whizzed by his quivering shoulders?

Or, for that matter, would some nubile young thing still go on coiling herself around my spouse at parties if she knew that she was, quite possibly, dooming herself to decade upon decade of Hunt the Other Sock?

But I have to admit, looking around at my contemporaries, that the ones who pop off down the primrose path from time to time do seem to weather life a great deal better than the heavy eaters, the hypochondriacs, the boozy flushers and the brave go-it-aloners. (All except one radiant-looking chum who says she gets it all from playing tennis.)

I suppose the ideal safety valve would be to hang on to one's comfy old marriage partner, warts and all, but to seek out some splendidly ascetic second string companion who would hold one's hand and yearn in a disciplined, *tidy* sort of way. Although I imagine one would have to be very old and warty not to want the relationship to lead *somewhere*. I have a friend who found herself a lovely extra fella with long slender hands and pale corduroy jackets.

'What is it that makes you seem so different from all the other men I meet?' she asked breathlessly.

'Perhaps it's because I don't lead with my genitals,' he replied drily, with a beautifully controlled but probing look into her eyes.

'The only trouble is,' she wailed, months and months of eye contact later, 'that he doesn't *follow* with his genitals either!'

In my thoughtful kitchen sink moments (especially when I'm bleaching my teacloths or scouring oily washing up bowls) I often toy with the idea of heading off into old age totally surrounded, like Colette or a character from Iris Murdoch, with doting elderly lovers. But I can't help wondering who's going to be matching, soaking and mending their socks while all these fumbling old replays are going on.

I just don't seem to have the right mental attitude for extra-marital primrose picking. Ah well ... anyone for tennis?

83 Banks

My Life and I, *Good Housekeeping*, October 1979

I became aware that my world was beginning to crumble when our bank lost my husband's £50 deposit.

'Look David, they've left that £50 off our bank statement!' I cried, when book-balancing day came around.

'Never mind,' he said, puffing away contentedly at his pipe. 'I'll get them to check their books the next time I go in. Here, see – it's entered in our deposit book with the amount and date and everything.'

'Where's your copy of the deposit *slip* then?' snarled the lady at the complaints desk, a ratty soul I think they employ specially for this sort of thing.

I have a nice husband, a good, reliable man but he does have one tiny fault. He is inclined to clean his pipe with any little pieces of paper he finds about his person. So what more natural than that he should make a neat little narrow tube out of his copy of the deposit slip to waggle peaceably through his pipe stem. And that was that. No slip, no recourse. We came away with the impression that somewhere backstage a computer had swallowed the whole distasteful mess and, once down the tubes, we'd had it.

I don't know what old Ratty said to the computer after we left but shortly after this, it sent us two totally out-of-date credit cards. Then our holiday currency arrived two weeks after we'd actually left the country.

'Here comes the troublemaker,' we distinctly heard Ratty hiss, as David once again made his way to the Complaints' Corner.

Then we changed banks.

The next one had beautiful flower arrangements on low tables. When, in the course of conversation, I made it known to the manager that I've never, *ever* been in the red, he sprang to his feet and shook me warmly by the hand. I don't know if this fact caused them to file me under 'Trusty' but shortly afterwards I received in the mail a mysterious, bulky parcel containing dozens of bundles of assorted foreign currency with the names of local inhabitants attached. 'So this is what New Zealand bank notes look like!' we cried. 'And these are your actual drachmas. And guess what? Miss Harrison of "The Beeches" must be off to Mesopotamia!' Then we realised that the banks were closed for the weekend.

'Just hang on to it all in a safe place until Monday,' said an accountant friend. At one minute past opening time on Monday I sidled backwards to the counter, beady-eyed and sweaty-palmed, with the loot carefully secreted about my person.

'Oh yes, we wondered where all that lot had got to,' said their chap, tossing it nonchalantly over his shoulder.

I know that there *are* people around who maintain that, overall, the world is steadily improving. But in my youth, banks were unquestionably the absolute cornerstone of all that was fine and true and upstanding.

I grew up on stories called 'The Tale of the Missing Halfpenny' in which all the staff stayed resolutely at their desks until midnight, if needs be, until the books tallied precisely and the missing halfpenny came to light.

'He's got a splendid job with a *bank*!' my mother was always saying stirringly to me and to my brother, as all sorts of totally admirable young men strode soberly past our gate. Since my brother was about three at the time and I was around seven, we were much too young to be actively seeking employment and/or a husband. But doubtless she wanted to get the pair of us thinking along the right lines as early as possible.

Nowadays, however, one has only to mention the word bank to just about anybody and all sorts of strong views and soul-searing experiences come to light. Is there anybody, anywhere, for example, who can honestly say that they find the catch-us-open-if-you-can banking hours convenient?

'Attitudes have changed so much,' sighs a friend. 'They used to treat me as if they really valued my account. But now I get "Our computer never lies – and if it does, hard luck!"'

'They should be firmly reminded,' says another, spirited soul, 'that they are, after all, only money shops!'

One lady I work with has an unnerving tale to tell. It just so happened that her husband had the same name and initials as another chap who banked at the same branch. And this other chap emigrated. And my colleague and her husband discovered one fine day that all their money, their holdings, their valuables, *everything*, had been transferred to Australia.

Or take my next door neighbour who sometimes gives me a lift to work in the mornings. Occasionally he rings me up and says could we start out earlier as he has to drive round to the bank and get some cash out of the machine? This machine is set into the wall outside his particular branch, for the greater convenience of customers who can't get to the bank during opening hours. He has said this to me on perhaps ten different occasions. So off we go and he leaps from the car and punches out his magic number, at the same time feeding his magic card into the appropriate slot. It is a very de-luxe machine, of amazing technological complexity and, on one memorable occasion, the required cash did magically appear.

On all other occasions the machine has eaten his card/punched him back/flashed up a sign saying 'A/C closed'/spat his card back already been jammed with someone else's card/

shredded his card completely/flashed up a sign saying 'Go Away!'/trapped his finger.

'I hate banks!" he screams, jumping back into the car, shaking all over. And I must say I do see his point.

84 M Is For Mystery

My Life and I, *Good Housekeeping*, November 1979

I suppose eventually the mysteries of metrication will all fall into place and I shall plunge confidently into 96-centimetre bras and Christmas cake recipes calling for 125ml of chopped walnuts. But for the present, it joins one whole area of my brain labelled 'M for Mystery'. A growing area, as life becomes more mechanised, computerised and standardised. Why must it become so standardised? Another mystery. How, for example, will adding six assorted letters and numbers to the tail end of my address cause a letter (I am assured) immediately to zoom to its destination? Who, or what, decodes it faster than a chap reading the word 'Surrey'? And why, in that case, does my weekly airmail letter to my mother, which in the Golden pre-postal code Age, regularly took three days, now take somewhere between ten days and three weeks? Life is full of mystery.

There is a magic door to our local supermarket that suddenly glides open at my approach. Well yes, I know that lots of doors do that these days. But in this particular case I do not have to step on a magic rubber mat for it to do so. Nor, search as I may, can I find any trace of a magic electronic eye. Or even a little chap secreted about the place, working a lever. I've looked for him. On many an occasion I've sidled around that entranceway, clutching my bags of groceries, and peering very thoroughly indeed at every inch of flooring, wall and ceiling. But not one sign can I find of what it is that triggers off that sliding door. It occurs to me, as I write this, that the sight of a heavily laden woman, lurking about in doorways, scowling thoughtfully at walls, may possibly have hitherto been on your mystery list. Unless you happen to be that man in the beret and cycle clips who silently joined in, the other morning, and shuffled around behind me glaring at any bricks I'd missed.

I wish he'd been around the day I saw the UFO. I've always been given to understand that if you stand around in a public place staring up at the sky, everyone else's eyes will just naturally be drawn upwards. So when I looked up and saw this red object flying steadily north to south over our local shopping centre one fine October afternoon, I assumed that all the other shoppers would grind to a halt and share the experience. But they didn't. They all just hurried past and stared at *me*. It was a great relief when my husband turned up and saw it too.

We *still* can't find anyone else who shared the experience with us. 'Pale red and silky, it was, rather like a flag-draped jeep,' we tell everyone. 'No it *wasn't* a kite or a plane or a weather balloon or a trick of the light.' David even adds that it had glaring head-lights. If you know my husband, you'll agree that he *never* says things have headlights, glaring or otherwise, unless they really do. If you also know me, you'll understand how much I wish I could say it was a great big, weird, scary, musical, sky-filling, mind-bending close encounter of some kind. But it wasn't. It was just an ordinary sort of red silky jeep-shaped thing (okay David, with headlights) chugging north to south over our shopping centre.

'Probably Father Christmas doing an early trial run,' said a waggish chum. But I know what I saw. And it is still the greatest mystery of my entire life. Of course, not all the mysteries I encounter have such exciting potential. Most are closer to the prosaic. Such as why, when I ask the butcher for a pound of mince, he *always* weighs it and says: 'Pound and a quarter near enough?' By the law of averages he should surely *sometimes* get it right. Or even try to palm me off with less.

And for mysteries I could also do without, how about the fierce lady last week who scrambled aboard my bus. All the seats were full and I was the lone standing passenger, holding on to a pole about half way along the aisle. Glaring intently, she pressed herself tightly against me and lunged for the same pole. When my arm went dead I shuffled a bit further along to another pole. More glaring and lunging. So I moved down the other way. Along she came. I think the other passengers quite enjoyed the sight of two women, one angry, one bemused, apparently doing some sort of slow gavotte from pole to pole, but I still don't know why we did it.

Or take that mysterious caller who used to ring us at the same time every evening for ages. We got so used to picking up the phone and hearing these pent-up wheezy noises that we eventually got quite chummy in a one- sided sort of way.

'Huuuuh-heeeeh,' he used to pant.

'Hi there, Heavy Breather,' we'd reply cheerily.

He tended to ring off quite quickly after this. Nor did he seem to care for David's clever technique of picking up the telephone and saying absolutely nothing. What a shock to a heavy breather to dial at random and apparently get connected to another one.

But the most hurtful mystery of all concerns my son's school lunch box. For one whole term, those who took their own lunches were plagued by a mini-thief who went round rifling these boxes. What I'd like to know is why this rotten kid always stole the shop-bought cakes from Dan's box and left the home-made ones. Perhaps some of life's mysteries are better left unsolved.

85 It'll Do For The Cottage

My Life and I, *Good Housekeeping,* March 1980

Winter clamps down with an iron hand, and indoors I wander from room to room trying to figure out why the central heating has gone berserk.

The living room and master bedroom are the comfortable 68°F I intended. The den is snug. Both Anna's and Dan's rooms are as cold as the tomb. They look at me with round, accusing eyes. Is 'hardening off the children' yet another of Mum's weird ideas? The downstairs cloakroom is as hot as newly-baked biscuits – it even smells scorched in there – and, as I pause at the kitchen sink, a blast of warm air billows up my skirt from the curiously misplaced air register I'm standing on. I keep this one closed but the hot air goes on blasting away anyway.

Outside, frost bites the edges of the kitchen window and to take my mind off wintery things, I decide to think summer thoughts …

Last year we became the owners of a lakeside summer cottage and joined the many Canadians who escape the city heat by trekking off into the countryside at weekends and for holidays. As a result of this a new phrase has entered our vocabulary, well known and well used by all summer home owners, namely – 'It'll do for the cottage.'

Canadians are, generally speaking, luxury lovers. Their homes hum and ping and shine. Deep shaggy carpeting spreads richly across golden oak floors. Logs crackle in natural stone fireplaces. Showers work and Tiffany lamps abound.

But once they get away from all this in the summer, the rugged pioneer approach takes over.

We bought our white clapboard cottage already furnished, obviously from a long line of 'It'll do's' and I wouldn't change its essential character for the world. Not even the three-legged armchair, the chipped and faded plates which state on the back that they are 'as presented to His Majesty during his visit in 1936', nor the mouse-nibbled maroon patterned carpet which blends so fetchingly with the orange patterned net curtains.

Actually I do have a pair of very nice Heals curtains going spare, which would just fit the living room windows. I could also rustle up a neutral, unchewed carpet. But that would break all the unwritten rules of cottage decor which state – silently but quite firmly – that this is pioneer living, boy, and we don't go in for any of that new-fangled Conran, taste-for-the-masses stuff out here in the bush.

No, by golly; the farmers' almanac and last year's calendar of a boy with his dog are good enough for us. Plus a toaster that has to be set permanently on 'very, very light'. Move the indicator even one sixteenth of an inch towards 'medium brown' and the whole thing bursts into flames. True I have been heard to murmur plaintively: 'But couldn't we even buy just one new, flat-bottomed frying pan?' as the menfolk jiggle their manly fry-ups in old, beaten metal objects which wobble and stick and grow blacker and warpier by the minute. But somehow the spirit of pioneer life prevails.

The moment the word gets around among friends that we've joined the weekend cottage set, gifts pour in. Not alas new toasters or fancy skillets. Hereabouts it seems the world has been waiting for the chance to fetch out all these old boxes of mixed china; the cruets that don't quite pour right; these old cushions we don't use much; some quite good assorted pillow-cases that just need a stitch: this old television which is quite a piece of furniture isn't it? And it can get one channel fairly clearly if the weather's right.

Suddenly our lives are filled with endless happy unloaders telling us cheerily that: 'It's a bit chipped/clogged/lumpy/torn/gigantic, but – it'll do for the cottage!' And strangely enough the cottage accepts all these offerings and we resign ourselves to life with the painting-by-numbers portrait of the girl in the bonnet, the varnished brown orange box that doubles as a bookcase, the enormous cylindrical washing machine, with *gears*, which was the Rolls-Royce of its day. (A lot of cottage equipment gets described as the Rolls-Royce of its day.) While anything new or citified or well-designed immediately looks out of place.

The cottage does concede me a few tiny victories. I am glad to discover that my two first-ever crocheted bedspreads (which didn't do all that much for our town bedroom) seem to hit exactly the right note on our new/old twangy metal Art Deco beds. (No, this style hasn't finally come back in. At the cottage it never went out.)

But when I raced in with armfuls of new oatmeal upholstery tweed for the two faded tartan divans out in the porch room, even I had to admit that it just didn't look right. Too stylish. (Dangnabbit, there she goes, getting all new-fangled again!)

And really, what does it matter, when in that same porch room, you can look out through picture windows twenty feet from the water's edge and watch a pair of ospreys? Or hear the loons calling. Or see fireflies to-ing and fro-ing at night, like tiny Hobbits with torches.

Or, after a hot, hard-working week, plunge blissfully into shorts and tee shirts and clamber down on to our own rickety jetty to watch the blue heron flap by. And swing at last in my (sneakily tasteful) Habitat string hammock which for years I've been lugging around, looking for two likely trees.

Now we are surrounded by enough sturdy maples and

willow and birch to lash ourselves aloft. Chipmunks come and sit below us and chatter for peanuts. Swallows zoom overhead. And I've even managed to track down a lovely new, un-read Iris Murdoch.

Ah, summertime! Such a far, far cry from frost, snow and chilblains and erratic hot air vents.

86 If Only …

My Life and I, *Good Housekeeping,* April 1980

I shall long remember the rage my son felt, as an eight-year-old, watching a tv commercial for a job at the Ford motorworks. 'Fifty pounds a week,' said their chap, 'a car purchasing scheme, four weeks paid holiday a year … etc, etc.'

'It's not *fair*,' burst out Dan, rushing upstairs in a paddy. 'I bet that job'll be *gone* by the time I get married!'

I suppose we all have a picture in the back of our minds of how life ought to be. A rather stylised picture, perhaps, based on how it was – or seemed – when we were young. Or how it should have been. Or how it is on our favourite telly programme. 'If only …' we sigh.

And instead, here we are, thrust by circumstances into situations totally unsuited to our (exquisitely sensitive, highly sophisticated, really rather rare) personalities.

I particularly find myself thinking this when I attend Daniel's sporting fixtures. As regular readers may recall, I have never really seen myself as your typical sports buff. So how is it that I've somehow become a keen supporter? Not perhaps a *really* typical hockey-mum. I can't *quite* bring myself to leap to my feet in the clinches, waving a sizeable hand bell and screaming 'Kill 'im: kill 'im!'

But I do astonish myself (not to mention nearby spectators) by clasping my hands to my bosom from time to time and warbling 'Oh well *played*, chaps!'

How many others of us, I wonder, when gritting our teeth and peeling our forty-ninth potato of the week, indulge in Walter Mitty dreams of how it might have been. '… I say! What *fun* to rustle up a meal for ourselves after all that wining and dining in Bangkok!' we trill, as with long white pampered fingers we reach caressingly for the Moulinex …

'Heavens! I'm hardly in the same category as *Chekhov!*' we murmur modestly, as we autograph yet another best seller …

'My goodness, Your Royal Highness,' we blush fetchingly, 'to think that you've been saving yourself for little me! …'

But then it's back down to earth with a thump and a splash as Number One Son clumps in from school with the latest gasp-making news: 'Hey, guess what? There *are* vampire bats and they give you rabies!'

I am not alone in this growing awareness that my lifestyle is somehow turning out to be a far, far cry from what I feel deep down it should have been.

I dropped in on an acquaintance the other day just as she was plunging her arm right round the U-bend in her loo, to retrieve the Incredible Hulk from yet another adventure.

'How *elegantly* you manage even the most prosaic chores!' I exclaimed.

'Well, actually,' she replied moodily, 'I'm a trained ballet dancer. Or *was* until all this lot caught up with me. Indeed I often feel, the way things are these days, as though I'm spending my entire life wading through treacle!'

And it isn't just the ones whose careers have fizzled out who get brooding attacks of what might have been …

'What would you be doing now, if you had your time again?' I asked a successful and respected author. Without hesitation he replied, with a faraway gleam in his eye, 'Oh I'd be the captain of a small but sturdy vessel, chugging around some native islands somewhere, trading in copra.'

Personally I often yearn – especially when I'm once again patching the knees on every single pair of Daniel's jeans – even the new ones I bought last week – for the 'if only' world of ivy-covered academic cloisters. There I'd be, taking tea with my own private Einstein, tossing theories back and forth in ever expanding circles. What bliss!

Others, caught in the commuter crush or trundling wearily round crowded supermarkets may well wonder whatever happened to that dream of buying a farm and growing roses in their cheeks. Not to mention socking away their egg money and creating tomato chutney recipes of county renown.

Of course if you happen to be already down on the farm, up to your 'ips in mud, then you may well be wishing you were squeezed on to the 8.30 to Waterloo.

When I am not mentally arguing the toss with Einstein, I do sometimes set my sights a little lower down the academic scale. Just one simple diploma would do, I tell myself, in – say – horticulture. (Well you have to start somewhere.) I even picked up a leaflet the other day on a two-year horticultural course being provided by a local college.

'Hey, look at this,' I told my family. 'I'd simply love to further my education and I've always fancied – er – outdoor things.'

Then David read the leaflet and pointed out that this particular course would provide me with a diploma in – among other less specifically useful attributes – 'graveyard work'.

One of the phrases we all know we must avoid like the plague is 'When I was a girl ...' To heck with that. When I was a girl, digging six-foot holes in the ground was fairly instinctive, common-sense work for old chaps with, not unnaturally, somewhat dour expressions.

Undaunted, when my next attack of the 'if onlys' struck, I confided to a very clever professor I know that I'd really rather like to pick up my education where I left off and perhaps take a degree in English.

'Good heavens, what on earth for?' he asked. 'You'd lose all your writing style in the process!'

Ah well, maybe some of us *are* wading through the right pools of treacle.

87 With My Clipboard Underneath My Arm

My Life and I, *Good Housekeeping*, May 1980

I once walked into the offices of *Good Housekeeping* when a staff member was trying out a psychological quiz.

'Quick!' she said. 'Assume that your house is on fire and the people and pets are all out. What's the first thing you'd grab?'

'Er – my passport,' I replied, which surprised even me. But I suppose it does tie in with a deep-rooted need to feel free to roam around life's corners. When I got home I tried the same question on a very fashion-conscious friend.

'Oh I'd save my clothes,' she said without hesitation. Which was slightly unnerving since I'd forgotten to add the bit about people and pets.

If I were asked the same question today I know what my answer would be. Unhesitatingly. My clipboard. Because, in under six weeks I shall become not just: 'Hi Mum, what's for dinner today?' Not just: 'I've been talking to your wife, David – you certainly picked a rum one, ho, ho, ho!' Not even just: 'Hey, your Mum's a real goer – considering her age!'

In six weeks time, on what I fervently hope will be a fine and sunny June morning, I shall become the Mother of the Bride. And, since the reception is to be held at home, I am also hoping to become the successful master-mind (mistress-mind?) behind it all. Hence the clipboard. It lives in the crook of my arm. It lists guests and champagne glasses and new shoes for me and a haircut for Daniel. It lists curried turkey and sugared almonds and potato salad and we need more teaspoons.

It lists heartfelt notes to the printer of the invitations. Anna is marrying a Canadian of Dutch extraction. Even I had to really sit down and learn how to spell his surname. And, since my own married name is Rapkins and I've just received a parcel of cheque books from the bank, each one individually printed 'Parkins', one can't be too careful. I already knew this anyway. My telephone bill, for years now, has been addressed to Papkins. The central heating was billed to Hopkins until we asked them to change it. Which they did. To Hopgood. This is all absolutely true. So much so that we have seriously talked of papering the downstairs loo with the variations we receive over the years. Ratkins is the slightly sinister and most common version. The nastiest, so far, is Rapeskins. How poor Anna will fare as Mrs Tjepkema I dread to think.

Other anxious notes encompass such peripheral activities as 'Check garden sprinkler'. This is a major necessity since I bought an enormous sack of something for the lawn called 'Weed & Feed'. Looking like one of those peasant ladies in 'The Gleaners' I girded it up on my hip and paced steadily to and fro, flinging great swathes of assorted magic pellets out across the greensward. I think I must have started too early in the season, because it is now brownsward. Not the ideal setting for a summer bride.

Meanwhile indoors Anna stitches the lace for her wedding dress and our good friend and chief bridesmaid Betty helps with fittings, while I hug my clipboard and I make a note to 'measure green garlands'. I plan to loop these, with posies of white flowers, along white-covered tables.

Betty has also volunteered to bake the wedding cake. She and Anna plan to ice it together. 'We can always practise a bit first,' says Anna, with amazing confidence. She even giggles as she says it. How did I, the last of the Really Great Worryers, ever find myself with such a blithe, nonchalant daughter?

I shan't easily forget my own youthful attempt to ice my first cake. How deftly I squeezed and smoothed and added clever curlicues. How proudly I led everyone kitchenwards with a merry *ta-ra!* And how silently we all gathered round this big, tacky brown lump sitting in a pool of not-so-Royal icing which, as we watched, slid silently down over the cake-stand and crept, glacier-like, across the table.

But now I smile bravely and lend Anna my GH cookbook with the cake decoration chapter carefully marked. I also secretly buy a little silver flower holder and plan to purchase a garland of silk flowers and several lengths of ribbon. If all else fails we can cover the results in cascading blossoms and satin streamers. More notes for the clipboard.

Out on the lawn (oh lor, I'd better put an asterisk next to 'check sprinkler') we'll serve punch on the William Morris tablecloths. More notes ... borrow a couple of extra punchbowls. While on the subject of drink, must remember to visit super French wine place we discovered recently ...

'It may not be open,' we are warned with a typical Gallic shrug. It seems that several bins of wine have been accidentally labelled at a tenth of their original price. And one customer demanded the right to buy them all at the marked price and did. So the proprietors fired three staff members for 'gross imbecility' and everyone went on strike.

But we are in luck and the wine store is operating on two floors. I prowl hopefully along the back shelves, hoping to find a few overlooked champagnes marked at lemonade prices but all seems to be disappointingly back to normal.

'What's the usher supposed to do, Mum?' says Dan, trying on his new cotton safari suit – a very carefully chosen half-way cross between old blue jeans (his choice) and the slick polyester Jimmy Osmond look (nobody's choice except the local store buyers).

'Well I suppose ushers *ush*," I say as I measure his trouser hem against the instep of his new shoes (two more ticks on the list). 'Actually you sort of *shunt* them around in church – oh, and one other thing this particular usher might do – just make sure, as we make our stately way up the aisle, that the mother of the bride hasn't still got a rather tatty clipboard clamped desperately underneath her arm...'

Notes on the text

KATE MACDONALD

1 My Dollyrocking Days Are Over

Courrèges: directional and expensive 1960s clothes designer.

housekeeping accounts: Betty's household budgeting evidently expected her to not overspend on clothes for herself by including her clothing budget in what the family needed for food and paying bills.

Mondrian: Dutch artist whose distinctive geometric paintings in white, yellow, red and blue were used by Yves Saint Laurent in his clothes designs for women in the mid 1960s.

Pre-Raphaelite: women's fashions in the circle of advanced nineteenth-century artists called the pre-Raphaelites tended towards the flowing, pleated and uncorseted and were much more forgiving to the figure than mainstream Victorian norms.

dickie front: a false shirt front used as a design feature, and to house fastenings like buttons.

Mod: music-focused youth movement whose fashions for women included miniskirts, white lipstick and straight tunic dresses that ignored the body's shape.

6 At A Disadvantage

muu-muu: loose flowing long gown of Hawaiian origin, designed for unrestricted relaxation.

The House of Usher: from the eponymous horror short story by Edgar Allen Poe.

Alan Badel: English stage and film actor, known for *This Sporting Life* (1961), *The Lover* (1963) and *Children of the Damned* (1964).

7 Party Time Is Here Again

Pola Negri: brooding screen siren from the silent movie era, famous for projecting sexuality.

advocaat: does indeed look like custard and is made from eggs, brandy and sugar, usually between 15% and 20% proof.

directoire: very old-fashioned ladies' underwear consisting of long knickers to the knee ending in an elastic cuff.

8 There Is A Verb To Chine

brawn: a jellied potted meat made from a boiled pig's head.

chine: the backbone or spine of a carcass; also a name for the narrow valleys along the south coast of England caused by stream erosion near the sea. Bournemouth has at least eight.

13 Hairdressing Is A Gift

Lionel Bart: famously bouffant English stage and film actor and director.

14 On The Scent

Sacha Distel: one of the few French singers to make an impact on British pop culture in the 1960s.

Richard Wagner: German composer of great nineteenth-century operas whose ideas were favoured by the Nazis.

Swarfega: a standby in the British garage, a green gloopy petroleum jelly used for cleaning oil off the hands.

16 Living-Room Overhaul

Tebrax: brand-name for a shelving system.

Conran: one of the most fashionable names in British interior decoration in the early 1970s.

17 Saturdays

Breakfast Special: a pop music radio programme from BBC Radio 2.

19 Sports Day

Crimplene: proprietary name for a polyester non-crease drip-dry dress fabric, ubiquitous for cheap women's daywear in the 1960s.

Ann Packer: British athletics gold medallist in the 1964 Olympics, and an Oxfordshire girl like Anna.

Angela Brazil: prolific and popular novelist of girls' school stories from the early twentieth century.

Queensberry rules: the rules for the conduct of boxing matches laid down by the Marquis of Queensberry and published in 1867.

21 Home Economics

gas mantles: easily breakable mesh hoods surrounding the jet of a wall-mounted gas lamp.

Welsh nuts: a smokeless fuel made from lumps of anthracite.

25 Life At The Launderette

green stamps: a forerunner of supermarket points, Green Shield stamps were given away at garages and shops depending on how many pounds you had spent, and could be exchanged for glassware, saucepans and other household goods.

28 A Pattern For Life

Ned Kelly: Australian outlaw and folk hero from the nineteenth century.

Madame Arcati: an eccentric spiritualist medium in Noel Coward's play *Blithe Spirit*, revived for a production in London's West End in 1970 with Beryl Reid in that role.

Dorcas: a early disciple of Jesus, described in terms of her piety, hard work and selfless giving to others.

Madame Pompadour: Madame de Pompadour was the flamboyant, cheerful and very popular mistress of eighteenth-century French monarch Louis XV.

34 Gathering Momentum

Dr Spock: famed advisor on baby health and care from the 1950s to the 1970s.

Jack Jackson: English band leader from the 1920s, whose Record Roundup music programme on the BBC Light Programme (later Radio 2) ran from 1948 to 1977. By the date of this column he would have been antediluvian in music terms.

Viva Zapata: a 1952 Western starring Marlon Brando as Mexican revolutionary Emiliano Zapata wearing a distinctively drooping moustache.

Phyllosan: iron supplement tablets which had been fortifying the over-forties since the 1940s.

Bio-Strath: natural food supplement tablets made from yeast.

scatter pins: groups of small decorative brooches.

35 On With The Dance

Pan's People: the house dancers for BBC variety TV programmes and *Top of the Pops*, the Thursday night pop music show, a fixture on British TV screens from the late 1960s to 1976.

37 Mod Con vs Old Con

treadle: a non-electric sewing machine powered by a foot pedal, which rocks and backwards and forwards in a gentle pumping action, or treadling.

tension: the two sewing machine threads above and below the fabric need to have the same tension, which can be eased or tightened as needed.

40 Accident Prone

Graham Hill: champion motor racing driver and road safety campaigner.

41 The Jumble Sale Cycle

shooting brake: a large car with plenty of room to carry baggage, children and dogs, very similar to an estate car.

42 Lady of Leisure

Min cream: a multipurpose wax-based household polish.

46 Weekend Diggers

courgettes: in the 1970s courgettes were better known as young marrows; to call these vegetables by a fancy French name indicated wealth, sophistication and wide travel horizons.

ten pole: traditional unit of measurement for land, still used for allotment gardens. Ten pole is equivalent to 250m², about the size of a tennis court.

47 Dressmaking

whip and run seams: also called overcasting or oversewing, when the folded edges of the seams are stitched together on the right side, to be flattened out.

bust darts: a stitched fold in the fabric, one on each side of the chest, to form a curve in the profile of the garment, into which the bust will fit and not force the garment out of shape.

two left fronts: a common mistake in cutting out, when the pattern piece has not been placed on a double layer of fabric to ensure that one piece is the mirror image of the other, but merely cut out twice, producing two pieces of the same shape.

nap: on textured fabrics this raised surface can be smoothed flat in one direction, and change shade when unsmoothed in the opposite, wrong direction. If the nap is different on two pieces sewn together, then one of them has not been cut from the correct orientation of the fabric.

baste: tacking, or stitching the pieces temporarily together with a long running stitch. This stage is frequently missed out by experienced sewers.

bring notches together: paper sewing patterns use notches, black triangles sticking out from the cutting line, as a signpost to help the sewer fit the pattern pieces together the right way round. Experienced sewers rarely skip this step as getting the notches matched correctly can be crucial.

small oo's: these are also signposts in a paper pattern, but in the body of the pattern piece, showing where pockets or darts need to be placed.

interfacing: a stiffening layer of thicker material to reinforce collars, waistbands and cuffs.

seam allowances: the 2cm-wide border area between the cutting line on the pattern and the anticipated seam line. Can be crucial when sewing around a curve.

54 Whatever Made You Choose *Him*?

Sheila Hancock, Ian Carmichael, Frank Muir, Cilla Black, Valerie Singleton, Richard Baker, Alf Garnett: Sheila Hancock (*Annie*, *Sweeney Todd* and the Royal Shakespeare Company) and Ian Carmichael (Bertie Wooster, Lord Peter Wimsey) were British actors; Frank Muir was a BBC comedy writer and radio raconteur; Cilla Black was one of the most successful British pop stars of the 1960s; Valerie Singleton was a longstanding BBC television and radio presenter; Richard Baker was a BBC television reporter and newsreader; Alf Garnett was the lead character in the BBC television sitcom *Till Death Us Do Part*, and was a byword for an unreasonable ranting curmudgeon.

57 Magic Motoring Moments

trafficator: the direction indicator stick.

59 Sorting Out The Rubbish

Blue Peter: long-running children's BBC television programme, famed for its DIY activities.

60 Pot Luck

Colcannon Supreme: colcannon is an Irish dish of cabbage cooked in milk and mashed with potatoes.

61 A Question Of Confidence

Zena Skinner, Delia Smith, Fanny Craddock: all three women were British professional television cooks and authors of hugely influential cookbooks.

Tommy Cooper: Welsh comedian, who specialised in performing as a failed conjuror, in variety shows and on television.

63 Sportin' Life

rec': abbreviation for recreation ground, a public space for community sports.

halt: archaic term for a person with a limp, deriving from Luke 14.21, 'the poor, the maimed, the halt and the blind'.

pebble lenses: glasses so smeared and dusty they looked as though the lenses were made from quartz rather than glass, so that she can't see very much.

64 You're Just the Person

matelot: slang for a sailor.

66 Oddawa

Lido Di Jesolo: a beach resort north of Venice.

Milky Bars: she's acting out a classic 1970s British television advert for white chocolate Milky Bars, featuring the Milky Bar Kid.

70 Happy Families

Good Lifer: the very popular BBC sitcom *The Good Life* began in 1975, about Tom Good's earnest insistence on living self-sufficiently by growing and rearing all their food in their suburban back garden, to the dismay of his wife and the derision of their neighbours.

The Waltons: long-running American television series about a large and loving homesteading family set during the Depression and the Second World War.

71 Moving In And Making Friends

carriage-style: large detached houses with the living quarters built above the garages, mimicking the stable-blocks of nineteenth-century estates where the grooms slept above the carriage buildings.

73 A Smile, A Purr And A Sigh

Evel Knievel: American motorbike stunt performer, who held records for jumping over cars and buses.

74 Bounding Through Life

Valentino: not the Italian couturier, but the 1920s silent movie film star Rudolph Valentino who had been a byword for silent male passion.

Mrs Miniver: the leading character in the eponymous 1940 novel by Jan Struther, and the 1942 film played by Greer Garson, who represents stalwart, elegant English womanhood.

Auntie Mame: the character played by Rosalind Russell in the 1958 film based on the 1955 novel, who is a big-hearted and exuberant aunt who takes in her orphaned young nephew and introduces him to her wildly inappropriate friends and way of life.

76 Finding A Job

hunt and peck: two-finger typing.

78 Dressing For The Occasion

Jean Varon: British designer in the 1960s and 1970s most well-known for designing costumes for Diana Rigg in the 1960s television series *The Avengers*.

86 If Only ...

paddy: a temper tantrum.